Peace Education

Peace Education

Pravat Kumar Dhal

SHIPRA

(First Published in India in 2019)

Rs. 1250, US$ 50

ISBN: 978- 81-938382-3-5

2023 Impression

Peace Education

Published by:
SHIPRA PUBLICATIONS
LG 18-19, Pankaj Central Market
I.P. Ext., Patparganj, Delhi 110092, India
91 11 47322068; 2223 5152; 96500 28065
info@shiprapublication.com
www.shiprapublication.com

Preamble of the Constitution of UNESCO

"Those who want war prepare young people for war: but those who want peace have neglected young children and adolescents so that they are unable to organise them for peace".

Maria Montessori

Preface

Peace is considered as a holistic endeavour that aims at the comprehensive development of persons. Peace encourages the practice of values such as love, truth, justice, equality, tolerance, harmony, humility, togetherness, and self-control. Peace education seeks to nurture the knowledge, skills, attitudes, and values that comprise a culture of peace. It is a long-term proactive strategy to nurture peaceful persons who resolve conflicts non-violently in educational institution. Peace education enhances the physical, emotional, intellectual, and social growth of children within a framework of human values.

Peace education aims at promoting a culture of peace. It can make learning a joyful and meaningful experience. Peace must be linked with our values. Inner peace is identified as the seed of peace, which creates nice personality. The concern for equality, social justice, poverty, violation of human rights and developing non-violent social system are the epitomes of peace education. Peace education needs to develop the characteristics like: tolerance, compassion, cooperation, justice, equality etc. within the students, teachers and members concern in the institution. Teacher is the real hero of the educational enterprises. He can make free the educational institution from various conflicts seen in present situation. He must be well aware about this approach. External material world cannot provide peace to human being. To generate a peaceful world let us start an inner journey!

At present we are facing the crisis of depletion of world resources, greenhouse effect, global warming, natural disasters and, in the social front: terrorism, poverty, unknown diseases, nuclear war, intolerance, jealousy, suspicion, threats posed by modern armaments, vast inequalities of opportunities, wealth and power round the globe, rapid increase in population, and even the AIDS epidemic. These devious activities are intolerable for human being. Hence human being wants to be free from the negative momentum and in the other way he has been searching peace and harmony in the society. It is his innate tendency. Having experienced it many advanced countries are facing towards peace. There are thousand organisations working for world peace. This is the need of the hour. Would we cooperate with this nice idea to protect our lovable beautiful world! Otherwise at any moment this fine earth will be turned in to assess.

Looking the above matter, Peace Education has been introduced as a subject of study in teacher education curriculum. It is a wonderful subject. This book is written to meet the need of the hour.

Prof. Pravat Kumar Dhal

Contents

Abbreviations

AE	Access and Equity
AEP	Adolescence Education Programme
AIE	Alternative and Innovative Education
AVAs	Assistance to Voluntary Agencies
BATNA	Best Alternative to a Negotiated Agreement
BOS	Black Board Operation Scheme
CEDAW	Convention on Elimination of all Forms of Discrimination against Women
CERPE	Centre for Research on affairs of Education for Peace
CGH	Construction of Girls Hostels
CPA	Common Wealth Plan of Action
CRC	Convention on the Rights of the Child
CWM	Collected Works of the Mother
DASA	Direct Admissions of Students Abroad
DPEP	District Primary Education Programme
DRP	Deep Rationality Theory
EGS	Education Guarantee Shame
EL	Educational Loans
EPE	Earth and Peace Education Association International
FEO	Fair Equality of Opportunity
GH	Girls' Hostel
GHA	Global Harmony Association
GNRC	Global Network of Religions of Children
GPS	Global Peace Science
HAP	Hague Appeal for Peace
ICCJ	International Council of Christians and Jews
ICT	Information and Communication Technology
IDMI	Scheme for Infrastructure Development of Private aided/Unaided Minority Institutions
IEDSS	Inclusive Education for Disable at Secondary Stage
IGNTU	Indira Gandhi National Tribal University
IID	Institute of Interfaith Dialogue
INDEST	Indian National Digital Library in Engineering, Science and Technology
JSSs	Jana Siksha Sansthanas
KGBV	Kasturiba Gandhi Balika Vidyalaya

KLS	Knowing how to, and Succeeding at, Extensive Living well
MDM	Mid-Day Meal
MS	Model School
NCERT	National Council Educational Research and Training
NCFSE	National Curriculum Framework for School Education
NCTE	National council of Teacher Education
NCUs	New Central Universities
NGO	Non-governmental Organisations
NPE	National Policy on Education
NPEEE	National Programme of Earthquake and Engineering
NPEGEL	National Programmes for Education of Girls in Elementary Level
NRP	National Research Professorship
PCS	Peace Culture System
PD	Physically Disabled
PPP	Public Private Partnership
QIS	Quality Improve in School
RMSA	Rastria Madhyamika Sikshya Abhiyan
RUSA	Rastria Ucchatar Siksha Abhiyan
SABCL	Sri Aurobindo Birth Centenary Volume
SAP	Scheme of Apprentice Training
SE	School Education
SIDA	Society for Inter-religions Dialogue
SPQEM	Strengthening for Providing Quality Education in Madrassas
SRCs	State Resource Centers
SSA	Sarva Siksha Abhiyana
TDM	Technology Development Mission
TVE	Technical and Vocational Education
UDHR	Universal Declaration of Human Rights
UN	United Nations
UNDDA	UN Department of Disarmament
UNESCO	United Nations Educational Scientific and Cultural Organisations
UNICEF	United Nations Children's Fund
VAW	Violence against Women
VSE	Vocationalisation of Secondary Education
WCCUs	World Class Central Universities
WFK	Wisdom as Factual Knowledge
WPS	Women Peace Securities
WSPN	Women's World Television by Satellite for Peace Network

1
Introduction

Peace Education is defined as "the process of promoting the knowledge, skills, attitudes, and values needed to bring about behaviour change that will enable children, youth and adults to prevent conflict and violence, both overt and structural; to resolve conflict peacefully; and to create the conditions conducive to peace, whether at an interpersonal, intergroup, national or international level."
—UNICEF

1.0 Introduction

Our earth is a planet where problems keep rising every day and man is constantly worried about finding probable solutions. We are facing the crises of depletion of world resources, greenhouse effect, global warming, natural disasters and, on the social front: terrorism, poverty, unknown diseases, nuclear war, intolerance, jealousy, suspicion, threats posed by modern armaments (conventional, chemical, biological and nuclear), vast inequalities of opportunities, wealth and power round the globe, rapid increase in population, and even the AIDS epidemic. All these distinctively modern crises have been made possible by modern science dissociated from the spirit. Isaac Asimov rightfully says *"the saddest aspect of life right now is that science gathers knowledge faster than society gathers wisdom"* (Asimov, 1988, p. 281). If we are to avoid in this century the horrors of the last one—wars, death camps, dictatorships, poverty, hunger, illiteracy, malnutrition, environmental damage—we urgently need to learn how to acquire more wisdom, which in turn means that our institutions of learning need to become more responsive, sympathetic, people-centric, practical and rationally effective. In the words of Abdul Kalam (2010, p. 199), "Enlightened citizenship has three components: education with value system, religion transforming into spiritual force, and creating economic prosperity through development." If we examine the crisis of our times, which is behind all our ills and maladies, it is the crisis of science without consciousness, which is restricted to acquire knowledge and more knowledge. Hence, Kalam (2010, p. 249) said, "Science is the best boon that God has bestowed upon mankind. Science with reasoning becomes the capital of society.... The convergence of science and technology with spirituality is touted to be the future for both science and technology, and spirituality." The irrationality of knowledge-inquiry further damages our ability to find solutions. The crux of our crisis is that we are living in man-made, non-dynamic, intellectual systems where we teach social science but not social philosophy, technology but not humanities, facility and rights but not responsibility and reason, while we exploit natural resources without any thought of conserving them. The root of the problem is the rebellious nature and the ignorance of mankind. Hence, American Philosopher Glenn Martin (Semashko, 2013, p. 296) aptly called it, "Our new planetary paradigm, and the fundamental revolution in science and paradigm shift in human consciousness."

Now we are living in a digital age, where it seems everything can be possible in a hurry. We have produced super computers, Akash tablets, i-pad, i-phone, e-learning, e-governance, etc. No doubt it helps to quicken our services. It also helps us to destroy our lovely world. If we ask a child for any calculation, he replies within a few seconds, having not known the addition, multiplication or division. He must have a busy schedule! There is no time for leisure, introspection and also no time for inner journey and having wisdom. Is it not reflected in the poem of W.H. Davies, "Leisure" (Davies, 1925)? The visions of progress include new consumer markets and unbridled profits, nuclear weapons, human cloning, satellite television, polluting factories, waste levels, pragmatic corruption, etc. Under their influence our modern educational system has assigned no respect or space to locally wise persons, wise languages, wise customs and wise institutions that existed outside the framework of formal/non-formal schools in the globe. Educational systems are still engaged in destroying the system by borrowing and superimposing deadened educational methodologies. The mind is moving faster than a storming wind, making a thousand wrongs. Rather, it is wise to stop and think for a few minutes and think deeply: "Let there be peace on earth and let it begin with me." (See Jackson & Miller, 2009)

"*Om poornamadah poornamidam*
Poornaat poornamudachyate
Poornasya poornamaadaya
Poornamevaavashishyate
Om Shantih!Shantih! Shantih!"

—*The Upanishad* (Sri Aurobindo, 1996)

(*Meaning:* That (pure consciousness) is full (perfect); this (the manifest universe of matter; of names and forms being illusion) is full. This fullness has been projected from that fullness. When this fullness merges in that fullness, all that remains is fullness.)

The present scenario of the society is effected with conflicts and violence; which needs to establish peace culture in the society. Observing this need, the National Curriculum Framework (2005) by NCERT has emphasised that education must develop awareness in individuals to their social environment. The concern for equality, social justice, poverty, violation of human rights and developing non-violent social system are the epitomes of peace education. Peace education needs to develop the characteristics like: tolerance, compassion, cooperation, justice, equality etc. within the students, teachers and members concerned in the institution. Teacher is the real hero of the educational institution. He must be well aware about this approach. Feeling this emergency UNESCO has been inspiring to world of education since 1948. In our country, NCERT has been organizing a number of workshops and discussions regarding this issue to develop the peace culture. It is observed that educational institutions are the proper centers through which peace culture will be created in the society. Hence educational institutions have to take binary role; i.e., eliminating violence and conflicts and establishing peace culture in the institution and society also.

1.1 Aims and Objectives

Human being wants a peaceful world. Education has paramount importance to provide peace to human civilisations. Peace education welcomes all-inclusive approach to a holistic way of living. It fosters in order to make the globe a better and more human value. It encourages learners about outermost and innermost values that shape them and their activities in the globe through peace pedagogy. It develops faith, commitment, courage, interdependence and compassion among the learners and stakeholders of society. It helps in eradicating human ills, injustice, inequality, prejudice, intolerance, destruction of environment and violent conflict. It prepares the world a better, healthy, safe, peaceful and united one. It sharpens awareness about co-existence and holistic relationships between people and between nations. It generates awareness among the stakeholders about commonality and diversity of human culture, population explosion, destruction of eco-system, gender issue, racism, poverty, war and terrorism, mutual relationship, global cultures, rights of living beings, etc. Peace education brings virtue, a positive attitude, tendency to do well, trust and justice.

On completion of the course the student teacher will be able to:

- Understand the importance of peace education.
- Familiarize them with the pedagogy of peace.
- Enhance understanding about strategies of peace education.
- Appreciate the role of peace in life, society and nation.
- Acquaint himself with the concept of peace in different religions
- Identify the factors those blocking the path of peace.
- Develop the means to combat the challenges in the path of peace.
- Create a national cum international platform of peace education.

- Encourage the global understanding for establishing peace on the earth.
- Sensitizing teachers about the concerns for peace and education for peace.
- Helping teachers to understand their role as peace educators so as to model the requisite behaviours, attitudes and values.
- Developing knowledge, attitudes, values and skills among teachers for conflict resolution.
- Enabling teachers to introduce stress-management techniques to cope with the academic failure of pupil in examination, corporal punishment, excessive competitiveness, and emotional matters related to adolescence etc.
- Enabling teachers to learn ways of integrating peace in the school curriculum and teacher-learning activities in and out of the classroom.

1.2 Meaning, Concept, Need and Significance

1.2.1 Meaning and Definition of Peace Education

Each individual in the earth wants peace. Peace is an eternal and inherited entity of human being. Any strategy or educational system helps to enhance tolerance, understanding, empathy, cooperation and respect for the difference in others among the individuals could be known as peace education. Peace education is also considered as a planning or strategy of eliminating the conflicts and violence caused by in justice, inequality and human rights, violations, and implementing the ways and means of reducing the same through appropriate teaching and learning tactics by means of producing responsible global citizen to attain and spread the peace in the world.

Peace education is a remedial measure to protect children from getting into the ways of violence. It aims at the total development of the child, which leads to peace in society also. It inculcates higher human and social values in the mind of the child. In essence it attempts to develop a set of behavioural skills necessary for peaceful living and peace-building from which the whole of humanity gets benefitted. Peace education is more effective and meaningful when adopted according to the social and cultural context and the needs. It should be enriched by its cultural and spiritual values together with the universal human values. It should also be globally relevant.

Peace begins with the individual and spreads to the family, to the community, to the nation, and to the world. Peace education builds love, friendship and international understanding. Peace means being one with life itself—that is having no fear or bitterness. J. Nehru said, "Peace is not a relationship with nations, it is a condition of mind brought about by serenity of soul. Peace is not merely by the absence of war. It is also a state of mind. Lasting peace can come only to peaceful people."

Nature of creator and creation is peaceful. But due to adverse circumstances and activities it is deteriorated. "Peace education should contribute towards changing the world. Peace education should reduce the willingness of individuals to resort to violence, and uncover and eliminate structures of violence in human relations, in all areas of society and between states." (Oscar Brilling *et al.,* 1999). It should be enriched by cultural and spiritual values together with the universal human values. It "is a planning strategy of eliminating to conflicts and violence caused by inequality, injustice and human rights violations; and implementing the ways and means of reducing the same through appropriate teaching and learning tactics by means of producing responsible global citizens to attain and spread the peace in the world."

Peace is a state of mind. It is calm and quietude of mind. It is not simple happiness or sensory pleasure; what we get from singing, playing, food, habit, vital activities and sensory feelings. It can be realised through descending of higher consciousness in the body, mind and spirit. Some yogic exercises, positive thinking, reading spiritual literature (*swadhyaya*), concentration, mental silence, prayer, sharing of consciousness, spiritual realisation can help to attend in the state of peace. It is called inner peace.

Truth, beauty and goodness provide us peace. Purity of body, mind and vital leads us to achieve higher consciousness. Aspiration of higher objectives like Truth, Beauty and Goodness; rejection of impurities within body, mind and vital and surrender of everything within ourselves to the Divine leads us to transformation of consciousness; that provides us permanent peace. Our education should be oriented through above processes to achieve peaceful existence in this fine lovable world. Like all flowers in a garden grow freely in harmonious manner, all the human beings in the lap of mother earth should grow freely without any hazards in a harmonious way. This is the law of nature or Creator. Human being should follow it seriously. Each individual, society and nation has a special role to do. Nobody can overlap other. If it happens then, it raises conflict, war, riots, destruction etc. It may be through mutual sharing and cooperation; we can achieve more. But never try to supersede other. Who does this he/she may be a devil—the source of negative kingdom; which is covered with darkness. Our history teaches us a lot about such type of kingdoms in the world and how divine force smashed them forever from the world scenario. The Divine wants peace, knowledge, love, beauty, power, truth and light. Peace education should provide these. Peace education teaches us egoless life. Sri Aurobindo says, "In peace there is besides the sense of stillness a harmony that gives a feeling of liberation and full satisfaction. It is from the Silence that the peace comes; when the peace deepens and deepens, it becomes more and more the Silence." (Letters on Yoga). Shall we aspire it and live accordingly!

Some definitions of peace education are as under:

"Peace is not merely the absence of war but the presence of justice, of law, of order-in short, of government." —Albert Einstein

"Peace is not the absence of war. Peace is the virtue, an attitude, tendency to good, trust and justice." —Spinoza

"A Peace education is an attempt to respond to problems of conflict and violence on scales ranging from the global and national to the local and personal. It is about exploring ways of creating more just and sustainable futures." —R.D. Laing (I 978)

"Peace education is holistic. It embraces the physical, emotional, intellectual, and social growth of children within a framework deeply rooted in traditional human values. It is based on philosophy that teaches love, compassion, trust, fairness, co-operation and reverence for the human family and all life on our beautiful planet."

—Fran Schmidt and Alice Friedman (1988)

"Peace education is skill building. It empowers children to find creative and nondestructive ways to settle conflict and to live in harmony with themselves, others, and their world. …Peace building is the task of every human being and the challenge of the human family." —Fran Schmidt and Alice Friedman (1988)

"Peace Education is defined as "the process of promoting the knowledge, skills, attitudes, and values needed to bring about behaviour change that will enable children, youth and adults to prevent conflict and violence, both overt and structural; to resolve conflict peacefully; and to create the conditions conducive to peace, whether at an interpersonal, intergroup, national or international level." —UNICEF

"Peace education is a mechanism for the transformation from a culture of violence to culture of peace through a peace of conscientisation." —Freire (2006)

"Peace education is the attempt to promote the development of an authentic planetary consciousness that will enable us to function as global citizens and to transform the present human condition by changing the social structures and patterns of thought that have created it." — Betty Reardon

"Peace education is grounded in active citizenship, preparing learners for assiduous participation in a democracy, through problem-posing and problem-solving education, and a commitment to transformative actions in our societies." —John Dewey

"The peace need not be grave or joyless—there should be nothing grey in it—but the gladness or joy or sense of lightness that comes in the peace must be necessarily something internal, self-existent or due to a deepening of experience—it cannot, like the laughter of which you speak, be conveyed by an external cause or dependent upon it, e.g. something amusing, exhilarating etc."

—Sri Aurobindo, Letters on Yoga

"To live within, in constant aspiration towards the Divine—that renders us capable of regarding life with a smile and remaining in peace whatever the external circumstances." —The Mother

"Each one has to find his peace from within. And peace to be real must be unaffected by outside circumstances."—M.K. Gandhi

Peace is not the product of terror or fear. Peace is not the silence of cemeteries. Peace is not the silent result of violent repression. Peace is dynamism. Peace is generosity. It is a right and it is a duty."

—Fr. Oscar Romero

"I believe that love, kindness, compassion, tolerance, and peace can be implanted in the psyche of man only: when fear, paranormal illusion and ignorance are removed. We can then shift our attention more to matters of peace, rather than to matters of war."

—Peter Ratzinger

1.2.2 Concept of Peace in Education

Education is a nation's tryst with destiny. "Peace is a prime requirement for progress and national integration. Conflicts dissipate our collective energy and destroy the framework for a better quality of life, even when the material resources for it are available" (NCERT, 2006). Peace as a noble and necessary ideal is considered by every society in every age. The great spiritual teachers of the past were peace lover, peace finder, and peace achiever. "Education for peace calls for a significant reduction, not an increase, in curriculum load. Peace embodies the joy of living. Learning, from the peace perspective, has to be a joyful experience" (NCF, 2005). Joy is the essence of life. In today's society, hurry and worry sour the joy of learning and reduce learning and the harmony of life.

Peace is linked with a commitment to justice. Injustice subverts peace. The most crucial injustice in our context are discriminations and disabilities based on caste and gender, both of which continue to rob millions of children of their right to education and dignity in school. "Caste and gender-based injustices continue to subvert education as a fundamental right" (NCERT, 2006). Addressing and rectifying these aberrations is a core agenda in education for peace. Denial of access to basic education perpetuates political, economic, and social injustice against the underprivileged, prejudices them, and excludes them from the mainstream of national life. (*op. cit.*)

Doing justice to teachers is crucial to implementing education for peace. "Education for peace seeks to nurture the knowledge, skills, attitudes, and values that comprise a culture of peace. It is a long-term proactive strategy to nurture peaceful persons who resolve conflicts non-violently" (*op. cit.*). Further, education for peace is holistic. It embraces the physical, emotional, intellectual, and social growth of children within the periphery of human values. The concern for equality, social justice, poverty, violation of human rights and developing non-violent social system are the hallmarks of peace education. The approach to peace education involves transforming the environment to imbue it with tolerance, compassion, cooperation, justice, equality etc. so that these qualities, essential for peace building are nurtured among students.

The National Curriculum Framework (NCF, 2005) by NCERT asserts that education must be able to promote values that foster peace, humanness and tolerance in a multicultural society. The aims of education enunciated in the NCF include developing commitment to democracy and the values of equality, justice, freedom, secularism, and concern for others well beings. Educational institutions must enable children to make choices and decisions about what is right and best for common good, promoting their ethical development and capacity for value-based decisions making. Education for peace is about empowerment of self so that individuals are equipped with knowledge, competencies and skills of conflict resolution; such individuals will have self-awareness, values of tolerance, compassion and competence to deal with crisis in creative manner.

In India, the concept of peace includes:

(i) The absence of tensions, conflicts, and all forms of violence including terrorism and war.
(ii) The creation of a society free from structural violence. The duty to practice justice: social, economic, cultural, and political.
(iii) The absence of exploitation and injustice of every kind.
(iv) International cooperation and understanding.
(v) Ecological balance and conservation. The adoption of lifestyles conducive to the wholeness of creation.
(vi) Peace of mind.
(vii) Peace implies the capacity to live together in harmony.

Peace is a dynamic concept because it is related to human beings. Democracy, freedom and equality for all are not enough; social justice and inequalities have to be understood and attended to. Human rights and responsibilities need to be respected. Inner peace or intra personal peace is reflected in the behaviour viz. physical, social, emotional, health, productivity, and relationships. The outside changes in the productivity, relationships, however, begin from individual, which are pro-peace. The extension of the meaning of peace to include health, yoga, meditation and fitness, communication skills, stress management, family relationships, democratic and constitutional values, ethics, justice, equality and equity. Some reflections of the peace are:

— Changing the self has possibilities for peace.
— Words have a tremendous capacity to influence others.
— Our efforts to promote peace howsoever small they may be spread all over.
— Sensitivity to the situation, changing one's own self, readiness to sacrifice, and endless cooperation are the keys to peace in the society.

The members of a society need to be oriented toward peace rather than towards violence. 'At the same time, social, economic, and political systems have to be reoriented to peace' (NCERT, 2010). The discipline of peace must shape our way of life. Education is vital for the effectiveness of peace in life. Peace education will provide peace in life. Let it be so!

1.2.3 Need and Significance of Peace in Education

This is the age of unprecedented violence: locally, nationally, and globally. It is a serious matter that schools, which are meant to be the nurseries of peace, become transmission points for violence. It is seen everywhere that day to day the children are becoming more violent in action, speech and deeds. "The more "achievement-oriented" a person is, the less able he tends to be in relating to people, even dear ones, sensitively, reciprocally, and responsibly. Lopsided development, marked by deficient social imagination, makes children vulnerable to violence" (*op. cit.*).

"In a survey conducted for this position paper, 18 per cent of the children interviewed were found to take pleasure in various acts of violence. They enjoyed stoning little pups and kittens, breaking flower buds off plants, holding butterflies between their fingers, older children engaged in eve-teasing and ragging to the extent that it sometimes became fatal" (NCERT, 2006, p. 3).

The citizens of tomorrow need to be empowered to choose the way of peace rather stray into the blind alleys of violence. Peace is a prime requirement for progress and national integration. Conflicts dissipate our collective energy and destroy the framework for a better quality of life. Every society in every age has acknowledged peace as a noble and necessary ideal. The great spiritual teachers of the past were, in their own ways, educators for peace.

Inner peace is the seed of collective peace. Peace implies the ability to respond to the surrounding suffering and other's needs in ways that affirm faith in the light beyond the darkness. *The ability to respond justly and affirmatively to the needs and sufferings of others is the hallmark of authentic inner peace.* It is not an exclusive obsession with peace for oneself, but a commitment to peace for all.

Peace education seeks to nurture the knowledge, skills, attitudes, and values that comprise a culture of peace. It is a long-term proactive strategy to nurture peaceful persons who resolve conflicts non-violently. Along with, peace education enhances the physical, emotional, intellectual, and social growth of children within a framework of human values. Peace is considered as a holistic endeavour that aims at the comprehensive development of persons. Peace mandates the practice of values such as love, truth, justice, equality, tolerance, harmony, humility, togetherness, and self-control (*op. cit.*).

Peace is the inset tendency of human being. Each human being has two tendencies; devil and divine. If one selects former one he will be a demon or having negative behaviour. If he selects latter one, he will be divine having positive behaviour. Positive behaviour means showing the behaviours approached by everyone. That is sociable, '*satyam*', '*sivam*' and '*sundaram*' *or Truth, Beauty and Goodness*. It is '*satwic*' in nature. Those are meant for wellbeing of individual, society as well as nation. It is ethical, spiritual, godly, pious and follows moral ideas. '*The Ramayana*', '*The Mahabharat*', '*The Gita*', '*The Savitri*', '*The Bible*', '*The Koran*' are great scriptures in the world which show the above path. There are thousands of scriptures in the world which are in similar nature. It leads to peaceful, happiest, truthful, harmonious, and faithful life. This is the path of knowledge, justice, power, light and love. It may establish the kingdom of God in this beautiful earth.

On the other way, Devil (negative) work means—the work which is negative in nature; that is un-lawful, falsehood, arbitrary, selfish, jealousy, arrogant, hatred, etc. Those are not suitable for others. It may be egoistic meant for self-satisfaction. A few people are satisfied with such activities. It may be both '*rajasic*' and '*tamasic*' in nature. It makes him restless, unstable, worried, unconscious and negative in behaviour. It leads to suffering, sad, disappointment, hopeless, faithless, disease and death. Destruction of earth by any means is the result of such activities.

Environment and society have significant role to create peace and harmony. Positive environment helps to move in positive direction i.e. direction of peace and negative environment helps him to move in negative direction i.e. the direction of suffering, hopeless, despair, troublesome, and sad. Now choice is imperative. Hell or heaven! The former path has gone to hell and the later one to heaven. The people in society will select which will help for him. Major people want positive direction. But unconsciously they also do mischievous activities and fall in trouble. Hence to maintain a harmonious and peaceful life the first condition is to be conscious in each component of human being, i.e. mind, vital, body, psychic and soul of human being. In consequence mind will achieve knowledge, vital-being will achieve power, body will achieve beauty and psychic will achieve '*ananda*'. Life will be peaceful and harmonious with the beautiful world.

Peace education aims at promoting a culture of peace. It can make learning a joyful and meaningful experience. Peace offers a contextually appropriate and pedagogically gainful point of coherence for all values. Inner peace is identified as the seed of peace, which creates nice personality. Education for peace, as a pioneering move, must be implemented with vision and determination.

To NCERT (2006), major frontiers of education for peace are:

(a) Bringing about peace-orientation in individuals through education;
(b) Nurturing in students the social skills and outlook needed to live together in harmony;
(c) Reinforcing social justice, as envisaged in the Constitution;
(d) The need and duty to propagate a secular culture;
(e) Education as a catalyst for activating a democratic culture;
(f) The scope for promoting national integration through education; and
(g) Education for peace as a lifestyle movement.

1.3 Barriers—Psychological, Cultural, Political and Socio-economical

In the path of peace and harmony there are several types of barriers. These are: psychological, cultural, political, socio-economical, etc. Each type has separate cause and effect. Those are not congenial for development of civilisation. Hence sound knowledge about some constraints of each component should be known by everyone.

(a) *Psychological*—Man is a psychological being. Psychological barriers happen due to unsound mind. If mind becomes unstable, unrest, worried, tension, confusion due to any reason it leads to devious work. People suffered a lot in various ways. Mischievous activities like loot, murder, conflict, war, terror happened. In this situation one cannot do right things in right manner for right purpose. Hence, in any way the first condition is calmness of mind. In calm mind one can get inspiration within. He can understand everything, take right decision and solve the faced problem smoothly.
(b) *Cultural*—Sometimes different cultures create barriers. It is seen that various riots, war, conflict have happened due to religion, dress code, speech, jealousness among communities, dogmatic belief, and superstition, etc. There may be other factors also. 'Jehad' is the deformation of religious belief. Mother India embraces every religion and culture in her lap. Her constitution is all-inclusive. But sometimes due to ignorance and fulfilling the ego desire several misshappenings have been occurred. Would we be free from it! A conscious approach of understanding may save us from all odds. Let us remember the message of our old scripture:

"Sarve bhavantu sukhinah,
Sarbe shantu niramaya
Sarbe vadrani pasyantu,
Ma kaschid dukh vag bhabet!"

(c) *Political*—It should be remembered that every profession has some ethics. Now-a-day politics is going on having no ethics; which is the root cause of conflict and indiscipline. In consequence it raises barrier in the path of peace and harmony. Through the politics man wants to fulfill his cherish: sex, money and power—the three vital elements of the life. For this narrow goal he can do anything, any misdeed; which creates disharmony in society. It should be changed towards help to weaker section of society, progress of village and people, establishment of advanced institutions and offices in rural area and in a nutshell for wholesome development of human civilisation. To achieve this politician has to be sincere, dedicated and a conscious learned citizen.

(d) *Socio-economical*—Man is a social being. He cannot live without society. He is born and brought up by family as well as society. Hence the economic condition of family and society has great influence in his life. If the social environment is not conducive he cannot move forward. All sorts of pollution, explosion, erosion, climate change, etc. will happen. To combat these challenges cooperation, collaboration, sympathy, fellow feeling, kindness, forgiveness, dedication, following truth, holiness, positive thinking, love, open to God, etc., are the essential qualities men have to follow. It will lead towards peace and harmony.

"Om saha naavavatu sahanau bhunaktu
Saha veeryam karavaavahai
Tejasvi naavadheetamastu maa vidvishaavahai
Om shantih shantih shantih"

—*The Krishna Yajurveda Taittiriya Upanishad* (2.2.2)

Meaning: May He protect us both (teacher and the taught)! May He cause us both to enjoy the bliss of Mukti (liberation)! May we both exert to discover the true meaning of the sacred scriptures! May our studies be fruitful! May we never quarrel with each other! Let there be threefold peace.

1.4 Factors Responsible for Breaking Peace

There are several factors responsible for breaking of peace. Some of them are discussed here.

Factors Responsible for Breaking Peace

↓

Depression | Unemployment | Terrorism | Exploitation | Suppression | Complexity

(a) *Depression:* When an individual faces any problem or tragedy for long time and feels that there is no other way to become free from that problem; in that case he undergoes depression. This is a mental state. Depression also creates other negative symptoms. In this case there are several techniques an individual can follow to overcome the depression, for example: laughing, viewing movies, listening music, meditation, visiting holy places and people and sharing with teachers or close friends, etc. These techniques have immense value to live peacefully in society.

If anybody is in depression stage he cannot achieve peace. Here one has to find the cause of depression. If it is removed anyhow, then he can move towards the path of peace. Otherwise, if one finds psychic, concentrates on it and realise it then he can achieve peace. If we move in the path of peace we have to be free from any mental aberration; because distorted mind cannot move in this path.

(b) *Unemployment:* It may be a cause in external world; but one has to understand that is it possible to provide job for each people, obviously not! We have to find the path of earning that means vocation or profession. As per our inner call we may choose it and succeed. If we do the work as per our interest we will get peace. If we do any work with burden we cannot achieve peace. Hence whatever we do, we shall do with '*shradha*' (love). In our ancient scripture it is written that '*shradhaban lavate param*'. And who will achieve the divine he will get 'sukha and shanti' (pleasure and peace).

(c) *Terrorism*: Nowadays we are facing a separate notion i.e. terrorism. It is a false notion to be great in one day. Terrorism cannot provide peace in the world. It destroys our nice world. If ego of a group of people is thwarted then they started such type of revolution. Revolution may be good in positive way. It is not approachable at all in negative direction, i.e. through murder, bombing, destruction, firing, etc. It creates social tension rather than peace in the society. Each person has to be aware about it. "Values are used socially to present claims, to evaluate other people, to evaluate oneself, to attack others, to gain revenge, to gain instrumental advantage. So people have to give importance to upbring the child with value clarification in each and every life stage and situation to prevent them from becoming terrorists."

(d) *Exploitation*: In a pond a small fish is preyed by a big fish. Everywhere a small insect is preyed by a big insect. Likewise human being is exploited by others. This epidemic is contaminated throughout the globe. One country exploits other country, higher officer exploits lower employees. House owner exploits servant. This happens only due to fulfilling his ego-desire, selfishness and brutal characteristics.

These are activities of devils or animals. But human being is much more than this. Hence, he has to follow the divine path: respect others, mind others as him, help others, cooperate others and reflecting kindness to downtrodden, backward classes and providing opportunities to deprived ones. This is the way of democracy and peace also. After seventy years of independence Indians are facing such problem. Not only in India but the entire globe is facing such a great challenge. Peace education can provide a good platform for combating the above challenge.

(e) *Suppression of individuality:* Day after day human being is facing with a lot of problems. When an individual or group dominates or suppresses other, he feels suffocation or tragedy for long time and feels that there is no other way to become free from that problem, at that moment he undergoes suppression. Sometimes he may agitate or reacts. Suppression helps to create other negative symptoms. He cannot feel free himself. He loses his independency or individuality. He feels unrest. In this case he may apply defense mechanism to protect himself.

(f) *Complexity:* Human being is complex in nature. If he creates more complex problems then automatically the world will become complex. In the name of advanced civilisation we are creating more complexes. Hence every day the news comes of war, bombing, loot, murder, throwing virus, negative politics, corruption, etc. These are the constraints of peace and harmony. In this case it is essential to become simple like a child. The world is moving in a single plan. Simplicity is the way towards the divine. Complexity destroys the civilisation. God can protect them who are simple and not harmful to nature and society. Simple living leads to peaceful life.

1.5 Religion and Peace

It refers to the study of religion's role in the development of peace. It is observed that in various times religion has taken role of blessings and curse also. Nathan C. Funk and Christina J. Woolner (1993) categorize these approaches into three models:

The first is "peace through religion alone". This proposes to attain world peace through devotion to a given religion. Opponents claim that advocates generally want to attain peace through their particular religion only and have little tolerance of other ideologies.

The second model, a response to the first, is "peace without religion". Critics claim that it is overly simplistic and fails to address other causes of conflict as well as the peace potential of religion. It is also said that this model excludes the many contributions of religious people in the development of peace. Another critique claims that both approaches require bringing everyone into their own ideology.

The third and final approach is known as "peace with religion". This approach focuses on the importance of coexistence and interfaith dialogue. Gerrieter Haar suggests that religion is neither inherently good nor bad for peace, and that its influence is undeniable. Peace with religion, then, emphasizes promoting the common principles present in every major religion.

A major component of religion and peace building is faith-based non-governmental organisations (NGOs). Douglas Johnston (1985) points out that faith-based NGOs offer two distinct advantages. The first is that since faith-based NGOs are very often locally based, they have immediate influence within that community. He argues that "it is important to promote indigenous ownership of conflict prevention and peace building initiatives as early in the process as possible" The second advantage Johnston presents is that faith-based NGOs carry moral authority that contributes to the receptivity of negotiations and policies for peace.

1.6 Peace in Different Religions

1.6.1 Hinduism

The truth in 'Sanatan' Dharma is based on the Vedanta. This is the eternal religion. It is rising up before the world. It is developed through Rishis, Saints and 'Avataras'. India will be great only for this religion. It embraces all religions. It is universal religion. In '*Uttarpara Speech*' Sri Aurobindo says:

This is the one religion that can triumph over materialism by including and anticipating the discoveries of science and the speculation of philosophy. It is the one religion which impresses on mankind the closeness of God to us and embraces in its compass all the possible means by which man can approach God. It is the one religion which insists every moment on the truth which all religions acknowledge he is in all men and in all things and that in him we move and have and have our being. It is the one religion which enables us not only to understand and believe the truth but realize it with every part of our being. It is one religion which shows us now we can best play our part in that Lila, its subtlest laws and its noblest rules. It is the one religion which does not separate life in any smallest detail from religion, which knows what immortality is and has utterly removed from us the reality of death.

The core of Sanatana Dharma is spiritual. There are major and minor differences between Hindus of various sects, schools, communities and races still there is also a general unity of spirit of fundamental type and form and of spiritual temperament which creates in the vast fluidity an immense force of cohesion and a strong principle of oneness.

Sanatana Dharma founded itself on the conception of timeless, nameless and formless, Supreme. It admits the aspects of God. To this religion the image is a symbol and support and can throw it away when its use is over. In its totality it has been a free and tolerant synthesis of all spiritual worship and experience. It observes the one truth from all its many sides, it shuts out none. It gives itself no specific name and bound itself by no limiting distinction. Though it has separate designation for its constituting cults and divisions, it remained itself nameless, formless, universal, and infinite.

Sanatana Dharma is founded upon three basic ideas. First comes the idea of the eternal, the infinite. To discover and unite with this permanent, this infinite, this eternal is the highest height and last effort of its spiritual experience. For its second basic idea is the manifold way of man's approach to the eternal and infinite. The infinite is full of many infinities and each of these infinities is itself the very eternal. God manifests himself and fulfills in the world in many ways, but each is the way of the eternal. For in each finite we can discover and through all things as his symbols we can approach the infinite.

The third idea is the divine. It can be approached through a universal consciousness and by affecting deeply through all inner and outer nature. It can be met by each individual soul in itself, in its own spiritual part. The essence of this dharma is "to aim at so growing and solving that we can grow out of the ignorance which veils this self-knowledge from our mind and life and become aware of the divinity within us" (SABCL, Vol. 14, p. 138).

1.6.2 Buddhism

'Hatred is never appeased by hatred in this world; it is appeased by love.' (Dhammapada I 5) Buddhism developed from the teaching of Siddhartha Gautama, called the Buddha (563 - 483 BC), who believed that human suffering can be overcome by overcoming the desire. The first precept of Buddhism is 'non-harming' (ahimsa). Buddhists reject violence. Some Buddhists have been very active in promoting peace. Some Buddhist monks burned themselves to death in self-sacrificing protest against the war. Buddhism follows sincerely non-violence. Buddhism has respect to ethics. At Bodhgaya people from Bhutan, Nepal, Ceylon, Thailand, Myanmar, China, Bangladesh, Tibet etc. are always gathering for prayer and meditation.

Confucianism and Taoism, which both developed in China, also share similar principles with Buddhism. For example, they seek to adjust human life to the inner harmony of nature (Confucianism) and emphasize mediation and non-violence as means to the higher life (Taoism). "The founders of these religions, Confucius and Lao-Tsze, lived in the same period as Buddha, the 6th century BC (PPU)*.

---

* PPU-Peace Pledge Union, 2018.

1.6.3 Sikhism

Guru Nanak (1469-1534) was the first Sikh Guru wrote this hymn:

> 'No one is my enemy
> No one is a foreigner
> With all I am at peace
> God within us renders us
> Incapable of hate and prejudice.'

He too emphasized the importance of non-violence and the equality of all humans whatever their religion. He was particularly concerned to reconcile Hinduism and Islam. Guru Gobind Singh (1666-1708) was tenth and last Guru of this path. In order to strengthen the courage and military discipline of the Sikhs at a time of great persecution, he organized the Khalsa - the Sikh brotherhood. His idea may be followed as below:

> 'When all efforts to restore peace prove
> useless and no words avail,
> Lawful is the flash of steel,
> It is right to draw the sword.'

"A central teaching of Sikhism is respect for people of all faiths.(*Op. cit.*)"

1.6.4 Baha'i Faith

The Baha'i Faith requires believers to avoid prejudice in daily life, to be friendly to people of all religions, social statuses, nationalities or various cultural traditions. At the nation's level, it calls for negotiation and dialogue between country leaders, to promote the process of world peace.

Bahaullah discouraged all forms of violence, including religious violence, writing that his aim was to: "quench the flame of hate and enmity" and that the "religion of God is for love and unity; make it not the cause of enmity or dissension." He warned of the dangers of religious fanaticism describing it as a "world devouring fire", prohibited holy war, and condemned the shedding of blood, the burning of books, the shunning of the followers of other religions and the extermination of communities and groups. Bahaullah promoted the concept of the oneness of the world and human beings describing the Earth as "but one country, and mankind its citizens". Bahaullah identified the elimination of disunity as a necessary pre-requisite to peace. "The well-being of mankind, its peace and security, are unattainable unless and until its unity is firmly established." Yet infinite in the diversity is the national characteristics of its federated units. (https://en.wikipedia.org/wiki/religion_and_peacebuilding#cite_note)

1.6.5 Judaism

"They shall beat their swords into ploughshares and their spears into pruning hooks: nation shall not lift up sword against nation, neither shall they learn war any more". (The Old Testament: Isaiah 2:4) Peace is the central teaching of rabbinical Judaism (teachings based on the writings of early Jewish scholars). However, Judaism is not a pacifist religion. The idea of Holy War occurs in the Hebrew Bible, but it was not about making others Jewish, but about survival.

The idea of 'Just War' is clearly expressed both in the Old Testament (Deuteronomy 20:10-15, 19-20) and in the later rabbinical tradition. So while revenge and unprovoked aggression are condemned, self-defense is justified. Defending modern Israel and dealing justly with the Palestinians places thoughful Jews in difficult dilemmas.

1.6.6 Christianity

Christianity has long tradition. It has been taken up all three positions on war: Pacifism, Just War and Crusade or Holy War. Jesus' teachings in the Sermon on the Mount (The New Testament: Matthew 5-7) are very clearly non-violent: for example, 'blessed are the peacemakers, for they shall be called the children of God' (Matthew 5:9) and 'love your enemies' (Matthew 5:44).

Pacifism was the teaching and practice of the Christian Church until the Roman Emperor Constantine (274-337) made Christianity the official religion of the Empire. Pacifism then largely gave way to the development of the 'Just War' doctrine. The majority of present-day Christians supports the idea that war is regrettable but unavoidable and should be fought according to 'Just War' rules.

1.6.7 Islam

'Islam' means 'submission' or 'surrender' to the will of God (Allah). Prophet Mohammed (c.570-632), was exponent of this path who recorded his understanding of the word of Allah in the Islamic sacred book, the Qur'an. Regarding Jihad one scholar wrote, 'Jihad means to 'strive' or 'struggle' in the way of God.' Jihad has two further meanings:

- the duty of all Muslims, as individuals and as a community, to exert themselves to realize God's will, to lead good lives, and to extend the Islamic community through such things as preaching and education, and 'Holy War' for, or in defense of Islam.

However, it is more correct to say that there are four different kinds of Jihad (PPU):

- personal spiritual and moral struggle in order to overcome self-centeredness and follow the teachings of the Qur'an;

- calm preaching and
- righteous behavior that witness to the unbeliever about the way of Islam; and
- war against those who oppress or persecute believers.

All faithful Muslims are thus involved in a continuous 'greater jihad' which is largely non-violent. 'The lesser jihad', war, is commanded by Allah but must be carried out according to strict rules. (*Op. cit.*)

1.6.8 The Humanist View

In recent time, religion has played a decreasing role in many societies, particularly in the West. Many people have consciously rejected the notion of a spiritual and sacred religion or God. This does not necessarily mean the rejection of ethical principles. Some people have developed a philosophy of 'humanism'. This is based on humanitarian ideals, such as individual responsibility for one's actions, respect for others, co-operating for the common good, and sharing resources.

Some humanists would accept the 'Golden Rule', a term first used by Confucius: 'Do as you would be done by', or 'Treat others as you would wish them to treat you'. Some see the natural or logical conclusion of such a principle to be the rejection of all war and violence. Others, who have reservations about pacifism, argue for 'Just War' rules similar to those based on religious law.

1.6.9 Pacifism

The Peace Pledge Union campaigns against war and promotes peace. It challenges the values and attitudes which are a serious obstacle to action for peace. As a non-sectarian organisation it welcomes co-operation with a variety of other groups, religious or non-religious, who share its aims. The opposition to war and violence as a means of settling disputes. Pacifism may entail the belief that the waging of war by a state and the participation in war by an individual are absolutely wrong, under any circumstances.

1.7 Some Thoughts in Different Faiths

> "Let us embrace the beauty of every culture and faith to create peace in our world."—Mitra Sen, Canadian teacher, filmmaker, and creator of Peace Tree
>
> "The peace we seek in the world cannot appear until its flame is first lit in our hearts. It is a divine force that whispers gently but insistently, coaxing us ever deeper into the dark recesses of our souls, shedding its healing light and liberating us from our fears. It is a

wondrous journey of personal liberation that, for me, continues to this day."—Mony Dojeiji and Alberto Agraso González.

"Courage is the price that life exacts for granting peace."

—Amelia Earhart

"Peace is not the absence of war. It is the presence of justice and the absence of fear". —Ursula Franklin

"Hatred and conflict are often rooted in differences between people of different races and religions. We all need to respect people of different races as well as people of different faiths and religions. We need to unite by recognizing our common desire and need for a harmonious society—a society in which we and our children and families and friends and communities can all live our lives in peace and harmony. Regardless of our race or religion, we all want and need such social harmony."

"Without respect for people of different races or ethnicities or religions, how can we have a peaceful and harmonious society or world? And without a harmonious society, how can there be the necessary economic development and atmosphere conducive to spiritual happiness and self-realisation?" —Jagad Guru

"How do you want to create peace, if there is no peace inside yourselves?" —Thich Nhat Hanh:

Buddhist Monk and peace activist.

"Peace is the harvest of love as war is the fruit of hate."

—Poet, Joan Walsh

1.8 Interfaith/Inter-religious Dialogue

Inter-religious dialogue is organized to establish harmony among various religious people having existence of own faith. They understand and believe each other. Each religion has some great value and significance. Hence, every religion should respect other religion. Each religion has some good and bad practices. It is wise to leave bad practices and follow the good ones.

Global Harmony Association

Global Harmony Association (GHA) is based on Spiritual Culture for Harmonious Civilisation. It is called as "Citizens of Earth"! It aims at "Unite in harmony for love, peace, justice, fraternity and happiness"! Since 2005, GHA has been running as an international NGO uniting more than 500 members in 56 countries and more than one million participants from the GHA collective members in 80 countries. There are 37 board members from 14 countries. The founder and President of GHA is Dr. Leo Semashko, Russia. The Mission of GHA is: *To bring peace from harmony and to pave a conscious way for harmonious civilisation on scientifically based 'ABC of Harmony' through harmonious education*. (Web: www.peacefromharmony.org)

Institute for Inter-religious Dialogue, Iran

The institute works for the greater understanding amongst different religious faiths. It does so in part by maintaining a library with resources on different religions and sponsors language classes for those interested in studying Islam. What is more, it holds monthly meetings and is involved in local and international conferences to promote knowledge of other religions.

Institute of Interfaith Dialogue (IID)

IID works to bring together representatives from different faiths around the world to promote understanding. By learning about other faith traditions, it also builds understanding of one's own faith. It also promotes efforts at religious education to eliminate ignorance.

International Council of Christians and Jews (ICCJ)

The ICCJ is an umbrella organisation of Christian-Jewish dialogue organisations in nearly 40 countries around the world. The dialogues got going in response to the Holocaust. Recently, the ICCJ has been pursuing dialogue with Moslems as well. The organisation holds yearly conferences as well as ad hoc consultations

Society for Inter-religious Dialogue (SIDA), Indonesia

SIDA was a response to the lack of respect for other religious traditions and inter-religious violence in Indonesia in the late 1990s. It aims both to promote understanding and meetings as well as to fight against the hijacking of religious symbols for political gains.

United Religions Initiatives

Created in 2000, URI has thousands of members representing over one hundred religions, spiritual expressions, and indigenous traditions in more than fifty countries around the world. They are working to build solidarity and facilitate the spread of best practices to build cultures of peace. The centrepiece of the URI is Cooperation Circles, which are regional or virtual teams made up of diverse members who identify concerns and articulate a vision of peace.

2
Empowerment for Peace

> *Peace education is the attempt to promote the development of an authentic planetary consciousness that will enable us to function as global citizens and to transform the present human condition by changing the social structures and patterns of thought that have created it."*
> —*Betty Reardon*

2.0 Background

The World Commission on Culture and Development at its third meeting held at San Jose, Costa Rica, 22-26 February 1994, set itself three goals; the third of which was "to promote a new cultural dynamic: the culture of peace and culture of development". The Commission undertook to "endeavour to recommend the concrete measures that could promote, on a national and international scale, a culture of peace" and went on to state that: "a culture of peace, culture of democracy and culture of human rights are indivisible. Their effective implementation must result in a democratic management and. the prevention of intercultural conflicts."[1]

Address to a meeting of the World Commission on Culture and Development, Manila, 21 November 1994, The Commission for a New Asia notes that:

> "the most rapid economic transformation is most likely to succeed within the context of international peace and internal political stability, in the presence of social tranquility, public order and an enlightened and strong government; and in the absence of societal turbulence and disorder."[2]

This comment highlights the link between economic, political and social concerns. But there is a danger that it could be interpreted to imply that peace, stability and public order are desirable only as conditions for facilitating economic transformation rather than as ends in themselves. Such an interpretation would distort the very meaning of peace and security. It could also be used to justify strong, even if unenlightened, government and any authoritarian measures such as a government may take in the name of public order.[3]

It is clearly understood that the material development does not provide human happiness. If it is sought in ways that wound the human spirit. It can in the long run only lead to greater human suffering. The vast possibilities that a market economy can open to developing countries can be realised only if economic reforms are undertaken within a framework that recognizes human needs. The Human Development Report makes the point that markets should serve people instead of people serving markets.

The true development of human beings not only depends on economic growth but also a sense of empowerment and inner fulfillment. This alone will ensure that human and cultural values remain paramount in a world. People's participation in social and political transformation is the central issue of our time. This can only be achieved through the establishment of societies which place human worth above power, and liberation above political control. In this way development requires democracy; which can provide genuine empowerment to the people. "When this is achieved, culture and development will naturally coalesce to create an environment in which all are valued, and every kind of human potential can be realised" (Kyi, 2009). Mere material assistance is not enough; the poor must have the sense that they themselves can shape their own future. The success of national policies depends on the willing participation of the people. Democratic values and human rights, it is sometimes claimed, run counter to "national" culture, and all too often the people at large are seen as "unfit" for government. Nothing can be further from the truth. The challenge we now face is for the different nations and people of the world to agree on a basic set of human values, which will serve as a "unifying force in the development of a genuine global community" (Parvu, 2014). True economic transformation can then take place in the context of international peace and internal political stability. Only strengthening civil society shall not bring the development of peace culture. We would look to a future where human beings are valued for what they are rather than for what they produce. If the UN and its agencies wish to assist this development they must support these movements which seek to empower the people, movements which are founded on democracy, and which will one day ensure a culture of peace and of development.

2.1 Justice—Social, Political, Economic, Cultural and Religious

By history, it is meant the experience that society, social orders, convictions and values—including the meaning of justice—can and do change over time. They are not fixed, eternal entities.

By politics, it means the awareness that human beings bear a fundamental responsibility for shaping the social order, for debating the terms on which to organize their co-existence, and for creating and improving a 'just society'.

2.1.1 Political Guarantee of Social Justice

Though modern democratic societies have often been described in such negative terms—of relativism, skepticism, and the loss of values. There may be some truth in that; but it is not the full picture. Day to day we have gained an increased awareness of human responsibility. Hence, respect for human responsibility has more and more become the core principle of modern democracy.

Every human is a responsible agent in the society. This gives a clue to understanding the modern interpretation of human dignity. Politically human rights entails that every human being is equally entitled. Respect for human dignity is the fundamental normative principle on which all possible orders of justice are based. Rights and responsibilities must go simultaneously together.

2.1.2 Religion and Social Justice

There are some basic requirements that allow us to cope with the pluralism of various ideas of what social justice is. Human rights epitomize these basic, normative principles. The difficulties of the question of social justice are shared across religions: Hinduism, Judaism and Christianity, as well as Islam. "Justice is deemed to be a universal value, a kind of intrinsic calling in the human conscience, which cannot be defined. It certainly cannot be defined by one religion against another" (Bahmanpour, 2003). Having accepted the idea of universal values, the main cause of disagreement in our judgments is that we come from different backgrounds, with different perspectives.

2.1.3 Cultural Identity and Value System

The reality of life in all societies has become very complex. "There is no possibility any more of 'authentic cultural identity' in that sense. We live in a global society in which forces of various cultural origins interpenetrate. The notion of identity can too easily accompany a false notion of cultural purity that generates a highly dangerous form of authoritarianism" (Bielefeldt, 2003). Identity, purity, are very complex concepts when society is viewed, not from a personal or even sociological standpoint—because in those perspectives they are understandable—but from the point of view of its core norms and values. In some parts of our country it has created more deterioration in society.

In making sense of human rights, it has been very important to emphasize that people do not constitute a comprehensive value system. Human rights are not collectively a religion, nor *Weltanschauung* (world view), nor a closed ideology; nor even a complete set of values—if values are understood as a way to shape one's life according to ideals of what a good life is. In each society or culture there are certain values prevailed. It must be understood in holistic way.

A person can, for example, become a monk, and understand his life in a very ascetic way. Human rights do not preclude this option or any other particular lifestyle either. But disguise monk is dangerous. Instead, the whole programme is about establishing the conditions which ensure that everyone has basic equal rights, and can make his own choice, independent of any form of domination by others. Respect to others, helping nature, listening others, cooperation, work together, mutual sharing etc. are basic principles for peaceful co-existence in public life.

2.1.4 Economical Justice

According to Justice Khehar, although political parties talk about economic reforms and globalisation in their manifestos, they never link the achievements of economic growth with the constitutional goal of socio-economic justice for the SCs, STs and other weaker sections of society. He said the question is: "How to operate the economic system for the good of the people through constitutional means?" (Kolko, 2015) Chief Justice also felt that economic growth has to be increased with economic justice and economic harmony.

According to Dr. B.R. Ambedkar, it was incorporated in the Constitution to make social and economic justice a reality. There is no fetter on the discretion to choose the means for disposal of natural sources, but the object of the policy should clearly be to sub-serve "the common good" as per the mandate of Article 39(b) which lays down the guiding principle with regard to disbursement of material resources of the community.

Though Sardar Patel wanted to have "fundamental principles of governance", Dr. Ambedkar favoured flexible directives as the concept of economic justice was bound to change with time.

"We have left enough room for people of different ways of thinking, with regard to the reaching of the ideal of economic democracy," he said during the debate on the draft constitution. His foresight can be seen from the fact that Article 39(b) which once justified nationalisation of assets is now guiding the disbursal of material resources to ensure economic justice to citizens.

After 70 years of Independence we are facing same problems of haves and have-nots. Day-to-day rich is becoming rich. All the finances sanctioned by government cannot reach the grass root levels. The facilities generated for the poor people can not avail by them. Mass awareness, policies including enforcement of laws may be helpful to fill this gap. Economic improvement of common people shows the sign of economic justice. Otherwise it is meaningless.

2.2 Equality—Egalitarianism, Education for All, Equal Opportunity

2.2.1 Egalitarianism

Armeson (2002) said, "One might care about human equality in many ways, for many reasons. As currently used, the label "egalitarian"...holds that it is desirable that people's condition be made the same in any respect or that people ought to be treated the same in any respect." It is commonly understood that, an egalitarian might be one who maintains that people ought to be treated as equals, as possessing equal fundamental worth and dignity and as equally morally considerable. In this sense, a non-egalitarian would be one who believes that people born into a higher social caste, or a favored race or ethnicity. 'The core egalitarian ideal is treating people as equals' (Dworkin 2000).

According to Walzer(1983), "a society is just if and only if its practices and institutions are in accord with the shared values and cultural understandings of its people. Democratic egalitarianism becomes a requirement of justice in modern societies, because this egalitarianism is an underlying important element of people's shared values and cultural understandings." But this appearance may be misleading. John Locke (1690) holds that "everyone at all times and places has equal natural moral rights that all of us ought always to respect" . The contemporary moral philosopher Thomas Scanlon (1998), holds that "all people everywhere equally have the moral right to be treated according to the outcome of a procedure: what constitutes morally right and wrong action is set by the principles that no one could reasonably reject."

If individual agents and public officials are liable through limited cognitive ability, limited knowledge, or limited allegiance to morality to misapply ultimate principles, it might well be the case that these principles could be implemented to a greater degree if they were not employed directly as decision-making guides for individual and public policy choice (Hare, 1981). Following this train of thought, one might favor as guidelines for individual and public choice simple, easily understood, readily implementable rules which are to serve as proxies for the moral principles which are the ultimate norms. Or one might instead hold that the ultimate moral principles that fix what is right and wrong are well suited to be practical decision making guides.

Egalitarianism might be upheld as a moral requirement, or as morally optional, a desirable ideal that we might permissibly decline to pursue. When affirmed as morally required, egalitarianism typically figures in a theory of justice. It concentrates on egalitarianism as a morally required component of justice, but in considering arguments against a version of egalitarianism, it is worthwhile keeping in mind the possibility that the norm in question is morally desirable but not morally mandatory.

2.2.2 Equal Opportunity

In our society, it is commonly understood that a son of a rich fellow must enjoy the aristocracy. A poor son lives as poor. Then how equality will come! "A historically important form of equality associated with the rise of competitive market economies is the ideal of equality of opportunity. This ideal is also known as formal equality of opportunity or careers open to talents (Armeson, 2002)."

There are two ideals of equality of opportunity deserve to mention. "One is the requirement that student slots in colleges and universities and competitive private schools should be open to all applicants with applicants ranked by their ability to learn and other academic virtues and selected on these academic grounds on paying fees and tuition (*Op. cit.*)". Another is that public sector jobs—other than those reserved for elected officials along with their staff—should be open to all applicants with selection of applicants being made on the basis of the merits of the applications.The general idea of equality of opportunity is that the political economy of a society distributes positions that confer special advantages and these should be open to all applicants with applicants selected by merit. The merits of the applications for a position should track the degree to which the applicant's hiring or selection for interaction would boost the fulfillment of the morally innocent purposes of the association (*Op. cit.*).

"The ideal of equality of opportunity is the ideal of a political economy in which each person's prospects as producer depend only on his initial stock of resources plus his ability and willingness to provide goods and services that others value plus luck as market fluctuations are encountered (*Op. cit.*)." Moreover, in the role of consumer, each individual faces the same array of goods and services on sale to anyone who can pay the purchase price (and can satisfy the relevant nonmarket conditions of the seller or maker). Such characteristics of persons as their supposed race, skin color, ethnicity, sex, sexual orientation, and religion play no role in determining one's life prospects in this public sphere except in so far as these traits might happen to affect one's abilities and willingness to offer what others are willing to exchange for money.

Equality of opportunity could be fully utilised in a society in which wealth passed along by inheritance from generation to generation, that determines everyone's competitive prospects. Jobs and positions are open to all applicants, but the only applicants who have the skills can qualify for the desirable posts are the children of the wealthy family. They are entering in the training and acculturation that develops skills.A society that establishes and maintains a state educational system sustained by public funds already goes some way beyond equality of opportunity and toward provision to all of its members of some opportunity to develop skills that will enable them to succeed in competitions for desirable positions regulated by equality of opportunity. The same can be said of a society that enforces minimal standards of child rearing to which parents must conform. One can imagine a society doing more in this same spirit (*Op. cit.*).

The policies must be formulated in society that secure at least a minimally acceptable schooling and skill formation for all its members. In other way, to eliminate entirely the advantages that family wealth and social status confer on individuals in competitions regulated by formal equality of opportunity. John Rawls (1999, 1963; 2001) fair equal opportunity (FEO) holds that any individuals in society with the same native talent and ambition should have the same prospects of success in competition for positions that confer special benefits and advantages... In a society regulated by FEO, socialization is adjusted so that among people equally willing to work to become qualified for a particular career and equally endowed by genetic inheritance with latent ability needed for that career, all have the same chances of success in that career. FEO also opposes racial and sexual and similar prejudices that work to deprive disfavored individuals from enjoying opportunities to become qualified so that they would benefit from formal equality of opportunity.

The parents naturally want to help their children develop the talents needed for competitive success. Some parents control a lot of resources useful for this purpose; some parents have few such resources. If society were fully to achieve FEO, then either parental freedom to help their children in ways that give them a competitive edge would have to be curtailed or such help would have to be exactly offset by compensating infusion of social resources toward the education and socialization of children whose parents are less effective. (Fishkin 1983 and Brig house and Swift 2009)

2.2.3 Education for All

Education for All (EFA) is an international initiative first launched in 1990 to bring the benefits of education to "every citizen in every society." To realize this aim, a broad coalition of national governments, civil society groups, and development agencies such as UNESCO and the World Bank Group committed to achieving six specific education goals:

1. Expand and improve comprehensive early childhood care and education, especially for the most vulnerable and disadvantaged children.
2. Ensure that by 2015 all children, particularly girls, those in difficult circumstances, and those belonging to ethnic minorities, have access to and complete, free, and compulsory primary education of good quality.
3. Ensure that the learning needs of all young people and adults are met through equitable access to appropriate learning and life-skills programmes.
4. Achieve a 50 per cent improvement in adult literacy by 2015, especially for women, and equitable access to basic and continuing education for all adults.

5. Eliminate gender disparities in primary and secondary education by 2005, and achieve gender equality in education by 2015, with a focus on ensuring girls' full and equal access to and achievement in basic education of good quality.
6. Improve all aspects of the quality of education and ensure the excellence of all so that recognised and measurable learning outcomes are achieved by all, especially in literacy, numeracy and essential life skills.

In 2000, 189 countries and their partners adopted the two EFA goals that align with Millennium Development Goals (MDGs) 2 and 3, which refer to universal primary education and gender parity. The World Bank recognizes that achieving these goals requires supporting the full EFA commitment.

Why is EFA Important?

According to World Bank (2014), although there has been steady progress towards achieving many EFA goals, many challenges remain:

- Today, an estimated 250 million children around the world are unable to read and write, even after spending three or more years in school.
- In 2012, 58 million children were out of school; half of these children lived in conflict-affected countries.
- In sub-Saharan Africa, girls accounted for 56 per cent of out-of-school children in 2012.
- In 2011, only 60 per cent of countries had achieved gender parity in enrollment at the primary level and 38 per cent at the secondary level.
- In around one-third of countries, fewer than 75 per cent of primary school teachers are trained according to national standards.
- In 2011, around half of young children had access to pre-primary education, and in sub-Saharan Africa the share was only 18 per cent.

Achieving the Education for All goals is critical for attaining all eight MDGs—in part due to the direct impact of education on child and reproductive health, as well as the fact that EFA has created a body of experience in multi-partner collaboration toward the 2015 targets. Simultaneously, achieving the other MDGs, such as improved health, access to clean drinking water, decreased poverty, and environmental sustainability, are critical to achieving the education MDGs.

Government of India have launched 'Right to Education Programme' in this regard. There are several programmes implemented by our Government to achieve this objective.

Right to Education

The Government of India through its Eighty-sixth Constitutional Amendment Act, 2002 inserted Article 21-A in the Constitution of India to provide free and compulsory education of all children in the age group of six to fourteen years as a Fundamental Right. (MHRD, 2018)The Right of Children to Free and Compulsory Education (RTE) Act, 2009 represents that every child has a right to full time elementary education of satisfactory and equitable quality in a formal school which satisfies certain essential norms and standards (*Op. cit.*).

Article 21-A and the RTE Act came into effect on 1 April 2010. The title of the RTE Act incorporates the words 'free and compulsory'. 'Free education' means that no child, shall be liable to pay any kind of fee or charges or expenses which may prevent him or her from pursuing and completing elementary education. 'Compulsory education' means to provide and ensure admission, attendance and completion of elementary education by all children in the 6-14 age group. With this, India has moved forward to a rights based framework that casts a legal obligation on the Central and State Governments to implement this fundamental child right as enshrined in the Article 21A of the Constitution, in accordance with the provisions of the RTE ac The Government of India through its Eighty-sixth Constitutional Amendment Act, 2002 inserted Article 21-A in the Constitution of India to provide free and compulsory education of all children in the age group of six to fourteen years as a Fundamental Right. The Right of Children to Free and Compulsory Education (RTE) Act, 2009 represents that every child has a right to full time elementary education of satisfactory and equitable quality in a formal school which satisfies certain essential norms and standards.

Article 21-A and the RTE Act came into effect on 1st April 2010. The title of the RTE Act incorporates the words 'free and compulsory'. 'Free education' means that no child, shall be liable to pay any kind of fee or charges or expenses which may prevent him or her from pursuing and completing elementary education. 'Compulsory education' means to provide and ensure admission, attendance and completion of elementary education by all children in the 6-14 age group. With this, India has moved forward to a rights based framework that casts a legal obligation on the Central and State Governments to implement this fundamental child right as enshrined in the Article 21A of the Constitution, in accordance with the provisions of the RTE Act. (*Op. cit.*)

The Key Features of RTE Act are:

- Right of children to free and compulsory education till completion of elementary education in a neighborhood school.
- It clarifies that 'compulsory education' means obligation of the appropriate government to provide free elementary education and ensure compulsory admission, attendance and completion of elementary education to every child in the six to fourteen age group. (*Op. cit.*)
- It signifies 'Free' means that no child shall be liable to pay any kind

of fee or charges or expenses which may prevent him or her from pursuing and completing elementary education.

- It makes provisions for an illiterate child to be admitted to an age appropriate class.
- It specifies the duties and responsibilities of appropriate Governments, local authority and parents in providing free and compulsory education, and sharing of financial and other responsibilities between the Central and State Governments. (*Op. cit.*)
- It lays down the norms and standards relating to: Pupil Teacher Ratios (PTRs), buildings and infrastructure, school-working days, teacher-working hours etc.
- It provides for rational deployment of teachers by ensuring that the specified pupil teacher ratio is maintained for each school, thus ensuring that there is no urban-rural imbalance in teacher postings.
- It also provides for prohibition of teachers for non-educational work, other than census, elections to local authority, state legislatures and parliament, and disaster relief.
- It provides for appointment of trained teachers, i.e. teachers with the requisite entry and academic qualifications.
- It prohibits (a) physical punishment and mental harassment; (b) screening procedures for admission of children; (c) capitation fee; (d) private tuition by teachers and (e) running of schools without recognition, (*Op. cit.*).
- It provides for development of curriculum in consonance with the values enshrined in the Constitution, and which would ensure the all-round development of the child, building on the child's knowledge, potentiality and talent and making the child free of fear, trauma and anxiety through a system of child friendly and child centered learning (*Op. cit.*).

2.3 Women's Empowerment for a Culture of Peace and Non-Violence

"Women give life and appreciate life…they are organically against war, and they can really save the world if they are permitted to play an equally active part in government".—Tatyana Mamonova

2.3.1 Introduction

Peace is pre-requisite to lasting progress and sustainable development on our lovable Earth. It is a great challenge for both men and women to achieve it. In the world scenario, it is observed that women are neglected in all respects due to dominating nature of men. This is the general mindset of common masses. But our ancient culture teaches us, "*Yatra naryastu pujyante, Tatra ramunte devata.*" It means—where women is worshiped, Gods presence is there. The promotion of women to key positions in governments, municipalities, educational institutions, and as leaders in the society is barely needed. Then it will create a new PCS. It will not only abate the violence against them, but also gradually eliminate it. Furthermore, their contribution to the building of a World beyond War and Violence, would contribute to the process of sustainable development on our planet and to the wellbeing of the whole of humanity.

In this beautiful planet both women and men are like fruits and flowers of a single plant. Each has great significance. None should be neglected. By virtue of their biological and cultural characteristics women are in a unique position. They can carry out the task of peace creating culture easily. Women are good at creating literature and the arts, and at promoting peace values and peace culture. Women are more than half the citizens of the world. Researchers report that there is a close link between gender and the yearning for a culture of peace. In our new era of globalisation, it is necessary for women to be equal partners with men in the building of a world beyond war and violence.

There are several international organisations, NGOs, frameworks and treaties, recognizing the critical role that women play in the promotion and strengthening of peace worldwide. The importance of the "Action Plan on Women, Peace and Security" including building a culture of peace and culture for development, has great significance. Intercultural dialogue can enhance in achieving and building peace. UNESCO emphasised on the safeguarding of the gender inequality and overcoming cultural barriers that generate actions of violence against women (VAW).

What is Culture?

Participants at the workshop of UNESCO recognised that culture is not static; that it is always changing. According to the participant responses, culture can be defined as a way of life, clarifying who we are, our identity, religion and shared history. Culture ascribes the roles that each member in a community plays and the roles that men and women play. It provides a sense of belonging. Culture includes arts, dances and sports. The participants also agreed that land and identity are interlinked, and together define the governance system in communities, the relations between members of communities and between men and women. (UNESCO, 2013, p. 3)

Cultural Barriers to Women

There are several cultural barriers observed by women of different countries. Some of them are as following:

- Women are taught to be uncomfortable speaking in public settings then men;

- It is the common views that women are nurturers, neither decision-makers nor leaders;
- Men are more dominating than women;
- Cultural norms, taboos are mainly in favour of men;
- Women don't want to move away from comfort zone;
- Cultural relationships and gender roles are often confusing;
- Generally women are shy in nature.

Using Culture for Preventive Action

The following preventive actions may be taken for safeguard of women in society.

- Organizing awareness programmes for women protection;
- Employment of women can protect them;
- We can use media for security of women;
- Workshops and professional development;
- They can perform the activities like: dance, song and drama to maintain their livelihood;
- Change the responsibilities in some activities like: weddings, birthdays and funerals;
- In Indian family as custom women eats after eating of all family members;
- The family can help to solve problems of women;
- Home community provides security and safety to women;
- Brother and sister relationship—in India, brother protects sisters;
- Policies and laws can protect them.

2.3.2 Understanding Gender Equality

It is recognised that gender equality is achieved when a society provides the same opportunities, outcomes, rights and obligations in all spheres of life to both men and women. Equality exists when men and women are able to share equally in the distribution of power and influence, have equal opportunities for financial independence through work or through setting up businesses and enjoy equal access to education. To empower women there must be a focus on identifying and giving women more autonomy to manage their own lives. Women's empowerment is vital to sustainable development and the realisation of human rights for all.

There are different layers of discrimination and inequalities in all spheres of family life, which commonly results in a dictatorship within the family. The opinions of women and young people are generally not given much consideration. Communities reinforce traditional gender roles through the use of consensus, hierarchical structures and maintaining the status quo. Women often maintain community peace and harmony. Women often have inferior roles in the workplace. At all levels the abuse of power occurs.

Achieving Gender Equality Requires

Achieving gender equality requires several factors. Some of them have been pointed out below:

- Increasing access to education and through a stronger emphasis on values, gender equality and building positive cultural models;
- Increasing the education provided to each girl and boy will increase their understanding of complex social issues and improve their opportunities for economic empowerment.
- The introduction of specific content on gender equality, positive family and community relationships, legal literacy, human rights and peace would further strengthen young people's understanding and ability to become equal partners as men and women.
- Improved economic opportunities for women that enable a greater degree of economic independence;
- A more gender responsive system of justice: This involves supporting women's opportunities to access justice services and systems of support for victims.
- Legislative changes are required to ensure that women have equal rights in all spheres of life;
- Raising awareness among women and the wider community about their rights and providing legal, physical and emotional support to women who have suffered abuse and violence.
- Providing women with a better understanding of their reproductive rights, access to reproductive health services;
- To pay special attention to gender equality and to be consistent with international human rights instruments such as CEDAW.

Proposed Actions for Gender Equality and Peace

Experts in global level have given following proposed actions that can be taken to achieve the gender equality.

- Harmonisation of regional (e.g. peace and security regional action plan) and national plans;
- Continued support and strengthening of efforts to improve gender equality, peace building and non-violence;
- Increase efforts to raise awareness among rural women, through targeting women's leaders and networks in villages;
- Support capacity building training on human rights, peace building and gender equality for: village leaders, regional leaders, and women's leaders;

- Utilize a range of different strategies and media to ensure that awareness-raising efforts reach women and men from all walks of life;
- Improve monitoring of student sex ratios;
- Document and promote comprehensive models for integration of gender equality within whole education systems (policy, infrastructure, curriculum, teacher training);
- Improve financial and legal literacy in the formal curriculum;
- Strengthen and expand programmes on women in the informal sector, including markets and creative and cultural industries;
- Develop a strategic approach to supporting women's economic empowerment;
- Strengthen legislation that protects and promotes equal rights of men and women in all spheres of life;
- Strengthen service provision, particularly access to justice and access to protection;
- Improve access to services in remote and rural areas and in countries where these are less developed;
- Develop capacity of women and men field workers involved in documentation of cultural practices and expressions;
- Build capacity in cultural institutions and regional and national authorities on culture and sports, to integrate themes on EVAW and gender equality into their art and sports events;
- Engage communities and religious leaders in identifying and making decisions relating to transmission of intangible cultural heritage to future generations based on the principles of human rights and gender equality;
- Countries to share experiences through region-wide information and networking activities as well as periodic reporting of the ICH Convention.

2.3.3 Women and Peace Education

Women are the major educators of the children at home, and continue to be so as they grow up.

Researchers suggest that "boys are particular targets of aggressive marketing of guns and other violent toys, and are more desensitised to aggressive content than are girls. Children's Television and Media programmes are inundated with violent content, reinforced by stereotypic sex-role behaviour." All this has to be drastically changed.

"Education worldwide today is mostly run by women teachers, and this can provide an important channel for the revolution needed in the creation and establishment of a powerful and effective Peace Culture System (PCS) in schools. The boom and expanding dimensions of communication technology, at which women are so good, can offer various new opportunities and directions for the promotion of a new PCS that would include peace studies, literature, and education. In the framework of the PCS, international co-operation and cross-disciplinary research, promoted by electronic technology and information services, can indeed greatly enrich peace education."

Recognizing the importance of this new trend, UNESCO convened a conference on "The Impact of Information and Communication Technologies on Teaching and Teachers," (Khvilon, Patru, 1997), in order to strengthen international co-operation in pursuit of peace and international understanding. More conferences of this kind should be convened, and special attention should be paid to the possibilities of peace culture, literature and the arts in pursuit of the development of global peace. The links and partnerships between the teachers, both women and men that are created through such conferences, promote multicultural views, based on understanding and cooperation. Teachers and youths participating in such intercultural projects, acquire the potential to move beyond narrow ethnic and group identities, and acquire a wider knowledge and assume a new additional identification, as global citizens, and as promoters of peace culture.

2.3.4 Women in their Pursuit of Peace

There have been great changes in recent years, such as the advancement of girls and women in education and in all walks of life, including in the arts. There is a need at the start of this new millennium, for a different, modern view of education and culture, which would include equality of women and men, and the creation of new peace values and norms, in addition to the transfer and transmission of important knowledge from one generation to the next. In this new PCS modern framework and agenda, peace should be considered as a central value and should inspire and influence all aspects of culture, education, and of life.

The study of peace culture would demonstrate to young people, as well as to adults, that it is otherwise, and it should be applied to all subjects. In the teaching of history, for example, due attention should be given to the policies that lead to the successful conclusion of Peace Treaties, and not merely and mainly concentrate on the waging of the wars, as is often the mode in the present times. The two sides of the conflicts should be presented in an authentic and convincing way, and non-violent means should be taught on how to resolve conflicts. Historical novels are a very good vehicle to present peaceful conflict resolution, in a convincing manner… In the study of literature, lives of heroines and heroes, such as Mahatma Gandhi and Martin Luther King, who have advanced the cause of peace, and the creation of the culture of peace, should be extensively studied, and presented as models, both in educational curricula, and through cultural programmes and films for the wider public. One of the possible examples is the peace heroine, Thea Wolf, who was a woman of many admirable qualities. She succeeded in saving many lives from the Nazi Holocaust, through the Hospital in Alexandria, with the aid of Egyptian officials, such as the port authorities, and the police.

Women's literature and organisations, point out that the attitude towards education and culture, which is used and absorbed on a daily basis, have an important effect on the society as a whole, for the dilemmas that confront the educational and cultural systems are a microcosm of the contradictions and struggles of the whole of society. The promotion of a Culture of Peace and an innovative and revolutionary PCS, through education, is therefore of central importance in trying to establish the dynamics that mark the interplay between society and peace.*

Women and the Innovative Peace Culture System (PCS)

In modern time, the new PCS should be largely propagated through the electronic media, mainly TV, Cinema, Internet and Radio. The powerful satellites, such as the WSPN—the Women's World TV by Satellite Peace Network and Internet programmes, literature, films and the arts, that can become important factors for the promotion of moral, ethical and democratic values. Peace culture, peace literature and peace films and art, are means for fostering consciousness and sensitivity to the shortcomings and deficiencies in the world, as well as promoting the willingness to take creative action to build a better world.

Culture is important at all ages and to all classes in our global village, and even when the cultures vary widely, there are many features, which apply to all of them. One of the most important requirements is to understand the necessity of establishing a cultural Agenda that excludes violence, and promotes a culture of peace that would ensure the Sustainability of the life on earth. In the framework of the new PCS, departments of Literary Peace Studies should be nationally and internationally established and empowered. These should promote the publication of Peace Literature periodicals and journals, including Electronic Peace Journals, such as the IFLAC Pave Peace daily Digest at www.iflac.com. It is also important to establish "peace museums," as part of the PCS educational system, all over the world, which would organize, exhibit and present to the wide public the fruits of peace research, art, films and literature, as well as hold public lectures and symposiums on the development of the global peace culture. There are more than a hundred such museums already established in Japan, and other places in the world.

In the framework of the innovative PCS, there should be a wide distribution of grants for peace research and the encouragement of the writing

---

* Aharoni, Ada, Peace, *Women in Pursuit of Peace,* Literature, and Art—Vol. I.

of peace literature, film-scripts, and plays, as well as the organizing of Peace Drama competitions, awards, and prizes that would have an advantageous and high payoff.

Participation of Women in the Culture of Peace

UN Women Deputy Executive Director Lakshmi Puri at the High-Level Forum on the Culture of Peace, at UN Headquarters in New York, 9 September 2014 addresses as following.

The role and contributions of women and youth to the Culture of Peace has great significance. The women and young people represent the majority of the global population. Also women and young people are key drivers of the radical change of mindsets, institutions and cultures.

Women and their empowerment are crucial to advancing the culture of peace in all its sectors—education, sustainable economic and social development, human rights and equality, democratic participation, advocacy based on true knowledge but also wisdom, tolerance and understanding at all levels—in the family, community, country, region and globally. As the United Nations Security Council resolution 1325 and other Women, Peace and Security resolutions affirm, women must not only be protected from war and the violence unleashed thereby, but they must be seen as agents of conflict prevention, of peacemaking, and as reconcilers in peace building in post-conflict.

As stated by the Secretary-General (2014): "Through education, we teach children not to hate. Through education, we raise leaders who act with wisdom and compassion. Through education, we establish a true, lasting culture of peace." The women as mothers, grandmothers, and other family members often being the first teachers of children, can play a vital role in educating young people to value peace and not war. As Jane Addams said: "Peace is not merely an absence of war, it's a nurture of human life and, in time, this nurture will do away with war as a natural process."

As the global leader on gender equality and the empowerment of women, UN Women strives to promote women's ability to strengthen peace and dialogue within their communities. At all levels, they work to amplify the voices of women in peace activities and facilitate their access to peace and security decision-making. UN Women are supporting local organisations to build referral services and networks for survivors, such as reproductive health care, access to justice, livelihood support and psychosocial counselling. They also focus on improving the access to education of girls and all young people, providing a secure environment for them to learn, breaking down gender stereotypes in school curricula and teacher training programmes, advancing understanding, tolerance and solidarity, and ultimately spreading a culture of gender equality which will lead to a culture of peace.

For the goal on achieving gender equality and women's empowerment, these include targets on:

- Ending all forms of discrimination against all women and girls everywhere;
- Eliminating all forms of violence against all women and girls;
- Eliminating all harmful practices, such as child, early and forced marriage, and female genital mutilations;
- Recognizing and valuing unpaid care and domestic work, and promoting shared responsibility within the household and the family;
- Ensuring women's participation and leadership at all levels of decision-making in political, economic and public life;
- Ensuring universal access to sexual and reproductive health and reproductive rights;
- Undertake reforms to give women equal rights to economic resources (land, property, financial services, inheritance and natural resources);
- Enhance the use of information and communication technologies (ICTs); and
- Adopt and strengthen sound policies and legislation.

There can be no human rights, peace or sustainable development without gender equality and the realisation of women's and girls' rights. We need to put policy into practice.

2.3.5 Women's Empowerment

What is Women Empowerment?

'Women empowerment' in simple words can be understood as giving power to women to decide for their own lives or inculcating such abilities in them so that they could be able to find their rightful place in the society.

According to the United Nations, women's empowerment mainly has five components:

(i) Generating women's sense of self-worth;
(ii) Women's right to have and to determine their choices;
(iii) Women's right to have access to equal opportunities and all kinds of resources;
(iv) Women's right to have the power to regulate and control their own lives, within and outside the home; and
(v) Women's ability to contribute in creating a more just social and economic order.

Thus, women empowerment is nothing but recognition of women's basic human rights and creating an environment where they are treated as equals to men.

CEDAW requires two types of action by the state to achieve substantive equality in all spheres: (1) actions to achieve equality of opportunity between men and women, and (2) actions to correct the inequalities of power between men and women. The concept of substantive equality arose out of the recognition that formal equality may not be sufficient to ensure that women enjoy the same rights as men. CEDAW therefore demands that to achieve substantive equality it is necessary to take into account not only the biological differences but also the conditions generated by the social construction of gender that produce inequalities or disadvantages for women.

It is noted that the arts and culture sector encourages the development and dissemination of information, research and knowledge about women's fundamental roles in culture, production of cultural expressions and history. Women's stories, traditional knowledge and dynamism in culture and arts, all elements that provide meaning to individuals and communities, should be sufficiently promoted.

Some Strategies for Women Empowerment

The researchers in international level have highlighted certain strategies of women empowerment, which are given below:

(i) *Gender equality in the education sector:* Education plays a critical role in addressing some of the cultural barriers to strengthening the achievement of gender equality. The Ministry of Education (ME) highlighted some of the work that is in progress to improve gender equality in its education sector. The ME works with the ILO, UN WOMEN, UNESCO and UNICEF to integrate gender equality and the empowerment of women in its education curriculum.

(ii) *Reaching a larger group of stakeholders through creative arts and sports to address gender equality:* Formal education is one of the means to reach a large audience to advocate and raise awareness on the issue of gender equality. A large audience can also be reached through the use of creative arts as a way to communicate this important message, including through writing, music and paintings. Sports are a further area that, due to their popularity, can be harnessed to promote gender equality.

(iii) *Linking education strategies to broader peace education strategies to bridge the cultural barriers and address some of the issues relating to the empowerment of women*

(iv) *Legal literacy for students and communities:* The need to integrate advocacy materials on gender related issues, including justice, into the school system and the larger community was identified as a priority to underpin change. Efforts to raise awareness of women's rights and the laws which affect them need to be stepped up. This can be achieved through creating community advocates who undertake legal literacy training and then act as community outreach officers for their local communities.

(v) *Women's access to resources when separated or divorced:* It was also highlighted that family law should ensure that during a separation there is recognition of women's contributions to marriage so that these are taken into account when making any settlement.

(vi) *Using a cultural approach of reconciliation for cases of VAWG:* There is value in the use of reconciliation processes to mend relationships in communities affected by violence against women and girls (VAWG), however, that reconciliation processes should not be used as a barrier to anyone seeking legal justice nor to remove victims' choices in how they want to deal with a situation.

(vii) *Access to services for victims and survivors from outside urban centers through community focal points:* Experiences have shown, however, that some services can be made available through community facilitators, village committees or local leaders who have undergone training to be able to provide such services. This type of approach can greatly expand the services available for victims and survivors.

To design, promote and strengthen a culture of peace at the country and regional levels, several discussions were held in collaboration among the United Nations Educational Scientific and Cultural Organisation (UNESCO), the United Nations Entity for Gender Equality and the Empowerment of Women (UN WOMEN) and the United Nations Development Programme (UNDP) Regional Centers.

The UN discussion group recognize and support the existing international, regional and national instruments, strategies and frameworks that promote women's empowerment and a culture of peace and non-violence, which include:

- United Nations Security Council Resolutions 1325, 1820, 1889, 1960;
- The Convention on the Elimination of All Forms of Discrimination against Women (CEDAW);
- The Convention on the Rights of the Child (CRC);
- The UNESCO Convention for the Safeguarding of the Intangible Cultural Heritage;
- The Commonwealth Plan of Action for Gender Equality (WAMM-CPoA/2005-2015);
- The UN Secretary General's Seven Point Action Plan on Women's Participation in Peace building; and
- The UN Declaration on a Culture of Peace.

Role of UN for Women Empowerment and Culture of Peace

The United Nations was founded after the Second World War by countries committed to maintaining international peace and security, developing friendly relations among nations and promoting social progress, better living standards and human rights. Today, more than six decades later, these goals remain equally relevant.

There are many threats to peace and security, emanating from mindsets of intolerance and hatred, greed, terrorism, abject poverty, food insecurity and climate vulnerability. Women and girls are at greater risk of other threats to human security, such as sexual exploitation, disproportionate financial hardship in difficult economic times, and in some cases trafficking and prostitution. While many of these risks occur at the time of the conflict or instability, because of dislocations within the community, there is also increased domestic and family violence in post-conflict situations. Also in times of natural disasters, women and girls are more prone to sexual violence, for example related to displacement, due to the loss of their homes or traditional protection mechanisms through family or clan structures.

The UN is very aware of the high vulnerability of women and girls in these situations. The UN, at the global level, has adopted and passed several declarations and resolutions aimed at world peace and recognizing the critical role that women play in the promotion and strengthening a culture of peace worldwide. These international commitments and obligations include the United Nations Security Council Resolution 1325, 1820, 1889, 1960; the Convention on the Elimination of Discrimination Against Women (CEDAW), the Convention on the Rights of the Child (CRC); the Beijing Platform for Action, the Commonwealth Women Affairs Ministers Meeting Commonwealth Plan of Action for Gender Equality (WAMM-CPoA/2005-2015); the UN Secretary General's Seven Point Action Plan on Women's Participation in Peace building and the UN Declaration on a Culture of Peace. It is also pertinent to mention about N-Peace, which is a multi-country network of peace advocates in Asia seeking to advance Women, Peace and Security (WPS) issues.

The UN Declaration on a Culture of Peace recognizes that "the fuller development of a culture of peace is integrally linked to promoting democracy, development and universal respect for and observance of all human rights and fundamental freedoms; strengthening democratic institutions and ensuring full participation in the development process". The declaration also challenges the UN system to continue to play a critical role in the promotion and strengthening of a culture of peace worldwide.

UN Security Council Resolution 1325 calls for greater participation and incorporation of women's unique perspectives in conflict prevention, peace building and reconstruction; and protection of women's and girls' human rights during conflict. It stresses the need for prevention of conflict and all forms of violence against women and girls in conflict and post-conflict situations. Also, it highlights the need to meet women's and girls' specific relief needs, and to ensure that women's capacities to act as agents in relief and recovery are reinforced and recognised. UN Security Council Resolutions 1325, 1820, 1888, 1889 and 1960 provide a useful framework, ensuring that due consideration is given to gender equality and addressing violence against women, girls and boys.

In its essence, the culture of peace and non-violence is a commitment to peace building and mediation; to conflict prevention and resolution; to peace education and education for non-violence; and to tolerance, acceptance, mutual respect, intercultural and interfaith dialogue and reconciliation. A culture of peace will generate a mindset that is a prerequisite for the transition from force to reason, from conflict and violence to dialogue and peace. Global efforts towards peace and reconciliation can only succeed with a collective approach built on trust, dialogue and collaboration. We need to recognize the fact that women have a major role to play in promoting the culture of peace, particularly in strife-torn societies, and in bringing about lasting peace and reconciliation.

2.3.6 Women Empowerment in India

Need and Significance

In the world history women are the target of varied types of violence and discriminatory practices done by men. Due to centuries of domination and discrimination done by men over women; need of women empowerment arouse. Its influence in India is clearly visible.There are various types of customs, traditions and practices prevailed in our country India. Here it is a moral that, "*Yatra naryastu pujyate, tatra ramyante devatah.*" We consider female as goddesses; we love to our mothers, daughters, sisters, wives and other female relatives or friends. But sometime, some people torture women in this country.

Indian people have great faith in all kinds of religious beliefs. In every religion women are given a special place and every religion teaches us to treat women with respect and dignity. But somehow the society has become so complex that various types of ill practices, both physical and mental, against women have been prevailing for long time. For example: sati pratha, dowry system, parda pratha, female infanticide, wife burning, sexual violence, sexual harassment at work place, domestic violence and other varied kinds of ill practices; all such acts consist of physical as well as mental harassments.The reasons for such behaviour against women are many but the most important one are the male superiority complex and patriarchal system of society. Though to eliminate these ill practices and discrimination against women various constitutional and legal rights are there, but in reality it has less impact. Several self-help groups and NGOs are working in this direction; also women themselves are breaking the societal barriers and achieving great heights in all dimensions: political, social and economic. But society as a whole has still not accepted women as being equal to men and crimes or abuses against women are still on the rise. For that to change, the society's age-old deep-rooted mind set needs to be changed through social conditioning and awareness programs.

Constitution of India and Women Empowerment

The Constitution of India is one of the finest valuable equality documents in the world. It provides provisions to secure equality in general and gender equality in particular. Various articles in the Constitution safeguard women's rights by putting them at par with men socially, politically and economically. The Preamble, the Fundamental Rights, DPSPs and other constitutional provisions provide several general and special safeguards to secure women's human rights.

Preamble: The Preamble to the Constitution of India assures justice, social, economic and political; equality of status and opportunity and dignity to the individual. Thus it treats both men and women equal.

Fundamental Rights: The policy of women empowerment is well entrenched in the Fundamental Rights enshrined in our Constitution. For instance:

- Article 14 ensures to women the right to equality.
- Article 15(1) specifically prohibits discrimination on the basis of sex.
- Article 15(3) empowers the State to take affirmative actions in favour of women.
- Article 16 provides for equality of opportunity for all citizens in matters relating to employment or appointment to any office.

Directive Principles of State Policy: Directive principles of State Policy also contains important provisions regarding women empowerment and it is the duty of the government to apply these principles while making laws or formulating any policy. Though these are not justiciable in the Court but these are essential for governance nonetheless. Some of them are:

- Article 39(a) provides that the State to direct its policy towards securing for men and women equally the right to an adequate means of livelihood.
- Article 39(d) mandates equal pay for equal work for both men and women.
- Article 42 provides that the State to make provision for securing just and humane conditions of work and for maternity relief.

Fundamental Duties: Fundamental duties are enshrined in Part IV-A of the Constitution and are positive duties for the people of India to follow. It also contains a duty related to women's rights: Article 51 (A) (e) expects from the citizen of the country to promote harmony and the spirit of common brotherhood amongst all the people of India and to renounce practices derogatory to the dignity of women.

Other Constitutional Provisions

Through 73rd and 74th Constitutional Amendment of 1993, a very important political right has been given to women which is a landmark in the direction of women empowerment in India. With this amendment women were given 33.33 per cent reservation in seats at different levels of elections in local governance i.e. at Panchayat, Block and Municipality elections. Thus it can be seen that these Constitutional provisions are very empowering for women and the State is duty bound to apply these principles in taking policy decisions as well as in enacting laws.

Some Laws in Support of Women for Security and Empowerment

Here is the list of some specific laws which were enacted by the Parliament in order to fulfil Constitutional obligation of women empowerment:

1. The Equal Remuneration Act, 1976.
2. The Dowry Prohibition Act, 1961.
3. The Immoral Traffic (Prevention) Act, 1956.
4. The Maternity Benefit Act, 1961.
5. The Medical Termination of Pregnancy Act, 1971.
6. The Commission of Sati (Prevention) Act, 1987.
7. The Prohibition of Child Marriage Act, 2006.
8. The Pre-Conception and Pre-Natal Diagnostic Techniques (Regulation and Prevention of Misuse) Act, 1994.
9. The Sexual Harassment of Women at Work Place (Prevention and Protection) Act, 2013.

International Commitments of India for Women Empowerment

India is a part to various International conventions and treaties which are committed to secure equal rights of women. One of the most important among them is the Convention on Elimination of All Forms of Discrimination against Women (CEDAW), ratified by India in 1993. Other important International instruments for women empowerment are: The Mexico Plan of Action (1975), the Nairobi Forward Looking Strategies (1985), the Beijing Declaration as well as the Platform for Action (1995) and the Outcome Document adopted by the UNGA Session on Gender Equality and Development mad Peace for the 21st century, titled "Further actions and initiatives to implement the Beijing Declaration and the Platform for Action". All these have been whole-heartedly endorsed by India for appropriate follow up.

These various national and International commitments, laws and policies notwithstanding women's situation on the ground have still not improved satisfactorily. Varied problems related to women are still subsisting; female infanticide is growing, dowry is still prevalent, domestic violence against women is practiced; sexual harassment at workplace and other heinous sex crimes against women are on the rise.

Though, economic and social condition of women has improved in a significant way but the change is especially visible only in metro cities or in urban areas; the situation is not much improved in semi-urban areas and villages. This disparity is due to lack of education and job opportunities and negative mind set of the society which does not approve girls' education even in 21st century.

Government Policies and Schemes for Women Empowerment

In the year 2001, the Government of India launched a **National Policy for Empowerment of Women.** The specific objectives of the policy are as follows:

- Creation of an environment through positive economic and social policies for full development of women to enable them to realize their full potential.
- Creation of an environment for enjoyments of all human rights and fundamental freedom by women on equal basis with men in all political, economic, social, cultural and civil spheres.
- Providing equal access to participation and decision making of women in social political and economic life of the nation.
- Providing equal access to women to health care, quality education at all levels, career and vocational guidance, employment, equal remuneration, occupational health and safety, social security and public life etc.
- Strengthening legal systems aimed at elimination of all forms of discrimination against women.
- Changing societal attitudes and community practices by active participation and involvement of both men and women.
- Mainstreaming a gender perspective in the development process.
- Elimination of discrimination and all forms of violence against women and the girl child.
- Building and strengthening partnerships with civil society, particularly women's organisations.

The Ministry of Women and Child Development is the nodal agency for all matters pertaining to welfare, development and empowerment of women. It has evolved schemes and programmes for their benefit. These schemes are spread across a very wide spectrum such as women's need for shelter, security, safety, legal aid, justice, information, maternal health, food, nutrition etc., as well as their need for economic sustenance through skill development, education and access to credit and marketing.

Various schemes of the Ministry are like: *Swashakti, Swayamsidha, STEP*, KVV and *Swawlamban* enable economic empowerment. Working Women Hostels and Crèches provide support services. *Swadhar* and Short Stay Homes provide protection and rehabilitation to women in difficult circumstances. The Ministry also supports autonomous bodies like National Commission, Central Social Welfare Board and *Rashtriya Mahila Kosh* which work for the welfare and development of women. Economic sustenance of women through skill development, education and access to credit and marketing is also one of the areas where the Ministry has special focus.

2.4 Citizenship—Socialism, Secularism and Democracy

2.4.1 Citizenship—Socialism

From an educational perspective removing poverty and inequality are the critical issues that socialism needs to address in the Indian context. The peace approach to education must engage with these challenges. Inequalities are reinforced and perpetuated by a hierarchical worldview that legitimizes them. Education, conceived and implemented from such a perspective, could perpetuate inequality and the dis-empowerment of the underprivileged unless corrective measures are integrated into the educational enterprise. Here cognition of education as a fundamental right for all children below the age of 14 is a timely remedial step. The holistic perspective of peace is essential if the full scope of this potential revolution is to be appropriated. Poverty is eminently eradicable and this needs to be deemed a national priority. Some areas that need urgent attention include the need to:

- Minimize the disparities between the various streams of school education, as recommended by the Kothari Commission (1964-66);
- Standardize educational infrastructure and technology nationwide, especially keeping in mind the appalling urban-rural divide;
- Optimize the competence, motivation, and skills of teachers;
- Create favourable economic and social conditions to contain and gradually eradicate school dropout rates in rural and tribal areas;
- Priorities the education of the girl child;
- Eradicate traditional stigma and prejudices in respect of caste, poverty, and gender; and
- Propagate, through textbook writing and learning experiences, values like respect for the inherent and equal worth of all human beings and their rights and dignity irrespective of caste, colour, gender, economic status, and religion.

2.4.2 Citizenship and Secularism

The word 'secular' was incorporated into the Preamble of the Indian Constitution only in 1976, through the 42nd Amendment. But the similar idea was incorporated in our constitution before. For example, Article 14 enshrines the right to equality. This is further reinforced by Articles 15 and 16 that protect all citizens against discrimination based on religion and caste. Articles 19 and 21 guarantee freedom of speech and expression to all citizens. Article 27 prohibits the state from being partisan or partial towards any religion. Article 25 gives to all citizens' freedom of conscience, and the right to "practice, preach and propagate" there. The specific issues in respect of secularism that education for peace needs to address in the Indian context are:

- Respect for diversity;
- Scientific temper and the spirit of critical inquiry as opposed to blind faith;
- Consolidation of our common identity as Indians, fortified by a shared vision for India so as to minimize divisive sentiments and prejudices;
- Shift from exclusive religious loyalty to inclusive spiritual values.

2.4.3 Citizenship and Democracy

Education builds citizenship. A good citizen must be a good nation builder and a follower of democracy. In other way, democracy supplement for efficient citizen. Democracy shares views with each other with peaceful co-existence. Every citizen wants this. Hence citizenship and democracy are supplement to each other. Democracy is the best system available for managing conflicts. Differences of opinion, belief, ideology, culture, and so on, are a natural part of every society. Conflicts emerge from the disharmony of differences. We may choose, however, to approach these conflicts from a perspective of peace or from a perspective of violence. The solution is the eradication of conflict by the assimilation or elimination of those who are different from the dominant group. The peaceful solution involves developing respect for diversity or a positive attitude to difference, as well as engaging those who are different in a way that enables difference to co-exist without undermining the whole system.

Indian constitution directs through Article 29, religious and linguistic minorities are granted the right to preserve their identity and culture, and Article 30 confers on them the right to establish and administer institutions of their choice. It shows the development of which must be an educational priority for India. Education is basic to peoples' participation, which is the hallmark of democracy. Illiteracy disables democracy. Literacy in itself is not, however, sufficient to facilitate democratic participation. Peace is a pre-requisite for participation. Violence excludes and disables all, except those who wield power. In times of large-scale conflict or war, citizenship rights get deactivated. People can be empowered only in a state of peace. A democracy that fails to foster a culture of peace stands in danger of degenerating into dictatorship. Eradicating every kind of exclusion from the life, resources, and opportunities of the nation through education is a bottom-line peace agenda in democracy. Education for peace is a powerful and necessary means for this purpose. The major categories of exclusion are:

- *Poverty:* This is the factor responsible for gross inequalities between the various streams of education and high dropout rates in rural and tribal India. The gulf between the rich and the poor is further widening in the wake of LPG, and it is necessary to address poverty-related issues in education with urgency and courage.
- *Cast:* The caste system freezes our social capital and excludes millions of people from the march to progress. Various indices of under development such as social degradation and economic disempowerment, point directly to the tyranny of caste over our democratic culture. Education for peace can turn the eradication of the caste system into a peaceful revolution.
- *Gender:* The Convention on Elimination of All Forms of Discrimination against Women (CEDAW)—often described as an international Bill of Rights for women—defines discrimination against women as:

  "...any distinction, exclusion or restriction made on the basis of sex which has the effect or purpose of impairing or nullifying the recognition, enjoyment or exercise by women...on a basis of equality of men and women, of human rights and fundamental freedoms in the political, economic, social, cultural, civil or any other field." India is a party to the convention. We are, as such, obliged to promote a culture of gender justice. Even though various NGOs have done, and are doing, commendable work in this respect, we are still woefully short of bringing about the required systemic and attitudinal changes mandated by gender justice. Violence, vulgarity, and sex-related crimes are increasing. Women face insecurity and discrimination in the workplace, in the public space, and even at home. In many regions killing the female foetus, Bride burning and rapes are continuing. The work democratic logic underlying the Constitutional provisions for empowering minorities (refer Article 30 of the Indian Constitution). Making reasonable provisions to enable religious and linguistic minorities to preserve their culture and identity does not amount to 'minority appeasement' but provides for the health of democracy itself. Globally, a nation's commitment to the welfare and security of minorities is regarded as a mark of the robustness of its democratic culture.

2.5 Critical Thinking: Reasoning and Applying Wisdom and Co-operation

2.5.1 What is Critical Thinking?

According to Michael Scriven mad Richard Paul (1987), Critical thinking is the intellectually disciplined process of actively and skillfully conceptualizing, applying, analyzing, synthesizing, and/or evaluating information gathered from, or generated by, observation, experience, reflection, reasoning, or communication, as a guide to belief and action. In its exemplary form, it is based on universal intellectual values that transcend subject matter divisions: clarity, accuracy, precision, consistency, relevance, sound evidence, good reasons, depth, breadth, and fairness.

It entails the examination of those things implicit in all reasoning: purpose, problem; assumptions; concepts; empirical grounding; reasoning leading to conclusions; implications and consequences; objections from alternative viewpoints; and frame of reference. Critical thinking consists of various dimensions, issues, and purposes. Those are: scientific thinking, mathematical thinking, historical thinking, anthropological thinking, economic thinking, moral thinking, and philosophical thinking. *It is the awakening of the intellect to the study of itself.*

Critical thinking has two components: (i) a set of information and belief generating and processing skills, and (ii) the habit, based on intellectual commitment, of using those skills to guide behaviour. It varies according to the motivation underlying it. It may be used either in positive or negative way depends on the user. The development of critical thinking skills and dispositions is a life-long endeavour.

2.5.2 Conceptualisation of Critical Thinking

Further more, critical thinking is self-guided, self-disciplined thinking which attempts to reason at the highest level of quality in a fair-minded way. People who think critically consistently attempt to live rationally, reasonably, empathically. They are keenly aware of the inherently flawed nature of human thinking when left unchecked. They strive to diminish the power of their egocentric and socio-centric tendencies. They use the intellectual tools that critical thinking offers—concepts and principles that enable them to analyze, assess, and improve thinking. They work diligently to develop the intellectual virtues of intellectual integrity, intellectual humility, intellectual civility, intellectual empathy, intellectual sense of justice and confidence in reason. They realize that no matter how skilled they are as thinkers, they can always improve their reasoning abilities and they will at times fall prey to mistakes in reasoning, human irrationality, prejudices, biases, distortions, uncritically accepted social rules and taboos, self-interest, and vested interest (*op. cit.*) They strive to improve the world in whatever ways they can and contribute to a more rational, civilised society. At the same time, they recognize the complexities often inherent in doing so. They avoid thinking simplistically about complicated issues and strive to appropriately consider the rights and needs of relevant others. They recognize the complexities in developing as thinkers, and commit themselves to life-long practice toward self-improvement. They embody the Socratic principle: *The unexamined life is not worth living,* because they realize that many unexamined lives together result in an uncritical, unjust, dangerous world. (Linda Elder, Sept, 2007)

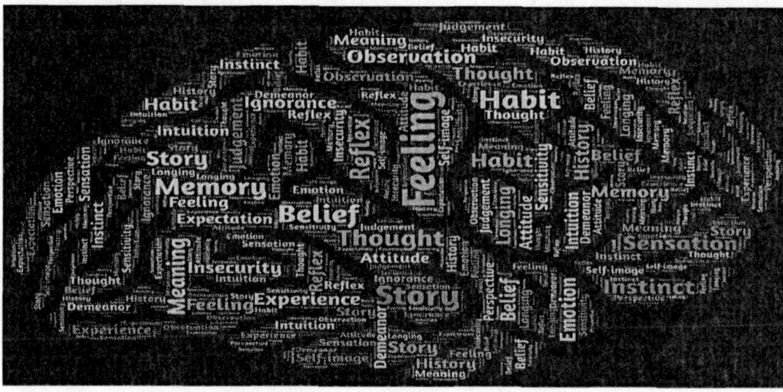

A Mapping of Critical Thinking

2.5.3 Why Critical Thinking?

A well cultivated critical thinker: raises vital questions and problems, formulating them clearly and precisely; gathers and assesses relevant information, using abstract ideas to interpret it effectively comes to well-reasoned conclusions and solutions, testing them against relevant criteria and standards; thinks open mindedly within alternative systems of thought, recognizing and assessing, as need be, their assumptions, implications, and practical consequences; and communicates effectively with others in figuring out solutions to complex problems. Critical thinking is, in short, self-directed, self-disciplined, self-monitored, and self-corrective thinking. It presupposes assent to rigorous standards of excellence and mindful command of their use. It entails effective communication and problem solving abilities and a commitment to overcome our native egocentrism and socio-centrism. (Taken from Richard Paul and Linda Elder, *The Miniature Guide to Critical Thinking Concepts and Tools,* Foundation for Critical Thinking Press, 2008)

2.5.4 Critical Thinking Defined by Edward Glaser

Edward Glaser (1941) defines critical thinking as follows "The ability to think critically, as conceived in this volume, involves three things: (1) an attitude of being disposed to consider in a thoughtful way the problems and subjects that come within the range of one's experiences, (2) knowledge of the methods of logical inquiry and reasoning, and (3) some skill in applying those methods. Critical thinking calls for a persistent effort to examine any belief or supposed form of knowledge in the light of the evidence that supports it and the further conclusions to which it tends. It also generally requires ability to recognize problems, to find workable means for meeting those problems, to gather and marshal pertinent information, to recognize unstated assumptions and values, to comprehend and use language with accuracy, clarity, and discrimination, to interpret data, to appraise evidence and evaluate arguments, to recognize the existence (or non-existence) of logical relationships between propositions, to draw warranted conclusions and generalisations, to put to test the conclusions and generalisations at which one arrives, to reconstruct one's patterns of beliefs on the basis of wider experience, and to render accurate judgments about specific things and qualities in everyday life. (Edward M. Glaser, *An Experiment in the Development of Critical Thinking,* Teacher's College, Columbia University, 1941)

Intelligence, knowledge, wisdom, discernment and good temperament are five distinct attributes a man or woman can possess. It is a common mistake to believe that they are interchangeable. They are not. Although they tend to be related, it is possible to have one without the others. How they interact with one another can determine the success or failure one experiences in life, to the extent we can control things, so it's important to learn how to maximize your advantages and mitigate your flaws by becoming self-aware.

Knowledge

Knowledge is pure, raw data and understanding of how something works. Knowledge is gained through study or experience. In some areas, such as statistics or facts, those with high analytical intelligence have an easier time acquiring it. For example; they read something once, understand it and add it to their database of information to draw upon in the future. In others, such as how to perform a trick play in basketball or a specific dance move in ballet, those with high body-kinesthetic intelligence will be able to pick it up and reproduce the required action with much less effort than their peers.

Whatever you ultimate goals are in life, acquire as much knowledge as possible because knowledge can trump intelligence in many, though not all, cases. If we run a steel mill and we can calculate our cost per tonnage more accurately than a competitor, it doesn't matter how smart he or she is, we have factual data that can lead to better, more optimised decisions.

Wisdom

Wisdom has long been recognised as a distinct, and unique, attribute that is rare among men. It has been personified and deified throughout all recorded history among most successful civilisations. Wisdom "is a deep understanding and realizing of people, things, events or situations, resulting in the ability to choose or act to consistently produce the optimum results with a minimum of time and energy. Wisdom is the ability to optimally (effectively and efficiently) apply perceptions and knowledge and so produce the desired results."

As philosophy defines it, wisdom is "making the best use of knowledge". If everyone had equal knowledge, the wisest person is the one who applied it in a way that got him what he wanted without a lot of work or effort. Put another way, wisdom is applying knowledge in the most optimal way to require the least amount of effort or expenditure on your part to achieve your desired goal. Wisdom is elusive. It is uncommon. Wisdom can trump intelligence and knowledge, though it is often heavily dependent upon the latter. Wisdom can be substantially augmented by a rational framework. The system proposed by Charlie Munger involving hanging your ideas on a latticework of pulled from the great disciplines in the hard and soft sciences has fundamentally altered the way.

Discernment

Discernment is "the ability to judge well". The word has taken on an inherent religious context over the past few centuries due to its use in scripture. Discernment is the still small voice inside that tells you when a course of action, which may appear wise, isn't quite right or that it would be damaging to your morality. Discernment can be summed up as knowing how to act in order to "avoid evil, do good", as most sources put it. By its very nature, discernment is tied inextricably to the moral underpinnings of a society. Consider that it is patently unacceptable in Christianity, Judaism and Islam to accept usury on lent money.

As Danny Morris and Chuck Colson wrote in *Discerning God's Will Together* "As important as the practices of discernment are, it would be improper to list them before the habit of discernment, because if the Holy Spirit has not been welcomed into the life of the discerner, practices of discernment will be empty and impotent. The habit of discernment constitutes a way of being, by which we are steeped in spirituality as a way of life…the habit of spirituality precedes the practices of discernment."

Temperament

Temperament is the master that drives the other four forces in life if left unchecked. Temperament is King, as it has the power to accelerate or demolish all efforts. The best definition is "the natural, default, innate bias toward action and thought" a person has. You know this already. Think of the people in your life. You know folks who have a natural state leaning toward happiness or depression, activist or victim, active or passive, pleasant or mean, selfish or generous, etc. You often hear family members say, "She's always been that way …" (Kennon, 2016)

There is a reason that so many of the people who are successful in certain fields are alike. The top scientists often have a lot of personality traits that are similar. That is because certain disciplines call for certain temperaments to be successful. Scientists with a bookish, insular, cerebral temperament are more likely to be successful because they would rather be thinking about chemistry and physics than tripping on acid at a rave party.

It doesn't matter how intelligent you are, how much knowledge you have, how deep your wisdom, or how powerful your discernment, if you have a natural temperament that inclines you to get your kicks by going out and getting drunk on the weekend, smoking yourself into an early grave, lying, cheating, stealing, or taking unnecessary risks, it is only a matter of time before you fail or die. Much of the success of the world's religions can be accounted for in the fact that they served as a mechanism for society to control those with ill-leaning temperaments.

It may be unfair, but there is a great deal of science that indicates temperament is the result of genetic brain chemistry. More specifically, scientists now know that temperament is heavily tied to the production of dopamine in the brain. People like me, who is perfectly content staying home and making a meal with friends and family on a Sunday afternoon have high levels of internal "happiness" drugs floating around in our heads. "When I see a beautiful pair of cufflinks, my heart rate accelerates, my voice rises, and my body temperature increases. I get an adrenaline rush and an emotional high."

Instead of whining about how unfair temperament is, find a way to overcome your own temperamental shortcomings and play to your strength. My brother, who is still deciding on his ultimate career, was wise enough to know that his temperament is sometimes inclined toward moodiness, so he doesn't want to become a doctor that has to deal with patients and "their stupid questions". If he goes into medicine, he would rather be a surgeon or something comparable where they have a highly skilled task to perform and then go on to the next item. (Joshua Kennon, (2016) *Philosophy*)

2.5.5 Reasoning and Applying Wisdom

Generally the human mind is always narrow and limited. So, constant effort is needed to widen it. An interesting reply to one readily brings others in its train and so the attentive child learns without effort much more than he usually does in classroom. The teacher should also teach him to enjoy good reading matter which is both instructive and attractive. In order to increase the suppleness and comprehensiveness of his mind, many varied topics and a single subject approached in various ways are needed, so that the child understands in a practical manner that there are many ways of facing the same intellectual problem, of considering it and solving it.

Sri Aurobindo identified different faculties of mind and their activities as following.

(i) *The Faculty of Imagination:* Imagination is a capacity to project oneself outside realised things and towards things realizable, and then to draw them by the projection. It has three functions, the forming of mental images, the power of creating thoughts, images and imitation or new combinations of existing thoughts and images, the appreciation of the soul in things, beauty, charm, greatness, hidden suggestiveness, the emotion.

(ii) *Training of the Logical faculty:* Logical reason should be trained by teaching the science of logic. The first step is to make the young mind interest itself in drawing inferences from the facts, training causes and effect. It should then be led on to notice its successes and its failures and the reason of the success and failure. The incorrectness, the carelessness in accepting a conclusion, the haste in drawing conclusion, open to doubt, prejudice should be rejected. Like this mind can be trained to reason as correctly as possible, by which the chances of error will be minimised.

(iii) *Exercise of Reason:* In man him-self there is a higher capacity called reason which is able to look at things calmly, coolly, reasonably. It develops judgment, vision, objectivity and the same time it has a very healthy action upon one's character. It helps one to avoid the ridiculousness of giving way to one's nerves and lets one behave like a reasonable person. A person who has established within himself a state of active, clear reasoning can face attacks of all kinds, emotional attacks or any trials whatever. The man without reason is a cork on a stormy sea. As long as there is an ego, there are desires, impulses, passions and preferences, attraction and repulsions, etc., reason is altogether useful. To be free from suggestion and adverse influences, one can must be exclusively under the influence of the divine.

Reason is a very respectful person. It has its limitations and prejudices. It keeps one from making a fool of one-self. It is neither the ideal nor the summit. It is only a kind of control and a guide for leading a good life, it keeps one from extravagances, excesses, inordinate passions, and above all from those impulsive actions which may lead to the abyss. One must be quite free from ego and perfectly surrendered to the Divine will be able to do safely without reason.

2.5.6 Organisation of One's Idea around a Central Idea

(i) Intellect and Pure Reason

The intellect is an instrument of expression and action. It is like an intermediary between the true knowledge and realisation here below, whose seat is in the higher regions above the mind. The intellect or the mind gives the form to the vital in the dynamism and life power and the material comes in last.

Intellect gives right thoughts, right conclusion, right views on things and persons, right indications about their conduct or course of action. It puts ideas in the form of thoughts, gathering and organizing the thoughts at the same time. When one is in contact with one's reason with the rational center of the intellect, the pure reason, it is a powerful control over all vital impulses. All that comes from the vital world can be very firmly controlled by it and used in a disciplined and organised action.

(ii) Ideals, Thoughts and Knowledge

Above the thoughts there are pure ideas; thoughts serve to express pure ideas. And knowledge is well above the domain of pure ideas. Pure idea is the translation of knowledge. Knowledge can be obtained only by total identification.

The best is to keep silent and look well at things, and little by little you make notes within yourself and keep the record without pronouncing any judgment. When you are able to keep all that within you, quietly, without agitation and present it very calmly before the highest part of your consciousness, with an attempt to maintain an attentive silence, and wait, then perhaps, slowly, as if coming from a far distance and from a great height, something like a light will manifest and you will know a little more of truth.[4]

Instead of being on this side, instead of looking at oneself, one enters the other person and looks. If one has a little bit imagination, a little more control over his thoughts, over his movements, one will have a real progress. In all that one does together with others. One can try to see the thing as the other person sees it, and put it with one's own way of seeing.

(iii) Organisation of Ideas around a Central Idea

It is always good to consider every problem from all possible stand points so as to avoid partiality and exclusiveness. In every case the natural and logical synthesis of all the points of view must be adapted. Great care must be taken in the choice of the central idea of mental synthesis, so that, you will make the totality of your thoughts into a dynamic and constructive force "The higher and the larger the central idea and the more universal it is, rising above time and space, the more numerous and the more complex will be the ideas, notions and thoughts which it will be able to organize and harmonies".[5]

If one trains oneself methodically, gradually one can follow a train of reasoning quite objectively. One can follow the logical deduction of one idea from another, and the normal, logical, organised movements. This habit is like the habit of methodically moving the muscles. It makes clear the thoughts and must be moved to obtain a certain result.

2.6 Learning to be and Learning to Live Together

In 1996, the UNESCO International Commission on Education for the 21st Century released an inspirational report "*Learning: the Treasure Within*" which presented a vision of education based on four pillars of learning: learning to live together, learning to know, learning to do and learning to be. The report emphasised that the survival of humanity is highly dependent on learning how to live together, beginning by understanding and accepting other people and their history, cultures, traditions and values.

The world has changed in many ways since then. Much has been accomplished, but a lot more needs to be done to translate the idealistic vision of education into actions on the ground. The clamour for education to foster more humanistic and sustainable lifestyles has highlighted a need to better understand how education systems—from the curricula, pedagogies, school environment and settings, assessments and extra-curricular activities—can concretely bridge theories and practices.

The Picture of Auroville, Pondicherry—where people of all nations in the world irrespective of caste, creed, sex and colours are learning and living together

Learning to Live Together is an interfaith and intercultural programme for ethics education that contributes to nurturing ethical values in children and young people. The launch of the Learning to Live Together Programme was held in Hiroshima, on the 24-26 May in 2008, during the Third Forum of the Global Network of Religions for Children (GNRC). This programme was developed during a period of three years through testing workshops organised by the Global Network of Religions for Children (GNRC) around the world with people of different faiths and secular backgrounds in close collaboration with UNESCO and UNICEF and tested through the GNRC to contribute to the realisation of the Right of the Child to full and healthy physical, mental, spiritual, moral and social development, and to education as set out in the United Nations Convention on the Rights of the Child (CRC), in article 26.1 of the Universal Declaration of Human Rights (UDHR), in the World Declaration on Education for all and in the Millennium Development Goals.

'Learning to Live Together' is a programme for educators (teachers, youth leaders, social workers) to nurture ethical values and spirituality in children and youth that will help them strengthen their identity and critical thinking, ability to make well-grounded decisions, respect and work with people of other cultures and religions, and foster their individual and collective responsibilities in a global community.

Learning to Live Together can be used with children and young people from 12 to 18, coming from different religions and cultures. The users can adapt it according to the context, the needs, the maturity of the children, and other aspects. It can be implemented in various contexts in formal, non-formal or informal settings.

Learning to Live Together is built in two modules, "Understanding Self and Others" and "Transforming the World together". It is based on four ethical values: respect, empathy, responsibility and reconciliation. The learning process focuses on methodologies based on experience, cooperation, problem solving, discussions and introspection.

2.7 Global Peace Science (GPS)

Global Peace Science (GPS) by Leo Semashko is the first in history the science of world peace, after more than two centuries of the birth of military science in the Adam Bülow's book in 1799. The GPS cognitive result is the first scientific extremely laconic formula of peace: "peace from harmony of SPHERONS through science", which determines a source, social actors and main way of global peace. The objective grounds and numerous details of this formula are disclosed in the book 13 chapters in different dimensions: social, philosophical, historical, structural, functional, political, economic, personal, educational, psychological, legal and others. The GPS practical and political resume is: Invincible soft force of global peace consists in absolute power of social harmony of the world's population, in its four SPHERONS, harmonious classes. Their harmonious power, scientifically organised in Spheral Democracy (SPHERONS' democracy) at all levels from local to global is able to put an end to militarism and endless wars of the irremovable ruling elite under the pall of its militarist "democracy".

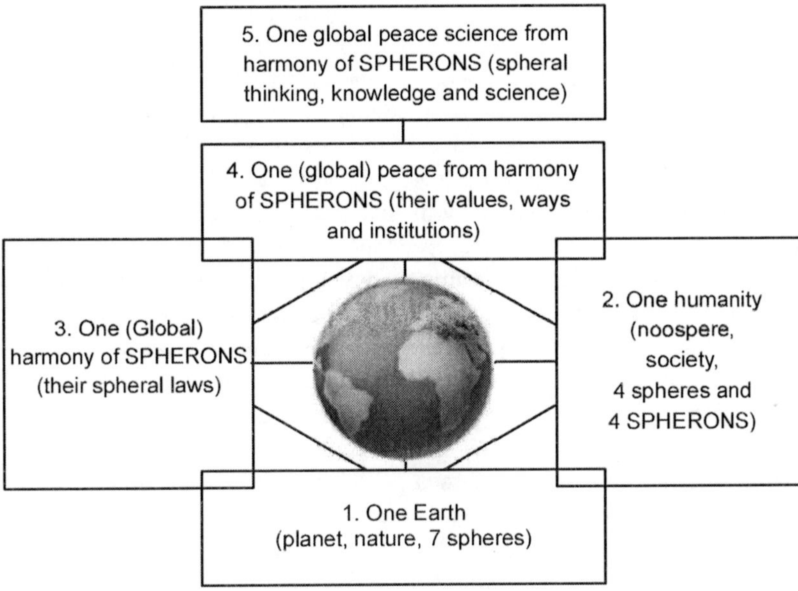

Global Peace Science

If Marx discovered in society the antagonistic groups as eternal sources of class struggle and wars, GPS discovered the eternal harmonious classes as sources of peace, in which the Marx's classes is only partial, disharmonious and temporary cases. GPS is a theoretical knowledge of global peace of SPHERONS confirmed by historical and statistical facts. Discovery of SPHERONS as the deep and constant global social structure is discovery a new social energy and soft force of harmony, able to harmonize all spheres of society and the individual. It is a scientific breakthrough to a new, harmonious civilisation and revolution of all social sciences overcoming its two centuries of lagging behind the military science. The GPS creation began almost 40 years ago, but strongly during 10 years in the GHA since 2005. The philosophical and sociological basis of GPS and SPHERONS discovery is Tetrism (four-dimensional pluralism) as unity of Tetra philosophy and Tetra-sociology—the science of social harmony, global peace and harmonious civilisation. The most complete it is presented in "The ABC of Harmony" (GHA, 2012). The book chapters is united in two parts: peaceful (future) and military (past) history of mankind, and three sections of the first part, which respectively unfold the architecture of GPS, global peace, and finally its evolution in the present time. The GPS unprecedented theoretical and practical qualities create a fundamentally new space of innovative technologies: social, informational, political and economic. This science is necessary for all conscious builders of global peace, especially leaders.

Social harmony provides the most favourable conditions of all possible and the most fruitful opportunities of all imaginable for life and development of each part of humanity, every nation and every human, as well as humanity in a whole. Therefore, all parts spontaneously seek harmony, and where it endsur:—there ends the existence and life itself. Therefore GPS defines the ultimate source of global peace in social harmony. All values and benefits of humanity are derived from harmony and impossible without it and beyond it. Life, love, peace, faith, justice, freedom, equality, brotherhood, happiness, humanism, human rights, sustainable development, survival and prosperity of mankind, of all its parts, nations and persons,—are consequences and attributes of social harmony. Their measure is determined by their degree of social harmony and they live only in the framework of this measure.

This measure is presented for the whole of humanity and for all levels in the social genome of harmony—SOCIONOME, which defines its fundamental actors—harmonious spheral classes—SPHERONS. Social harmony becomes conscious and most effective when they will transform from spontaneous to conscious actors that begin with the creation of scientific knowledge of social harmony. Thinking spheres and SPHERONS within SOCIONOME create a qualitatively new way of thought that determines the revolution of social thinking and breakthrough in social science. Along with this new knowledge arises global peace science (GPS). It expresses the scientific revolution of social thinking and a breakthrough in social knowledge, which retains and consolidates all previous peacemaking achievements, raising them to the level of innovative science of the 21st century. The principal value of *the ABC of Harmony* is the beginning of global peace science and source of its revolutionary thinking. But this was anticipated by Confucius, Buddha, Jesus Christ and many other prophets and thinkers of humanity. What Abdul Kalam wrote on the first of them, can be said about each of them:

The wise sage Confucius said,

> "*When there is beauty in the character,*
> *There is harmony in the home*".

The enlightened one, the Buddha added,

> "*When there is harmony in the home,*
> *There is order in the nation,*
> *When there is order in the nation*
> *There is peace in the world*". —Abdul Kalam

This is the most accurate definition and most brief formula of global peace from harmony at all levels from the individual to the whole world:

- beauty (measure)
- harmony (consent)

- order (coherence)
- peace (prosperity).

The source of global peace is measure and harmony in all spheres of humanity and the relevant order into its social, spiritual, political and economic life. GPS spiritualizes this formula of global peace from harmony through 2,500 years by discovering and unfolding the essence of its universal and eternal actors-harmonious spheral classes, SPHERONS.

Endnotes

1. "Draft Preliminary Outline of the World Report on Culture and Development". UNESCO, CCD-III/94/Doc. 2, Paris, 7 Feb. 1994, p. 16.
2. "Towards New Asia", p. 40.
3. "Practically any human behaviour can be, and historically has been, rationalised as threatening to damage the security of the nation": Scoble and Wiseberg (eds.), "Access to Justice", p. 58.
4. *Collected Works of The Mother*, Vol. 4, p. 47, Sri Aurobindo Ashram Trust.
5. *Collected Works of The Mother*, Vol. 12, p. 26, Sri Aurobindo Ashram Trust.

3
Development Perspectives

"Peace education is an attempt to respond to problems of conflict and violence on scales ranging from the global and national to the local and personal. It is about exploring ways of creating more just and sustainable futures."—R.D. Laing (1978)

3.1 Cognitive, Moral, Social Reasoning and Wisdom

Wisdom

Wisdom is the ability to think and act using knowledge, experience, understanding, common sense, and insight.[1] This implies a possession of knowledge, or the seeking of knowledge to apply to the given circumstance. This involves an understanding of people, objects, events, situations, and the willingness as well as the ability to apply perception, judgment, and action in keeping with the understanding of what is the optimal course of action. In short, wisdom is a disposition to find the truth coupled with an optimum judgment as to what actions should be taken.

The *Oxford English Dictionary* defines wisdom as "Capacity of judging rightly in matters relating to life and conduct; soundness of judgement in the choice of means and ends; sometimes, less strictly, sound sense, esp. in practical affairs: opp. to folly;" also "Knowledge (esp. of a high or abstruse kind); enlightenment, learning, erudition."[2] Charles Haddon Spurgeon defined wisdom as "the right use of knowledge".[3] Robert I. Sutton and Andrew Hargadon defined the "attitude of wisdom" as "acting with knowledge while doubting what one knows".[4]

Philosophical Perspectives

To Socrates and Plato, philosophy was literally the love of Wisdom (philo-sophia). This permeates Plato's dialogues, especially *The Republic*, in which the leaders of his proposed utopia are to be philosopher kings, rulers who understand the Form of the Good and possess the courage to act accordingly. Aristotle, in his *Metaphysics*, defined wisdom as the understanding of causes, i.e. knowing why things are a certain way, which is deeper than merely knowing that things are a certain way.[5]

The ancient Romans also valued wisdom. It was personified in Minerva, or Pallas. She also represents skillful knowledge and the virtues, especially chastity. Her symbol was the owl which is still a popular representation of wisdom, because it can see in darkness. She was said to be born from Jupiter's forehead.[6]

In the Inuit tradition, developing wisdom was one of the aims of teaching. An Inuit Elder said that a person became wise when they could see what needed to be done and do it successfully without being told what to do. In many cultures, the name for third molars, which are the last teeth to grow, is etymologically linked with wisdom, e.g., as in the English *wisdom tooth.*

Educational Perspective

Public schools in the US have an approach to character education. Eighteenth century philosophers such as Benjamin Franklin, referred to this as training wisdom and virtue. Traditionally, schools share the responsibility to build character and wisdom along with parents and the community.[7]

Nicholas Maxwell, a contemporary philosopher in the United Kingdom, advocates that academia ought to alter its focus from the acquisition of knowledge to seeking and promoting wisdom, which he defines as the capacity to realize what is of value in life, for oneself and others.[8] He teaches that new knowledge and technological know-how increase our power to act which, without wisdom, may cause human suffering and death as well as human benefit. Wisdom is the application of knowledge to attain a positive goal by receiving instruction in governing oneself.

Psychological Perspective

Psychologists have gathered data on commonly held beliefs or folk theories about wisdom.[9] These analyses indicate that although "there is an overlap of the implicit theory of wisdom with intelligence, perceptiveness, spirituality and shrewdness, it is evident that wisdom is an expertise in dealing with difficult questions of life and adaptation to the complex requirements."[10] Baltes *et al.* in 2002 through *Wisdom: its structure and function in regulating lifespan successful development*[11] defined "Wisdom is the ability to deal with the contradictions of a specific situation and to assess the consequences of an action for themselves and for others. It is achieved when in a concrete situation, a balance between intrapersonal, inter-personal and institutional interests can be prepared".[12]

Researchers in the field of positive psychology have defined wisdom as the coordination of "knowledge and experience" and "its deliberate use to improve wellbeing."[13] With this definition, wisdom is further defined as a multidimensional construct with the following facets:

- Problem Solving with self-knowledge and sustainable actions.

- Contextual, sincerity to the circumstances with knowledge of its negative and positive aspects (or constraints).
- Value based consistent actions with knowledge of diversity in ethical opinions.
- Tolerance towards uncertainty in life with unconditional acceptance.
- Empathy with oneself to understand one's own emotions (or to be emotionally oriented), morals, etc. and others feelings including the ability to see oneself as part of a larger whole[14]

Wisdom leads a person to overcome feelings of helplessness, powerlessness, anger or aggression by non-understanding of external elements and internal acknowledgement. It leads to a change from the experience of meaninglessness to meaningful goals, prospects for coping with critical life events and to engage constructively with complex life problems.[15] John Vervaeke has argued through *cognitive science of wisdom* that, when basic relevance realisation processes that underlie cognition is fed back onto themselves and made self-referential/differentiated reflection with the problems facing and its dimensions, leads to enhanced insight abilities associated with wisdom.[16]

Dr. B. Legesse *et al.*, a neuropsychiatrist at McLean Hospital/Harvard Medical School, offers "a theoretical definition that takes into account many cultural, religious, and philosophical themes is that wisdom represents a demonstrated superior ability to understand the nature and behaviour of things, people, or events." He states "this results in an increased ability to predict behaviour or events which then may be used to benefit self or others." He furthermore adds "there is more often a desire to share the accrued benefits with a larger group for the purpose of promoting survival, cohesion, or well-being of that group. The benefits do not result from malicious or antisocial intents or inequitable behaviour. Environmental factors, such as family, education, socioeconomic status, culture, and religion, are involved in generating the milieu in which the personal value system develops. Many of these same factors also influence how a given community decides whether wisdom is present or not. This model of wisdom relies on the individual's ability to generate a mental representation of the self (cognitive, emotional, and physical), the external world, and the dynamic relationship of the self with the external world." It is a popular notion that wisdom increases with age,[17] supported by a recent study showing that regardless of their education, IQ or gender, older adults possess better reasoning about societal and interpersonal conflicts.[18]

Sapience is often defined as wisdom, or the ability of an organism or entity to act with appropriate judgment, a mental faculty which is a component of intelligence or alternatively may be considered an additional faculty, apart from intelligence, with its own properties. Robert Sternberg has segregated the capacity for judgment from the general qualifiers for intelligence, which is closer to cognizant aptitude than to wisdom. Displaying sound judgment in a complex, dynamic environment is a hallmark of wisdom.

The word *sapience* is derived from the Latin *sapientia*, meaning "wisdom".[19] Related to this word is the Latin verb *sapere*, meaning "to taste, to be wise, to know"; the present participle of *sapere* forms part of *Homo sapiens*, the Latin binomial nomenclature created by Carl Linnaeus to describe the human species. Linnaeus had originally given humans the species name of *diurnus*, meaning man of the day. But he later decided that the dominating feature of humans was wisdom, hence application of the name *sapiens*. The words "sentience", "self-awareness", and "consciousness" are used in similar ways in science fiction.[20]

Isaac Asimov says *"the saddest aspect of life right now is that science gathers knowledge faster than society gathers wisdom"*(Asimov, 1988, p. 281). If we are to avoid in this century the horrors of the last one—wars, death camps, dictatorships, poverty, hunger, illiteracy, malnutrition, environmental damage—we urgently need to learn how to acquire more wisdom, which in turn means that our institutions of learning need to become more responsive, sympathetic, people-centric, practical and rationally effective. In the words of Abdul Kalam (2010, p. 199),"Enlightened citizenship has three components: education with value system, religion transforming into spiritual force, and creating economic prosperity through development. "If we examine the crisis of our times, which is behind all our ills and maladies, it is the crisis of science without consciousness, which is restricted to acquire knowledge and more knowledge. Hence, Kalam (2010, p. 249) said, "Science is the best boon that God has bestowed upon mankind. Science with reasoning becomes the capital of society…The convergence of science and technology with spirituality is touted to be the future for both science and technology, and spirituality." The irrationality of knowledge-inquiry further damages our ability to find solutions. The crux of our crisis is that we are living in man-made, non-dynamic, intellectual systems where we teach social science but not social philosophy, technology but not humanities, facility and rights but not responsibility and reason, while we exploit natural resources without any thought of conserving them. The root of the problem is the rebellious nature and the ignorance of mankind. Hence, American Philosopher Glenn Martin (Semashko, 2013, p. 296) aptly called it," Our new planetary paradigm, the fundamental revolution in science and paradigm shift in human consciousness."

Maxwell (2013), a wisdom blogger, wants a revolution in the aims and methods of science—and of academic inquiry more generally. In Maxwell's view, instead of giving priority to the search for knowledge, universities, colleges, schools and other institutions of learning need to engage and devote themselves to seeking and promoting wisdom by rational means, with wisdom being the capacity to realize what is of value in life, for oneself and others. Wisdom thus includes knowledge, understanding and technological know-how, but much else besides. A basic task ought to be to help humanity learn how to create a better world for us and for our children too. The revolution we need would change every branch and aspect of academic inquiry. A basic intellectual task of academic inquiry would be to articulate our problems of living (personal, social, global and environmental) and propose and critically assess possible solutions, actions, policies, political programmes and philosophies of life. This would be the task of social inquiry and the humanities. Tackling problems of knowledge would be secondary. Social inquiry would be at the heart of the academic enterprise, intellectually more fundamental than natural science.

In our common understanding, different perceptions of wisdom exist, ranging from the psychological to the moral, from the specific to the universal, from the practical to the mythical/spiritual. There are also many different spaces, times, and experiences (stories, songs, dances, games, festivals, work activities, health practices) for inheriting, generating and sharing wisdom. These rich and diverse understandings and spaces contribute to dynamic learning processes for developing our individual and collective reflections, creativity, sensitivity, and social responsibility for dealing with the inherent ambiguity, complexity and even absurdity of life.

We need to reset our journey not just from ignorance to knowledge but from ignorance to knowledge to higher consciousness, which alone can change the world, our living (personal, social, global) and give us a definite direction to solve problems. Creating a 'Wisdom Society' is the bounden duty of all, not of a chosen few. We need to live, learn and liberate by sharing our experience and caring for each other, at a little deeper, personal and humane level than being shallow, mechanical, cosmetic and superficial. Knowing each other will be more important than showing oneself as intellectually superior to another. Hence, conscious knowledge may be called wisdom. In India, it is assumed as '*pragyan*'. It is Godly knowledge or perfect knowledge. Spiritual leaders have had such wisdom.

Wisdom is one of those qualities difficult to define—because it encompasses so much—but which people generally recognize when they encounter it. And it is encountered most obviously in the realm of decision-making. Psychologists tend to agree that wisdom involves an integration of knowledge, experience, and deep understanding that incorporates tolerance for the uncertainties of life as well as its ups and downs. There's an awareness of how things play out over time, and it confers a sense of balance. It can be acquired only through experience, but by itself, experience does not automatically confer wisdom. Only now are researchers beginning to look into the social, emotional, and cognitive processes that transmute experience into wisdom. Wise people generally share an optimism that life's problems can be solved and experience a certain amount of calm in facing difficult decisions.

Various Aspects of Wisdom

Ryan (2013) has nicely derived such article regarding different aspects of wisdom. Some of those parts are likely given below:

Wisdom has been analysed by various philosophers, psychologists, spiritual leaders, poets, novelists, life coaches, and a variety of other important thinkers. This entry will provide a brief and general overview, and analysis of, several philosophical views on the topic of wisdom. Moreover, this entry will focus on several major ideas in the Western philosophical tradition. In particular, it will focus on five general approaches to understanding what it takes to be wise: (1) wisdom as epistemic humility, (2) wisdom as epistemic accuracy, (3) wisdom as knowledge, (4) a hybrid theory of wisdom, and (5) wisdom as rationality.

1. ***Wisdom as Epistemic Humility:*** Humility theories of wisdom are not promising, but they do, perhaps, provide us with some important character traits associated with wise people. Wise people, one might argue, possess epistemic self-confidence, yet lack epistemic arrogance. Wise people tend to acknowledge their fallibility, and wise people are reflective, introspective, and tolerant of uncertainty. Any acceptable theory of wisdom ought to be compatible with such traits. However, those traits are not, in and of themselves, definitive of wisdom.

2.`***Wisdom as Epistemic Accuracy:*** Many philosophers would hesitate to endorse this interpretation of what is going on in *The Apology*. They would argue that a failure to defend one's beliefs from Socrates' relentless questioning does not show that a person is not justified in believing a proposition. Many philosophers would argue that having very good evidence, or forming a belief via a reliable process, would be sufficient for justification. It should be noted, however, that although accuracy theories do not provide an adequate account of wisdom, they reveal an important insight. Perhaps a necessary condition for being wise is that wise people think they have knowledge only when their beliefs are highly justified. Or, even more simply, perhaps wise people have epistemic ally justified, or rational, beliefs.

3. *Wisdom as Knowledge:* An alternative approach to wisdom focuses on the more positive idea that wise people are very knowledgeable people. There are many views in the historical and contemporary philosophical literature on wisdom that have knowledge, as opposed to humility or accuracy, as at least a necessary condition of wisdom. Aristotle (*Nichomachean Ethics*

VI, ch. 7), Descartes (*Principles of Philosophy*), Richard Garrett (1996), John Kekes (1983), Keith Lehrer & Nicholas Smith (1996), Robert Nozick (1989), Plato (*The Republic*), Sharon Ryan (1996, 1999), Valerie Tiberius (2008), Dennis Whitcomb (2010) and Linda Zagzebski (1996) for example, have all defended theories of wisdom that require a wise person to have knowledge of some sort. All of these views very clearly distinguish knowledge from expertise on a particular subject. Moreover, all of these views maintain that wise people know "what is important." The views differ, for the most part, over what it is important for a wise person to know, and on whether there is any behaviour, action, or way of living, that is required for wisdom.

Aristotle distinguished between two different kinds of wisdom, theoretical wisdom and practical wisdom. Theoretical wisdom is, according to Aristotle, "scientific knowledge, combined with intuitive reason, of the things that are highest by nature" (*Nicomachean Ethics*, VI, 1141b). For Aristotle, theoretical wisdom involves knowledge of necessary, scientific, first principles and propositions that can be logically deduced from them. Aristotle's idea that scientific knowledge is knowledge of necessary truths and their logical consequences is no longer a widely accepted view. Moreover, it will combine scientific knowledge with other kinds of factual knowledge, including knowledge about history, philosophy, music, literature, mathematics, etc. Consider the following, knowledge based, and theory of wisdom:

3.1 *Wisdom as Extensive Factual Knowledge (WFK):* According to (WFK), a wise person is a person who knows a lot about the universe and our place in it. She would have extensive knowledge about the standard academic subjects. There are many positive things to say about (WFK).

3.2 *Wisdom as Knowing How to Live Well (KLW):* This view captures Aristotle's basic idea of practical wisdom.

3.3 *Wisdom as Knowing How to, and Succeeding at, Living Well (KLS):* That means; it has two aspects; which shows one can succeed and he can live well also.

In the preface of his *Principles of Philosophy*, Descartes insisted upon factual knowledge as an important component of wisdom. Descartes wrote, "It is really only God alone who has Perfect Wisdom, that is to say, who has a complete knowledge of the truth of all things; but it may be said that men have more wisdom or less according as they have more or less knowledge of the most important truths" (*Principles,* 204). Of course, among those important truths, one might claim, are truths about living well, as well as knowledge in the basic academic subject areas.

4. Hybrid Theory: One way to try to accommodate the various insights from the theories considered thus far is in the form of a hybrid theory. It is the amalgamation of four aspects:

- He should have extensive factual and theoretical knowledge.
- He knows how to live well.
- He is successful at living well.
- He has very few unjustified beliefs.

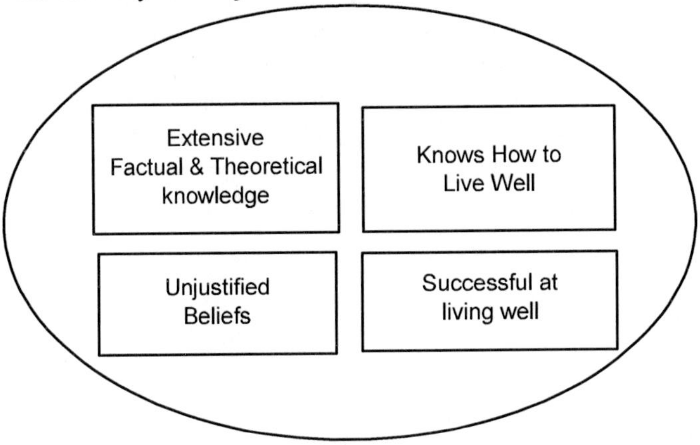

Hybrid Theory

Wisdom is a virtue and a way of living, and it requires more than smart ideas and knowledge. If we think of wisdom as the highest, or among the highest, of human virtues, then it seems incompatible with a deeply evil personality. This theory was also criticised.

***5. Wisdom as Rationality*:** The final theory to be considered here is an attempt to capture all that is good, while avoiding all the serious problems of the other theories discussed thus far. Perhaps wisdom is a deep and comprehensive kind of rationality (Ryan, 2012).

Deep Rationality Theory (DRT)

This theory shows that one is wise if and only if:

1. S/he has a wide variety of epistemically justified beliefs on a wide variety of valuable academic subjects.
2. S/he has a wide variety of justified beliefs on how to live rationally (epistemically, morally, and practically).
3. S/he is committed to living rationally.
4. S/he has very few unjustified beliefs and is sensitive to her limitations.

In condition (1), DRT takes account of what is attractive about some knowledge theories by requiring epistemic justified beliefs about a wide variety of standard academic subjects. Condition (2) takes account of what is attractive about theories that require knowledge about how to live well. For example, having justified beliefs about how to live in a practically rational way would include having a well-reasoned strategy for dealing with the practical aspects of life. It requires having good reasons behind one's actions, responding appropriately to, and learning from, one's mistakes, and having a rational plan for all sorts of situations and problems. Condition (3) ensures that the wise person live a life that reflects what she or he is justified in believing is a rational way to live. In condition (4), DRT respects epistemic humility. It requires that a wise person not believe things without epistemic justification. The Deep Rationality Theory rules out all of the unwise poets, politicians, and craftsmen that were ruled out by Socrates. The Deep Rationality Theory does not require knowledge or perfection. But it does require rationality, and it accommodates degrees of wisdom. It is a promising theory of wisdom.

3.2 Self-Development and Self-Identity

Self-development should be placed in the peace curriculum because 'self' is the locus of all thoughts, attitudes, or values, which give rise to a peaceful, or aggressive, or violent personality. If the individual self is calm, evolved and adequate without any insecurity, inferiority feelings or weakness or fear the peace comes, naturally to such a person since self exists in relationships. Improving communication skills,—both verbal and non-verbal could help develop the self.

Self-Development for peace included mainly three aspects Understanding and Developing Self through effective communication and listening skills, understanding prejudices and biases in Communication and developing positive social skills viz. cooperation. The teachers are to be introduced the concept of inner-self, and empowerment of self by opening to others, meditation and self-reflection. Importance of balance between inner self and outer self and how peace is possible through calming inner noise and conflicts within self would be realised. Yoga and pranayama are very useful for improvement of physical, mental, and emotional health and staying calm and composed in daily life. It helps for peace in mind and body.

Perception of Self in terms of one's cultural ties, regional, professional and personal qualities have a lot of influence over the prejudices, biases and judgments one makes on others. Awareness of one's own identity enables one to be fair while judging others and making evaluations about them. In order to be fair and free from prejudices towards others particularly those from different culture/regional groups, it is important for any individual, especially teachers to be aware of their own identity. So, that they become aware of their biases and prejudices toward students and do not allow them to interfere in their teaching learning relationship. Awareness is starting point in dropping the prejudices and developing tolerate and respect for cross-cultural populations. Intercultural harmony at school level could be nurtured by developing awareness of identity among teachers.

Identity, and its role in persuasion and mediation enable teachers to understand the nature of identity and the ways in which it influences our attitudes and values. Persuasion and meditation of conflicts requires consciousness of identity. Mediation requires understanding clearly the source and nature of conflict and the biases, which hold the conflict in peace. If the mediator also holds some prejudices and biases as the conflicting parties, he will not be able to comprehend the real issue and mediate. Identity is supported by our cultural ethos and gives rise to positive and negative attitudes towards others, at the same time it also enables us to relate with others and motivates us especially during childhood. The identity takes complete charge over our behaviour and thinking, it becomes our reference point for judging others right or wrong. It was discussed that awareness of identity is important so that it does not submerge the individual. The feeling of continuity, which is so characteristic of identity, needs to be understood in proper perspective in the sense that the subtle changes are accruing to all, which do not become apparent to the individuals. These characteristics of identity must be known to a person getting ready to mediate in conflict. Sense of continuity in the identity gives us distinction and a feeling of belonging but the changes in identity over time are significant and need to be understood.

Beside awareness of the nature of our identity, the time and place for mediation must be chosen with care. Mediation requires sensitivity and patience towards conflicting persons, their feelings, even prejudices, and biases need to be respected before any change could be expected. Mediation requires empathy with the people involved in conflict and respect for their concerns and points of view.

3.3 Controlling Bad Habits: Drug, Abuses, Theft, Indiscipline

Our society is democratic, egalitarian and secular society. But in ground level we are not free from biasness. We have different types of discriminations, feelings, ideas thoughts etc. Even major so called officials, administrators, politicians, thinkers, writers, academicians have such feelings. The root cause is ignorance. The negative ideas are not only created by lower strata's of people. It comes from also higher strata's of people in our society. But the common masses are affected by it. Whatever it may be these are happening due to ignorance.

Taking drug, creating abuses, organizing theft, or generating any type of indiscipline is social offence. Our people should be conscious about it. They should know merit, limitations, laws and orders of Government etc. Government should take measure precaution for various discriminations in the society. There may be various views, thoughts, ideas; but it should not harmful for society or common masses. Views from various dimensions enrich our culture.

People from all spheres are involved in these odd abuses. Sri Aurobindo says, "If you want to change the world, you change yourself first". Individual change leads to social change. Social changes enhance global change. Hence, awareness in every level is needed. The purpose of any society is wellbeing of humanity; not destruction. If anybody/any society wants this, he is not maker but breaker, destroyer of civilisation. Thanks God! Doclam conflict is resolved by India's diplomatic action. Otherwise it may progress towards the destruction of both countries China and India. Similar conflict between India vs. Pakistan, USA vs. Korea, Russia vs. Israel etc. is going on. These are conflicts due to ego and power. Nobody is superior in the earth. Everybody should maintain harmony like separate petals of a flower. Then this beautiful earth will be survived as God's creation. We should remember that this fine earth is not a puppet in few men's hand. It is the creation of unseen Godhead. Today or tomorrow, certain circumstances will compel everybody to move in righteous path rather odd ones. This is the law of God's Universe. If this is the destiny, then why not we be aware about it!

3.4 Obedience to Law, Order and Ethics

Generally it is seen that learners are obedient to teachers. Juniors in family obedient to seniors. All the components in the Universe run in a harmonious order. Otherwise it is not possible the existence of this fine earth. The nature, the moon, the sun, the planets, the stars all are moving in natural order. This is the essence of the Universe. Day and night, season cycle are possible only by the harmonious movement of the sun.

Law, order and ethics are created for peace and harmony of the human civilisation. It guides to individuals and society. It shows the direction how to move in a socially approved means. It protects human civilisation from various odds. Human being follows law and order and principles of ethics for better living and peaceful life. Who does not follow it, he creates indiscipline, conflict, riots, theft, accident etc. Consequently he has to face the catastrophes of nature. Hence, in a turmoil situation we should follow laws of ethics for betterment and peaceful life. Constitutional laws protect us from various evils in the society. If human beings do any misdeed, the result will be disharmony of the beautiful earth. Follow the ethics, obey the laws and order save the good civilisation!

Steve Johnson (1999) writes in *Issues in Ethics* (Vol. 10, No. 1 Spring) following points regarding this approach:

(i) Affective and Effective Approaches

In modern society, schools have neglected of moral education. Affective approaches such as values clarification, self-esteem building, moral decision making, and most recently, character education are to be inculcated in the education systems.

Values clarification was a popular affective approach that stressed individual self-reflection on values over the promotion of any specific values. While the program had a worthy objective, it did not deliver as intended. We realized there were choices we simply didn't want children to feel good about, and no increase in clarity would make the unacceptable acceptable. Contemporary educators are often delicate about anything that tastes of indoctrination. We can become downright imperialistic about academic honesty, respect for self and others, and violence-free schools.

While affective approaches have not contributed a reliable means for schools to develop ethics, they have made valuable contributions, especially in recognizing the importance of the emotions, as well as the intellect, and the importance of school climate in creating an environment where character can develop.

(ii) Limits of Moral Decision Making

Moral decision making concentrated on the study of ethical principles. Moral decision making assumed that under the right conditions, children would figure out ethical principles for themselves and generalize what they learned to their everyday moral opportunities. But the problems taught were rarely situated in the children's own real lives. The abstract principles were hard for students to retrieve in situations where, for example, they could save themselves pain by lying and they could not see a connection between their lying and the abstract ideals they had learned.

There are difficult situations where we need the assistance that formal ethical decision making offers. But ethics is not just about the hardest choices we will ever have to make; it is also about what we do all day every day. This brings up a simple observation about the moral life. Most of the time, we know what we ought to do. We're just having trouble doing it. Schools should be more concerned about helping students create the conditions in their lives where they will more consistently do what they know they should. Moral decisions encourage wellbeing of all. Schools should help to practice various skills which promote the moral decision making.

(iii) Creating an Ethical Educational Climate

Character education means creating a culture that calls for everyone in the school community to be the best people they can be. Character education programs that work are, a giant mutual-improvement process involving students, teachers, administrators, parents, and other stakeholders. Swami vivekanand emphasizes on character building in education. Idealistic views have great importance on character education. Ancient system of education (Gurukula) had stressed very much on this issue. Ascetic life depends on character formation. Hence, it is said:

> "If wealth is lost, nothing is lost,
> If health is lost, something is lost;
> If character is lost, everything is lost."

Faculties should identify the elements of curriculum that support the virtues and add other materials on ethics. Ethical decision making is taught and practiced throughout the school, but it is supplemented by training in reflection, coping skills, and cooperation. Positive thinking encourages ethical climate.

Faculties must work as credible role models of the virtues. In this way, they are joined by parents, who can receive help through the school in strategies for raising ethical children. These can include such important skills as maintaining a daily dialogue with a child; connecting with his or her friends; effective, consistent reinforcement of desired behaviors; and skillful reduction of undesired behaviors.

The work of character education in schools and homes always starts with the adults. When we talk about the moral decline of our youth, we are often just observing our own reflection in the children who learned what we modelled. As teachers and parents, we must demonstrate not only the right behavior but also the kind of thoughtfulness that makes a moral education more than the human version of obedience school. At its best, character education cultivates an appreciation for the power of story, reflection, and the essential tools of habit and reason in dealing with the complexities of daily life. Holistic means of thinking also creates ethical climate. Spiritual education leads to ethical climate.

3.5 Utilization of Moral Habits

It is observed that the present so called modern society is running with deprivation of morals. Neither parents nor schools can significantly impact the moral development of children. A child has to learn one of our major goals in influencing moral behavior. As much as parents and schools need to model what good moral character looks like, they also need to teach students how to deal with the things that get in the way of moral behavior. Students are most likely not to do what they know they ought when they are in angry and intensely emotional situations. Sometimes by the influence of peers, children are involved in mischievous activities. At that time, personal or academic honesty works against them. When they are involved in patterns of self-destructive, drug/alcohol-related, gang, or delinquent behavior; Students can learn practical ways to overcome these obstacles. They need training in anger control, social skills, conflict resolution, dealing with hostile people, and situational perception.

These habits can be greatly reinforced and encouraged with living books or examples. Tell the children stories of a famous persons, saints who exhibited truthfulness. Introduce him to a person he know who exemplifies personal initiative. Read a biography about a person who was careful with borrowed property, like Abraham Lincoln's walking miles to borrow and return books. Such living ideas will go far in motivating your child to develop moral habits. We can follow similar biographies of Gandhiji, SriAurobindo, Swami Vivekananda, Abdul Kalam etc.

"Sow a thought, reap an action; sow an action, reap a habit; sow a habit, reap a character." Here it is mentioned the category of moral habits.

Category of Moral Habits

- Integrity
- Obedience
- Personal Initiative
- Reverence (respect for other people and property)
- Self-Control (keeping back the expression of our passions & emotions
- Sweet, Even Temper
- Truthfulness
- Usefulness (offering valuable or productive service to others)

According to Phillip Barron (2004), I believe, as Aristotle did, that your moral character is just the constellation of the morally relevant habits you have. Fleshing out what makes a "morally relevant habit" may be where Aristotle and I depart.

Diana Mertz Hsieh (2000), in her speech *Moral Habits, The Art of Living Subconsciously* said, "...moral habits are necessary for effectively applying our ethical principles to the particulars of our lives. If we want to live the Objectivist ethics, we need to deliberately cultivate good moral habits. On the surface, moral habits seem to rub the Objectivist ethics the wrong way. After all, as Objectivists, doesn't rationality require that we consciously and deliberately make moral choices? Isn't it dangerous to act on habit, to leave moral decisions up to our subconscious, to our emotions? In fact, as we investigate the nature of moral habits, we will find very little tension between the principles of Objectivism and moral habits. Instead, what we will find is a powerful new tool to integrate into our daily lives."

What are habits?

According to him, habits are largely dominant and subconscious patterns of action established and maintained by repetition. So, habits are patterns of action with three distinguishing features: (1) dominance, (2) unconsciousness, and (3) repetition. Moral habits share all of these features of ordinary habits, plus one more: moral habits arise out of a commitment to particular moral principles. We might adopt the moral habit of consciously setting aside time to rest and rejuvenate in order to achieve the value of being more productive while working. We might adopt the moral habit of being aware of our emotional states in order to achieve the value of greater clarity of thought. In other words, moral habits are habits which aim to achieve moral values.

Moral habits automatize decisions for us, freeing us from the time and effort of deliberating most everyday moral choices. Our automatised moral principles spare us from explicitly deriving the principles relevant to a choice from the fundamental facts of human nature.

Moral habits dispose us to act morally. Good moral habits make virtuous action easy and natural, and render vice difficult and unpleasant. In forming habits, we condition our emotions to take pleasure in acting on principle and feel pain in acting against principle. That emotional feedback naturally inclines us towards the right thing to do. For example, a student with a strong habit of self-discipline about schoolwork will take pleasure in the writing of a difficult term paper, even if she'd rather be goofing off, because she's proud of "getting the job done." Conversely, the pleasure of goofing off would be seriously diminished by an unfinished paper looming in the background. The habit of self-disciple helps the student look beyond the short-term pleasure of goofing off and the short-term pain of writing a paper. The habit aligns her emotions with her long-term self-interest.

Habits work much the same way, simply in the realm of action rather than knowledge. Just as moral principles automatize moral knowledge, moral habits automatize moral actions. Of course, moral habits do not force us to act in one way rather than another. They do not prevent us from engaging in rational deliberation when a complex or unusual situation arises. But they do offer emotional incentives and emotional impediments. As Aristotle said, "to feel delight and pain rightly or wrongly has no small effect on our actions." (Nicomachean Ethics, 1105a)

Moral habits give us consistency between our words and our deeds. Moral habits connect our abstract moral principles to the concrete moral choices we face every day. As such, habits strengthen the bond between what we say and what we do. They strengthen our integrity. However, integrity concerns more than the "trickle-down" effect from our principles to our actions. It also concerns the "trickle-up" effect from our actions to our principles.

There are also particular moral habits we can develop to help us come to terms with a bad deed without resorting to rationalisation. We can be in the habit of making amends to injured parties. We can clearly admit our wrongdoing in a journal or to a trusted friend, so we have an objective record of our wrongdoing. We can imagine what we will do differently next time. Such habits serve as a coat of armour for our integrity against corrosive effects of rationalisation. To the sum, these three major benefits of moral habits are: (1) reduction of cognitive load, (2) the disposition to act morally, and (3) consistency between our words and our deeds, we can see how consciously developing good moral habits enrich and solidify our moral lives. However, every silver lining has a cloud. We need to understand the limitations of moral habits in order to take full advantage of them.

How can we determine which habits will help up better live the Objectivist virtues?

There have two methods proven particularly useful: (1) Nathaniel Branden's sentence completion and (2) brainstorming with other people. Nathaniel Branden uses programmes of sentence completion to stimulate self-awareness and development. In these exercises, we quickly and repeatedly complete sentences such as "If I bring five per cent more awareness to my emotions." and "If I commit to dealing with people fairly and benevolently." Using Branden's own programmes of sentence completion, as well as specialised sentence stems for Objectivist virtues, we will discover innumerable moral habits that will help us live better, happier lives. Sentence completion is an effective tool for breaking our moral principles down into moral habits. Another remarkably effective method of discovering good moral habits is brainstorming sessions with other Objectivists.

By thinking of virtues in terms of habits, those virtues take on a real and particular meaning in our lives. Using habits, we can set ourselves on a clear path of moral self-improvement. We've often heard, particularly from those new to Objectivism, the difficulties of translating Objectivist principles into real life. That moral habits concretize the virtues greatly helps in this process of translation from abstract to particular. The virtue of productiveness is thus mostly concerned with recognizing the value of productive work, rather than actually productively working!

David Kelley and others have begun to define virtues as commitments to acting according to our moral knowledge. Virtue is thus more than a mental act of recognition; it explicitly requires both awareness and action. We're doing the right things for the right reasons. Moral character similarly requires both awareness and action. It requires automatised knowledge of our values and principles. It requires automatised action in congruence with those values and principles. Our characters are the sum of what we think and what we do that is so ingrained in our subconscious, so a part of who we are, that we would not consider doing or thinking otherwise. Thus the automatised actions of well-developed moral habits are an integral part of good moral character. Specifically, habits shore up our moral character by helping us overcome weakness of will. Sometimes we are presented with extraordinarily tempting choices. The immediate pleasure to be gained overwhelms us, whether from drinking, gambling, jelly beans, or loose men. But strongly engrained moral habits remind us of the emotional feelings to come. They help prevent even the thought of such temptations.

Knowing how moral habits function in our lives, we can safely say that the potential damage to ourselves brought on by even occasionally violating our moral principles is not worth the potential benefit. We know that indulging in immorality weakens our moral principles through rationalisation. We know that, without a process of atonement for a violation of our ethical principles, we will change those principles to put ourselves in a better light. So the prudent predator, in predating, risks losing the very principles that are necessary for him live and live well in almost all circumstances. He endangers his only long-term means of achieving his values and supporting his life: his principles. In other words, the prudent predator example presumes that people can occasionally violate their moral principles without any harmful side-effects to those principles. But we know that is not true.

Moral Habits, The Art of Living Subconsciously Diana Mertz Hsieh (diana@dianahsieh.com) Lecture to 2000 TOC Summer Seminar 3 July 2000 (The results of the "Moral Habits Workshop" mentioned in this lecture are also available on www.dianahsieh.com.)

3.6 Role of Education in Promoting Human Rights, Values, Peace and Development

Preamble

Addressed at presentation of National Award to Teachers in New Delhi on

5th September 2004, the then president of India APJ Abdul Kalam said, Education is an endless journey through knowledge and enlightenment. Such a journey opens up new vistas of development. Of humanism where there is neither scope nor room for pettiness, disharmony, jealousy, hatred or enmity. It transforms a human being into a wholesome whole, a noble soul and an asset to the Universe. Real education enhances the dignity of human being and increases his or her self-respect and universal brotherhood in its true sense becomes the sheet anchor for such education. (p. 60, 2016)

Eternal vigilance is the price of democracy. It is the function of education to create and foster an ever vigilant community. As John Dewey observed long ago: "the devotion of democracy to education is a familiar fact. The superficial explain is that a government resting upon popular suffrage cannot be successful unless those who elect and who obey their governors are educated. Since a democratic society repudiate the principle of external authority, it must find a substitute in voluntary disposition and interest; these can be created only by education. But there is a deeper explanation. A democracy is more than a form of government; it is primarily a mode of associated living of conjoint communicated experience." (John Dewey, 1965, p. 87)

It is observed that education acts as a key lever of democratic machinery. The promotion, survival, and success of a democratic society largely rests upon a well-organised, self-disciplined, open-minded, rational, scientific tempered, secular oriented masses who have cultivated habits of discussions, faith in non-violence, peaceful methods of solving problems and faith in justice and equality etc. through education. Education should lead to the creation and promotion of self-reliant and self-sustaining society which can take care of their problems of health, hygiene, environment, communal tensions, children education, youth welfare, optimum utilisation of local resources etc. People should have an awareness of their problems, and needs, able to priorities them, plan strategies for their solutions, mobilize their resources, mobilize themselves to solve these problems and serve as bacon lights tom the younger generations.

Human Rights and Duties Education will aim at making the learners acquire conceptual clarity and develop respect for norms and values of freedom, equality, fraternity and justice with their philosophical, ethical, social, economic and political dimensions. A full understanding of UDHR and the relevant Constitutional-legal provisions and institutional mechanism for realisation and enforcement of rights in the country will constitute an objective. It will include awareness of civil society organisations and movements promoting human rights.

3.6.1 Role of Education in the Development of Human Rights and Values

3.6.1.1 Concept of Human Rights Education

The full realisation of human rights requires all human beings to be aware of their and other people's rights and of the means to ensure their protection. This is the task of human rights education which builds knowledge, skills and attitudes prompting behaviour that upholds human rights. (Navi Pillay, former UN High Commissioner for Human Rights)[21]

Human rights protect the dignity and freedom of every human being. States are required under international law to respect, protect and fulfil human rights, and therefore must ensure that education is aimed at strengthening the enjoyment of human rights and the full development of the human personality.[22] There is a growing agreement amongst members of the international community that human rights education plays a fundamental role in the realisation of all human rights. Human rights education is a lifelong learning process aimed at fostering:

- *Knowledge and skills*—learning about human rights standards and mechanisms, as well as acquiring the skills to put them into practice in daily life;
- *Values and attitudes*—developing values and reinforcing attitudes which uphold human rights;
- *Behaviour and action*—encouraging action to defend and promote human rights.[23]

Human rights education is described as education, training and information aimed at building a universal culture of human rights. Human rights education is not just about equipping learners with knowledge of human rights and the mechanisms that protect them, it is also empowering them to take action to defend and promote human rights, democracy and the rule of law.[24] Human rights education is therefore all forms of education, training, awareness raising, information, practices and activities which aim to empower learners to contribute to the building and defense of a universal culture of human rights in society.

At the individual and community level, human rights education facilitates the development of knowledge, personal and social skills; increases appreciation and understanding of differences and diversity; builds mutual respect for human dignity and shared values; encourages dialogue and promotes non-violence in the resolution of problems and disputes, with respect for each other's rights; and combats all forms of discrimination and violence, including bullying and harassment.

At the societal level, human rights education contributes to and fosters the establishment of sustainable and participative forms of democracy based on respect for human rights and good governance. Human rights education is therefore an ongoing investment for societies that value human rights principles such as respect, non-discrimination, participation, and the rule of law.

3.6.1.2 Understanding Human Rights Education

The term "human rights education" is often used in a broad sense to also include "education for democratic citizenship", "peace education", "global citizenship education", and "education for mutual respect and understanding", which are all based on internationally agreed human rights standards. These concepts are seen as closely interconnected and mutually supportive, differing in focus and scope, rather than in goals and practices.

There is consensus that human rights education encompasses three aspects:[25]

(a) Learning about human rights, which includes providing knowledge and understanding of human rights norms and principles, the values that underpin them and the mechanisms for their protection;
(b) Learning through human rights, which includes learning and teaching in a way that respects the rights of both educators and learners; ensuring that the context and the way learning is organised and imparted is consistent with human rights values (e.g. participation, inclusion, freedom of thought and expression, etc.), recognizing that the process of learning is as important as the content of the learning;
(c) Learning for human rights, which includes empowering persons to enjoy and exercise their rights and to respect and uphold the rights of others. Human rights education has to be learned through experience, through being exposed to human rights in practice.

What is Human Rights Education?

"Human rights education is all learning that develops the knowledge, skills, and values of human rights." As per provisions with in universal declaration of human rights and other international documents and treaties, human rights education can be defined as education, training and information aiming at building a universal culture of human rights through the sharing of knowledge, imparting of skills and molding of attitudes directed to:

(a) The strengthening of respect for human rights and fundamental freedoms;
(b) The full development of the human personality and the sense of its dignity;
(c) The promotion of understanding, tolerance, gender equality and friendship Among all nations, indigenous peoples and racial, national, ethnic, religious And linguistic groups;
(d) The enabling of all persons to participate effectively in a free and democratic Society governed by the rule of law;
(e) The building and maintenance of peace;

(f) The promotion of people-centered sustainable development and social justice.

Importance of Human Rights Education

Human rights education is central to the full and equal enjoyment of all human rights and encourage the development of sustainable national strategies and programmes in human rights education.

The recently adopted United Nations Sustainable Development Goals set as a target for States (Goal 4.7): "By 2030, ensure that all learners acquire the knowledge and skills needed to promote sustainable development, including, among others, through education for sustainable development and sustainable lifestyles, human rights, gender equality, promotion of a culture of peace and non-violence, global citizenship and appreciation of cultural diversity and of culture's contribution to sustainable development".

In 1993 the World Conference on Human Rights in Vienna reaffirmed human rights education, training and public information as essential for the promotion and achievement of stable and harmonious relations among communities and for fostering mutual understanding, tolerance and peace.[26] In 1994 the United Nations General Assembly declared the UN Decade for Human Rights Education (1995-2004)[27] and urged all UN member states to promote "training dissemination and information aimed at the building of a universal culture of human rights". As a result, governments have put greater effort into promoting human rights education, mainly through state education programmes. This commitment has been demonstrated in a number of plans and programmes developed and implemented by the United Nations.

Building on the achievements of the UN Decade, in 2004 the United Nations General Assembly proclaimed the World Programme for Human Right Education[28] to further the implementation of human rights education programmes in all sectors and at all levels. The aim was to promote a common understanding of basic principles and methodologies of human rights education, to provide a concrete framework for action, and to strengthen partnerships and cooperation from the international level to the local communities. It is a significant milestone in the framework for human rights education policy and implementation.

In 2012, the UN Secretary-General launched the Global Education First Initiative (GEFI) rallying a broad spectrum of world leaders and advocates to deliver on the promise of Education for All. Among the three priority areas of the initiative was the need to foster global citizenship. "Education must be transformative, cultivating respect for the world and each other. It should provide children with the understanding they need to cooperate in resolving the interconnected challenges of the 21st century", said Ban Ki-moon.

Human Rights Education in International Law

Every individual and every organ of society ... shall strive by teaching and education to promote respect for these rights and freedoms. (Preamble to the Universal Declaration of Human Rights 1948) Since that day, the international community has come to recognize and promote human rights and fundamental freedoms through a vast body of international human rights law. Among these rights, the right to education provides an entry point to the enjoyment of all human rights. It includes human rights education, the right to learn about those rights, and the ways and means to protect and promote them in our societies.[29]

A. *Conventions, Covenants and Treaties:* The right to a public education that promotes human rights, fundamental freedoms and respect for the content of specific treaties can be found in multiple international conventions and treaties, which form part of international law and impose obligations on States to ensure enjoyment of human rights, including the right to education and specifically human rights education.[30] Some examples are:

- Under the International Covenant on Economic, Social and Cultural Rights (1966) State parties recognize the "right of everyone to education", and agree that "education shall be directed to the full development of the human personality and the sense of its dignity, and shall strengthen the respect for human rights and fundamental freedoms." (Article 13)
- State parties to the International Convention on the Elimination of All Forms of Racial Discrimination (1965) "undertake to adopt immediate and effective measures, particularly in the fields of teaching, education, culture and information, with a view to combating prejudices which lead to racial discrimination and to promoting understanding, tolerance and friendship among nations and racial or ethnical groups." (Article 7)
- Under the Convention on the Rights of the Child (1989), State parties "agree that the education of the child shall be directed to:
  (a) The development of the child's personality, talents and mental and physical abilities to their fullest potential;
  (b) The development of respect for human rights and fundamental freedoms, and for the principles enshrined in the Charter of the United Nations;
  (c) The development of respect for the child's parents, his or her own cultural identity, language and values, for the national values of the country in which the child is living, the country from which he or she may originate, and for civilisations different from his or her own;
  (d) The preparation of the child for responsible life in a free society, in the spirit of understanding, peace, tolerance, equality of sexes,

and friendship among all peoples, ethnic, national and religious groups and persons of indigenous origin;

(e) The development of respect for the natural environment." [Article 29(1)].

- States parties to the International Convention on the Rights of Persons with Disabilities (2006) "recognize the right of persons with disabilities to education. With a view to realizing this right without discrimination and on the basis of equal opportunity, States Parties shall ensure an inclusive education system at all levels and lifelong learning directed to. the full development of human potential and sense of dignity and self-worth, and the strengthening of respect for human rights, fundamental freedoms and human diversity." (Article 24).

  Under this Convention, State parties also undertake to adopt immediate, effective and appropriate measures to raise awareness within society regarding persons with disabilities, to foster respect for the rights and Education International dignity of persons with disabilities, and to combat stereotypes, prejudices and harmful practices relating to persons with disabilities. Such measures to include fostering at all levels of the education system, including in all children, an attitude of respect for the rights of persons with disabilities. (Article 8)
- Under the Convention on the Elimination of All Forms of Discrimination against Women (1979), States "should take all appropriate measures to eliminate discrimination against women in order to ensure to them equal right with men in the field of education." (Article 10)

B. Declarations, General Comments and Recommendations: The obligation of States to ensure human rights education as an inherent component of the right to education has been developed and expressed in a number of declarations, comments, opinions, frameworks and standards developed by experts and committees of the United Nations. These so called 'soft law' sources give a strong indication that States must ensure enjoyment of human rights education.

General comments of the Committee on Economic, Social and Cultural Rights have given content to the right to education, and have read quality education (a component of one of the four "essential features" of the right to education) to include human rights education.[31] The Committee on the Rights of the Child also has issued general comments that further explains that the right to education includes a right to quality education and in particular human rights education.[32]

It is the responsibility of States to ensure that young people and adults have access to quality education. There should be equal opportunity and access to all levels of education, and equal participation and opportunities within education. No one should be disadvantaged due to perceived differences, including those based upon gender, race, ethnicity, sexual orientation, faith, cultural or economic background, disability or personal characteristics.[33] The rights of all people must be recognised equally. The non-discrimination principle does not prevent the taking of special measures to reduce or eliminate discrimination.[34] Addressing discrimination may require changes in legislation, administration and resource allocation, as well as educational measures to change attitudes.[35]

Every child has a right to an education that should provide the child with life skills, strengthen the child's capacity to enjoy the full range of human rights, and promote a culture which is infused by appropriate human rights values. The goal of education is to empower the child by developing his or her competencies, learning and other capacities, human dignity, self-esteem and self-confidence.[36]

A Picture of United Nations an Apostle of Peace in the Globe

The principles of inclusion and non-discrimination should be applied to curriculum content, educational processes, the pedagogical methods and the environment within which education takes place. An inclusive learning environment includes not only a spirit of shared understanding through dialogue and a respect for difference, but also a physically inclusive environment that ensures access and safe spaces for learning for all.[37]

Attention should be placed on issues relating to gender (as well as issues relating to other marginalised, disadvantaged or vulnerable groups), and, in particular, issues relating to stereotyping and impediments to participation in education for such students and education personnel. For example, gender discrimination can be reinforced by practices such as a curriculum which is inconsistent with the principles of gender equality, by arrangements which limit the benefits girls can obtain from the educational opportunities offered, and by unsafe or unfriendly environments which discourage girls' participation.[38]

The UN Declaration on Human Rights Education and Training is the first international instrument devoted specifically to the issue and a significant milestone in the UN framework for human rights education. Everyone has the right to know, seek and receive information about all human rights and fundamental freedoms and should have access to human rights education and training ... Human rights education and training is essential for the promotion of universal respect for and observance of all human rights and fundamental freedoms for all, in accordance with the principles of the universality, indivisibility and interdependence of human rights.[39]

The Declaration encourages a higher level of commitment among States to implement systematic and comprehensive programmes on human rights education and training within all educational sectors—formal, informal and non-formal. While States have the main responsibility "to promote and ensure human rights education and training"[40], the Declaration recognizes that "various other actors in society, including ... educational institutions, the media, families, local communities, civil society organisations, human rights defenders and the private sector, have an important role to play in promoting and providing human rights education and training."[41]

Human Rights Education in India

Indian Constitution 1950 embodies the human rights values. For the dissemination of HRE, the government of India constituted a committee under the chairmanship of home secretary comprising the secretaries of other ministers and department. When the National Human Rights Commission (NHRC) was setup in sep./oct. 1993, the coordination committee requested it to draft a national plan of action for human rights education. The task was over in 2001, when the national plan of action for HRE was finalised. The plan focused on strategies for human rights awareness-raising and sensitizing specific target groups such as students, officers in the administration of justice etc. Civil society as well as the NHRC is involved in the implementation of human rights education programmes. It is also reported that the secondary as well as higher education sector have undertaken certain activities relates to HRE which includes the preparation of curriculum, revision of text books and development of a number of training modules for teachers in English, Hindi and local languages by the National Council of Teacher Education (NCTE).

The concept of human rights of the state is included in the constitution. The Preamble, Fundamental Rights, Fundamental Duties, and Directive

Principles of the State policy are concrete steps toward the realisation of human rights. Whereas basic objectives have been defined in the Preamble, the protection of human freedom and liberties are emphasised in Fundamental Rights and Directive Principles of State Policy. The rights of the child have been given the greatest priority. Since rights and duties are inseparable, Fundamental Duties (Article 51) are also imperative. These provisions epitomize the collective will and aspiration of all Indians. The following provisions in Constitution safeguard human rights:

— Equality before the law (Article 14);
— Non-discrimination on ground of religion, race, caste, sex, and place of birth (Article 15);
— Equality of opportunity (Article 16);
— freedom of speech, expression, assembly, association, movement, residence, acquisition, and disposition of property, practice of any profession, carrying out any occupation, trade, or business (Article 19);
— Prohibition of traffic in human beings and forced labour (Article 23);
— Prohibition of labour in case of children below 14 years (Article 24);
— Freedom of religion (Article 25);
— No provision for religious instruction in any educational institution wholly maintained out of State funds (Article 28);
— Conservation of language, scripts, and culture (Article 29 [1]);
— Right of minorities to administer educational institutions (Article 30);
— State guarantee of social order (Article 38 [1], Directive Principles of State Policy);
— adequate means of livelihood, equal pay for equal work for both men and women, non-abuse of health of the worker, opportunity for children to develop in a healthy manner and in conditions of freedom and dignity (Article 39, Directive Principles of State Policy);
— Right to work, education, and public assistance in specific cases (Article 41, Directive Principles of State Policy);
— Provision for free and compulsory education of children up to 14 years of age (Article 45, Directive Principles of State Policy); and
— ensuring education and economic development of scheduled castes, scheduled tribes, and other weaker sections of society (Article 46, Directive Principles of State Policy).

Article 51A (1) of the Indian Constitution 1950, imposes a duty on all citizens to develop scientific temper, humanism and the spirit of inquiry and reform. The effective discharge of this duty will require HRE to give people enhanced awareness and greater openness.

In 1975, the National Council of Educational Research and Training (NCERT) formulated the first National Curriculum Framework which states:" The awakening of social consciousness, the development of democratic values and of a feeling for social injustice and national integration are extremely important. All subjects should be taught in such a manner so as to foster the spirit of scientific humanism." The National Curriculum Framework for primary and secondary education (NCERT 1988) identifies and addresses some of these concerns such as promoting values of democracy, secularism, equality, egalitarianism, removal of social barrier and creating a sense of common citizenship. National Curriculum Framework for School Education (NCERT 2000) reaffirms the 10 core components identified in the National Policy on Education (1986): To include the fundamental duties as laid down in Article 51 A of the constitution as core components of the curriculum was also emphasised by NFC (2000).

In recent years, Government of India has implemented several policies in the field of education for the above issue. These are:

- *Higher Education:* RUSA, NRP, NCUs, WCCUs, Degree Colleges in backward areas, Educational Loans, Construction of Girls Hostels etc.
- *Technical Education*: SAP, NPTEL, INDEST-AICTE, NPEEE, TDM, DASA, Integrate the PWD in main stream of Technical and Vocational Education
- *School Education:* SSA, DPEP, MDM, NPEGEL, EGS & AIE, IDMI, KGBV, BOS, SPQEM; RMSA, IEDSS, AEP, QIS, AE, GH, MS, ICT at school, VSE, Model school under PPP, SRCs, JSSs, AVAs etc.

A Rights Based Approach to Education

Aurora (2016) has nicely explained the Rights based approach in following manner. A human rights based approach is a conceptual framework that is normatively based on international human rights standards and operationally directed to promoting and protecting human rights. It seeks to analyze inequalities and redress discriminatory practices and unjust distributions of power that impede progress.[42] when applied to education it is synonymous with human rights education.

The human rights principles that inform a rights based approach include:[43]

- Universality and inalienability: Human rights are universal and inalienable.
- Indivisibility: Human rights are indivisible. Whether civil, cultural, economic, political or social, they are all inherent to the dignity of every person

- Interdependence and interrelatedness;
- Equality and non-discrimination;
- Participation and inclusion;
- Empowerment;
- Accountability and respect for the rule of law.

A rights-based approach can significantly add value to the processes and goals of education:[44]

- It promotes social cohesion, integration and stability;
- It builds respect for peace and non-violent conflict resolution;
- It contributes to positive social transformation;
- It produces better outcomes for economic development.

Human rights education lies at the heart of all efforts to develop a culture of human rights and a society that embraces dignity, inclusion, and equality. Human rights education contributes to social cohesion, democracy, conflict prevention and resolution, and understanding of diversity. It is a means to develop societies where the human rights of all are respected, protected and fulfilled. The provision of human rights education is a legal obligation on States under international human rights law, and one which is essential for the enjoyment of all other rights in a pluralistic democracy.

3.6.2 Role of Education in the Development of Peace and Harmony

In today's World, hurry and worry hinder the joy of learning and undermine learning and the harmony of life. Students' unrest is the common phenomena at present time. It influences unrest in home, village and life. Hence, everywhere there are disturbance, turmoil, unstable and problems keep rising every day and man is constantly worried about finding probable solutions. We are facing the crisis of depletion of world resources, greenhouse effect, global warming, natural disasters and, in the social front: terrorism, poverty, unknown diseases, nuclear war, intolerance, jealousy, suspicion, threats posed by modern armaments (conventional, chemical, biological and nuclear), vast inequalities of opportunities, wealth and power round the globe, rapid increase in population, and even the AIDS epidemic. This scenario needs peace education in all levels.

Peace education aims at equipping individuals with the values, skills, and attitudes they need to be wholesome persons who live in harmony with others and as responsible citizens. Values and attitudes are the building blocks of the culture of peace. Peace provides the joy of living. Learning, from the peace perspective, has to be a joyful experience. Life with joy is very meaningful. Religion, according to the National Curriculum Framework for School Education (NCFSE)—2000, is a source of value generation.

Value education is the vital component of peace education. Peace is a contextually appropriate and pedagogically included as coherence for values. Peace concretizes the purpose of values and motivates their internalisation. Peace education encourages educating for peace; which is, thus, the ideal strategy for contextualizing and making operative value education. Values are internalised through experience and influence. It is lacking in the classroom and exclusively cognitive approach to teaching.

The concept of peace includes:

(i) The absence of tensions, conflicts, and all forms of violence including terrorism and war.

(ii) The creation of a society free from structural violence. The duty to practice justice: social, economic, cultural, and political.

(iii) The absence of exploitation and injustice of every kind.

(iv) International cooperation and understanding.

(v) Ecological balance and conservation. The adoption of lifestyles conducive to the wholeness of creation.

(vi) Peace of mind.

(vii) Peace implies the capacity to live together in harmony.

On the whole it believes to live as "Vasudheva kutumbakam"

Peace begins with the individual and spreads to the family, to the community, to the nation, and to the world. The members of a society need to be oriented toward peace rather than toward violence. At the same time, social, economic, and political systems have to be reoriented to peace. The discipline of peace must shape our way of life. Education is vital tool for the effectiveness of peace in life. Peace education will encourage peace in life. Let it be so!

This is the age of unprecedented violence: locally, nationally, and globally. It is a serious matter that schools, which are meant to be the nurseries of peace, become transmission points for violence. It is seen everywhere that day to day the children are becoming more violent in action, speech and deeds. The more "achievement-oriented" a person is the less able he tends to be in relating to people, even dear ones, sensitively, reciprocally, and responsibly. Lopsided development, marked by deficient social imagination, makes children vulnerable to violence.

"In a survey conducted for this position paper, 18 per cent of the children interviewed were found to take pleasure in various acts of violence. They enjoyed stoning little pups and kittens, breaking flower buds off plants, holding butterflies between their fingers, older children engaged in eve-teasing and ragging to the extent that it sometimes became fatal." (NCERT, 2006, p. 3)

The citizens of tomorrow need to be empowered to choose the way of peace rather stray into the blind alleys of violence. Peace is a prime requirement for progress and national integration. Conflicts dissipate our collective energy and destroy the framework for a better quality of life. Every society in every age has acknowledged peace as a noble and necessary ideal. The great spiritual teachers of the past were, in their own ways, educators for peace.

Inner peace is the seed of collective peace. Peace implies the ability to respond to the surrounding suffering and other's needs in ways that affirm faith in the light beyond the darkness. *The ability to respond justly and affirmatively to the needs and sufferings of others is the hallmark of authentic inner peace.* It is not an exclusive obsession with peace for oneself, but a commitment to peace for all.

Peace education seeks to nurture the knowledge, skills, attitudes, and values that comprise a culture of peace. It is a long-term proactive strategy to nurture peaceful persons who resolve conflicts non-violently. Peace education enhances the physical, emotional, intellectual, and social growth of children within a framework of human values. Peace is considered as a holistic endeavour that aims at the comprehensive development of persons. Peace mandates the practice of values such as love, truth, justice, equality, tolerance, harmony, humility, togetherness, and self-control.

Peace is the inset tendency of human being. Each human being has two tendencies; devil and divine. If one selects former one he will be a demon or having negative behaviour. If he selects later one he will be divine having positive behaviour. Positive behaviour means showing the behaviours approached by everyone. That is sociable, '*satyam*', '*sivam*' and '*sundaram*' *or Truth, Beauty and Goodness*. It is '*satwic*' in nature. Those are meant for wellbeing of individual, society as well as nation. It is ethical, spiritual, Godly, pious and follows moral ideas. '*The Ramayana*', '*The Mahabharat*', '*The Gita*', '*The Savitri*', '*The Bible*', '*The Koran*' are great scriptures in the world which show the above path. There are thousands of scriptures in the world which are in similar nature. It leads to peaceful, happiest, truthful, harmonious, and faithful life. This is the path of knowledge, justice, power, light and love. It may establish the kingdom of God in this beautiful earth.

On the other way, Devil (negative) work means-the work which is negative in nature; that is un-lawful, falsehood, arbitrary, selfish, jealousy, arrogant, hatred etc. Those are not suitable for others. It may be egoistic meant for self-satisfaction. A few people satisfied with such activities. It may be both '*rajasic*' and '*tamasic*' in nature. It makes him restless, unstable, worried, unconscious and negative in behaviour. It leads to suffering, sad, disappointment, hopeless, faithless, disease and death. Destruction of earth by any means is the result of such activities.

It is said that environment and society have significant role to create peace and harmony. Positive environment helps to move in positive direction i.e. direction of peace and negative environment helps him to move in negative direction i.e. the direction of suffering, hopeless, despair, troublesome, and sad. Now choice is imperative. Hell or heaven! The former path has gone to hell and the later one to heaven. The people in society will select which will help for him. Measure people want positive direction. But unconsciously they also do mischievous activities and fall in trouble. Hence to maintain a harmonious and peaceful life the first condition is to be conscious in each component of human being, i.e. mind, vital, body, psychic and soul of human being. In consequence mind will achieve knowledge, vital-being will achieve power, body will achieve beauty and psychic will achieve '*ananda*'. Life will be peaceful and harmonious with the beautiful world.

Peace education aims at promoting a culture of peace. It can make learning a joyful and meaningful experience. Peace offers a contextually appropriate and pedagogically gainful point of coherence for all values. Inner peace is identified as the seed of peace, which creates nice personality. Education for peace, as a pioneering move, must be implemented with vision and determination.

To NCERT (2006), major frontiers of education for peace are:

(a) Bringing about peace-orientation in individuals through education;
(b) Nurturing in students the social skills and outlook needed to live together in harmony;
(c) Reinforcing social justice, as envisaged in the Constitution;
(d) The need and duty to propagate a secular culture;
(e) Education as a catalyst for activating a democratic culture;
(f) The scope for promoting national integration through education; and
(g) Education for peace as a lifestyle movement.

3.6.2.1 *Education meant for Individual cum Social Development*

Education is the key that unlocks the door to modernisation. Education system of today has come to be viewed as a major determinant of social, political and economic change. The World Bank has declared that the qualities of the nation's people have an important influence on its prosperity and growth, as human beings are source of ideas, decisions, actions and innovations. Besides entrepreneurial and administrative abilities, technological, scientific and professional skills are very important factors. Human being should be prepared to assume their role as responsible citizens, to develop a scientific outlook, and have an awareness of their rights and responsibilities, to sensitize them to ethical, social and cultural values which make them an enlighten nations; finally, to impart the necessary knowledge, skills, and attitudes necessary for the nation's development. Education is the most powerful agent in increasing the potential of human resources.

Education as a fundamental human right resorts to cultivating good attitude to an individual. The world and developing countries are giving highest concentration to education. But some of the measure developments in the last six decades which accounts for this new values attached to education and for shift in perspective regarding relation to society, the economy and the policy are: firstly the large scale entry into the world arena after decolonisation of the third world countries and the consequent increase in the demand for education in those countries and secondly, the increasing awareness even in the advanced countries, about the necessity to continuously educate people to cope with the technological advancement. The whole gamut of literature on social change, places a high premium on the role of education as the most important vehicle for social change. Since Plato and Aristotle, political philosophers have affirmed principles embodied in the phrases, "as in the State so is the School." In other words, political thinkers too recognised the nexus between the educational and political system.

During 20th century, as the age of democracy advanced, the faith in education as the liberator of mankind increased. According to John Dewey, "It is the business of school environment to eliminate so far as possible, the unworthy features of the existing environment from influence upon mental habitudes...As society become more enlightened it realised that it was responsible not to transmit and conserve the whole of its existing achievements but to strive for a better future society. The school is its chief agency for the accomplishment of this end." Conservatives essentially believed that the purpose of education was to preserve and transmit certain values, but the liberals believed that the school as an institution can play an important role in social reform for improving the lot of mankind. The Kothari Commission on education arrived at the conclusion that, "what is needed is a revolution in education which will set in motion the much desired social, economic and cultural revolution." The well-known de-schoolers such as Reimer, Ivan Illich, Holt and Goodman called for alternative strategies in education which can lead to transformation of society towards desirable objectives of freedom to enjoy life, liberty and pursuit of happiness for all. Evan Illich in particular argued that schooling is one of the major means by which status quo is preserved. Endorsing the view of Illich, Kurien, an Indian scholar, brought out nicely how knowledge "becomes the cleverest and most powerful ally to the status quo in all societies everywhere. "Nineteen centuries was deemed to the century of industries, while 20th century is the Century of Education. Bertrand Russell argued that, "education in the modern world tends to be a reactionary force, supporting the government when it is conservative and opposing it when it is progressive."

In the words of Harold Silver, a contemporary scholar, "education has been seen both as a means of selecting and perpetuating elites. It is discussed in terms of class domination and social control but also of social liberation and progress... It has become more and more prominent in political manifests and policies in economic calculation and family discussions, in bookshops and in the press. It has also become a major instrument of national policy.

Education systems and educationists have come together in educational movements, professional conferences and in attempts at educational policy at regional, national, and international levels. Education had become one of the most sensitive national responses to economic and political change."

3.6.2.2 Education and Economic Development of Nation

Education is regarded as directly promoter of economic advancement. The human invest revolution in economic thought initiated in 1960's by Theodore Schultz produced an electrifying effect on the trends theory and practice of education. Education has come to be regarded a panacea for all the ills in society.

The governments of the world, particularly third world, were convinced of the economic benefits of the education. The approach to education was changed; from consumption or a device for culture transmission to the most valuable investment of mankind, in man and 'human capital' swept into developmental plans of countries. "Educational plans were drawn as part of social and economic development plans."

Education and economic development are inter-linked. Education is regarded as a pre-requisite for economic growth. The acceptance of education as the master determinant of long-term economic growth, apart from all its other benefits in the development process, has become for many persons almost an instrument of faith. Schultz in a paper opined that "except for some pure rent (in earning) for differences in the inherited abilities most of the differences in earnings are a consequences of difference in the amounts that have been invested in people." Although investment in people consists of such other factors as food, security, health, the major component of investment in human being is in the form of more and better education.

Education is regarded as consumption good and production good at the same time. Educational experience can access to more different forms of consumption. In developing countries although some returns from investment in education may be expected at all stages of economic development, investment in educational facilities may produce much lower returns in some earlier stages of economic growth that the application of equal amounts of investment in other forms of capital especially capital constituting the material infrastructure of economy. It is deferred investment.

At certain periods, investment in a given set of non-human resources and at other periods investment in human resources bring about a higher sustained rate of growth of average income. Broadly speaking economic development is the result of two factors: the human factor and the non-human factor. It is the human factor which contributes to more than 50 per cent of economic growth which has taken place in different countries.

In conclusion, education is regarded as a pre-requisite for social change, facilitating reorientation of values through better understanding of environment, human, material and physical. According to National Policy of Education (1986) Government of India, the country has reached a stage in its economic and its technical development when a major effort must be made to derive the maximum benefits from the assets already created and to ensure that the fruits of change reach all sections. Education is the highway to reach that goal. Thus education is very important factor for individuals and their own family development, development of peace and harmony, rights and values, community improvement, and overall economic development of a particular country.

Endnotes

1. "Wisdom—Define Wisdom at Dictionary.com". Dictionary.com.
2. *Oxford University Press. Retrieved July 14, 2015.*
3. Wikiquote: Charles Spurgeon#Quotes
4. Carney, Brian M.; Getz, Isaac (2009). *Freedom,* Inc. Crown Business. p. 238. ISBN 9780307462473. Retrieved 8 March 2015.
5. Wikiquote: But note that two thousand years after Aristotle, Isaac Newton was forced to admit that "I have not yet been able to discover the cause of these properties of gravity"
6. "Myths about Roman goddess minerva. (n.d.)". Roman-colosseum.info.
7. "Character education: our shared responsibility". Ed.gov. 31 May 2005
8. knowledgetowisdom.org
9. Sternberg, R.J. (1985). Implicit theories of intelligence, creativity, and wisdom. Journal of Personality and Social Psychology, 49, 607-62.
10. Brown, S.C.; Greene, J.A. (2006). "The Wisdom Development Scale: Translating the conceptual to the concrete". *Journal of College Student Development.* 47: 1-19. doi:10.1353/csd.2006.0002.
11. http://psycnet.apa.org/psycinfo/2002-02382-024
12. Jeste, DV; Ardelt, M; Blazer, D; Kraemer, HC; Vaillant, G; Meeks, TW (October 2010). "Expert consensus on characteristics of wisdom: a Delphi method study".
13. Peterson, Christopher; Seligman, Martin E.P. (2004). *Character Strengths and Virtues: A Handbook and Classification.* Oxford: Oxford University Press. p. 106. ISBN 0-19-516701-5.
14. Harter, Andrew C. (2004). "8". In Peterson, Christopher; Seligman, Martin E.P. *Character Strengths and Virtues: A Handbook and Classification.* Oxford: Oxford University Press. pp. 181-196. ISBN 0-19-516701-5.
15. Ferrari, Michel (2012). *The Scientific Study of Personal Wisdom.* Springer Verlag. ISBN 978-9048192304
16. Vervaeke, John. "*The Cognitive Science of Wisdom*". Mind Matters Conference. Retrieved 13 April 2013.
17. Sternberg, Robert J. (2003). Wisdom, Intelligence, and Creativity Synthesized. New York: Cambridge University Press. ISBN 0-521-80238-5.

18. Grossmann, Igor; Jinkyung Na; Michael E W. Varnum; Denise C. Park; Shinobu Kitayama; Richard E. Nisbett (2010). "Reasoning about social conflicts improves into old age". *Proceedings of the National Academy of Sciences of the United States of America.* 107 (16): 7246-7250. Retrieved 1 May 2011.
19. Lewis, C.T. and Short, C. (1963). *Latin Dictionary.* Oxford University Press. ISBN 978-0-19-864201-5.
20. https://en.wikipedia.org/wiki/Wisdom#cite_sepience
21. http://path-to-dignity.org/film-english.
22. Universal Declaration of Human Rights (1948), Article 26.
23. http://www.ohchr.org/EN/Issues/Education/Training/Pages/HREducation TrainingIndex.aspx.
24. United Nations World Programme for Human Rights Education, Plan of Action First Phase, page 3.
25. United Nations Declaration on Human Rights Education and Training (2011), Article 2.2.
26. http://www.ohchr.org/EN/Issues/Education/Training/Pages/HREducation TrainingIndex. aspx.
27. Vienna Declaration and Programme of Action, adopted by the World Conference on Human Rights in Vienna (1993), Part I, para. 33 and Part II, para. 80.
28. UN General Assembly resolution 49/184 (23 December 1994).
29. UN General Assembly resolution 59/113 A (10 December 2004).
30. Human Rights Education in the School Systems of Europe, Central Asia and North America: A Compendium of Good Practice (2009).
31. Of Estonia, Latvia, Lithuania, Poland, Russia, Denmark, Norway, Sweden, Finland, Germany and the United States, all have ratified all the treaties mentioned below, except for the United States which has ratified CERD, and signed the ICESCR, CRC, CRPD and CEDAW.
32. See General Comment No. 13 (1999) of the Committee on Economic, Social and Cultural Rights on the right to education, paras. 6(b) and 50. The four essential features of the right to education are: availability, accessibility, acceptability and adaptability. Quality education is considered to be a component of 'acceptability'.
33. See Committee on the Rights of the Child, General Comment No. 1 (2001) on the aims of education.
34. See Convention on the Rights of the Child, Article 2. See also General Comment No. 1 (2001) of the Committee on the Rights of the Child on the aims of education, paras. 10-11.
35. See General Comment No. 5 (2003) of the Committee on the Rights of the Child on general measures of implementation of the Convention of the Rights of the Child, para. 30.
36. See General Comment No. 5 (2003) of the Committee on the Rights of the Child on general measures of implementation of the Convention of the Rights of the Child, para. 12.
37. General Comment No. 1 (2001) of the Committee on the Rights of the Child on the aims of education, para. 2.
38. See General Comment No. 1 (2001) of the Committee on the Rights of the Child on the aims of education, para. 19.

39. See General Comment No. 1 (2001) of the Committee on the Rights of the Child, para. 10 on the interpretation of Article 29(1) of the Convention of the Rights of the Child.
40. United Nations Declaration on Human Rights Education and Training (2011), Article 1.1 and Article 1.2.
41. United Nations Declaration on Human Rights Education and Training (2011), Article 7.
42. United Nations Declaration on Human Rights Education and Training (2011), Article 10.

4
Pedagogy of Peace

Peace education is grounded in active citizenship, preparing learners for assiduous participation in a democracy, through problem-posing and problem-solving education, and a commitment to transformative action in our societies. —*John Dewey* (1938)

4.0 Introduction

Peace education contains two sub themes; Whole School Approach and Pedagogy of Peace. The first sub theme 'Whole School Approach' was aimed at making teachers becoming conscious that the school environment is created not only by building, staff and students; it also includes dynamic interaction among teachers. The environments where there is freedom of expression, the authorities are perceived as accessible, fair and benevolent, produces assured and calm personalities and feelings of wellbeing. On the other hand the lack of communication in the school system among authorities, teachers, and students etc. may give rise to stress, anxiety and fear at all levels which threatens peace and wellbeing of everyone, It is therefore important that the whole school may be organised from the point of view of whole school approach.

The 'Whole School Approach' awakes of the fact that each and every activity of the school, and the teaching and non-teaching personnel and staff all contribute to peace. The environment of the school, the schedule, staff-principal relationships, teaching learà′:ning atmosphere in the class, the activities relating to art, music, craft, cleanliness, policies like, appreciation for participation, involvement of all etc. all have a role in maintaining peace. The responsibility of the school is meant for not only the school children, but also community around the school, and out of school children, and need to work for the wider society and extending school resources for the purpose. The teacher can mobilize classroom climate for peace. Improving classroom climate needs to become aware of the problems which disrupt peace, personality characteristics of the teacher which help in the management of the classroom climate, and reflection on the qualities, the teachers possesses for peace orientation and how they transform themselves.

There are different subjects; which carry separate values. Identifying values hidden in the subject matter and how these values relate to peace in real life situations is a significant issue. For instance values of measurement, accuracy in description, unbiased assessments etc. taught in science have implication for day-to-day interaction with people and process of arriving at a judgment about others. Similarly subjects like social sciences, and mathematics too have inherent values that could be easily related to peace in real life. The values of thinking logically, drawing conclusions, appropriate generalisations, making estimates, verifying results etc. have implications for peace in real life as well. The co-curricular activities such as: dance, play, debate, poetry, creative writing, NSS, etc. also help for peace making.

The behaviour of the teacher within the classroom could educate students, and relate their learning process. Outside the classroom learning is also a vital way of improving teacher-pupil relationships. Personality characteristics of the teacher help in the management of the classroom climate. The peace orient exercises helped teachers to think about the ways of peaceful teachers and need to orient their own self for such behaviour. Each subject has its inherent values. The teachers should aware of the potential of the subjects to convey the inherent values within. They should identify the values hidden in the subject matter and how these values relate to peace in real life situations. For instance values of measurement, accuracy in description, unbiased assessments etc. taught in science have implication for day-to-day interaction with people and process of arriving at a judgment about others. Similarly subjects like social sciences, and mathematics too have inherent values that could be easily related to peace in real life. The values of thinking logically, drawing conclusions, appropriate generalisations, making estimates, verifying results etc. have implications for peace in real life as well.

The teacher is the leader in the classroom. His teaching style influences not only, the learning outcomes but also molds the personality of the students. Teachers' communication style, disciplining style, aggressiveness, warmth, or caring attitudes will have long lasting impact on the emotional development of students. Democratic teacher, free of prejudice motivate all equally, while those who are arrogant and distinctive, will hamper self-expression and growth of pupils. Opinionated, autocratic teachers cannot nurture peace. Teachers have to be made mindful of their own style of being with children and reflect on its impact on them. The teacher should developing ideas for integrating peace in lessons to develop strategies for teaching lessons to orient teaching towards peace. They can develop lesson plans in their own subject areas and simultaneously highlight peace related value. They must be aware of the co-curricular strategies for peace. The teachers should be aware about various strategies for peacemaking such as dance, play, debate, poetry, creative writing, NSS, etc. There are various methods which can be adopted by teachers for generating peaceful climate.

4.1 Some Key Areas

Some of the key areas are identified below that need to be addressed to ensure that education for peace has a reasonable chance of succeeding.

4.1.1 Curriculum Load

It is observed that most of the present children are deprived up play and joy. They have no curiosity instead of mulishness. They are becoming rebellious. Heavy load of curriculum, text books, school bags, pressure of teachers and guardians make them rubbish. Along with:

- The approach to covering the syllabus;
- The exclusive tyranny of the cognitive degrades learning into a labourious, not a joyful experience for students;
- Inordinate parental ambition, in a context of intense competition.
- The underdevelopment of personality and inner resources results in the inability to cope with stress and strain;
- The children belong to poor family

The burden of curriculum load creates and activates impatience among the learners. Since peace education is to be integrated into the curriculum, it needs much the availability of adequate instructional time to teachers to practice this integration. Peace education calls for a vastly different approach to teaching as compared to what is prevailed now. Teachers have to be creative, innovative, and experimenting in their pedagogic approach. That can change the sense of burden and underprivileged. At MIRA, Oupada, Odisha, freeway education, education without bag, open library, open class room, organising events by students, writing diary, etc. are experimented by the author. The output is wonderful.

4.1.2 Textbook Writing

Textbooks convey attitudes and values obviously. Every aspect of textbooks—language, contents, and presentation, including illustrations has core value. It can create either peace or violence. It is, therefore, important to ensure that textbooks are written and designed from the perspective of education for peace. Care needs to be taken in writing textbooks to avoid violence in diction and illustrations. Illustrations, at times, for purposes of effect tend to err on the side of the violent and the melodramatic. Implicit forms of violence are common in textbook writing, and tend to reinforce prejudices and stereotypes of discrimination.

The directive of the National Policy on Education (1986) stated that 'sex stereotyping' in the school curriculum be scrupulously avoided. The integration of a peace perspective in textbook writing can help eradicate these anomalies.

Ideally, textbook writing should take into account the larger context in which the educational influence on students takes place. Authors should be aware of socio-economic inequalities, negative attitudes, discriminatory stereotypes, prejudices based on caste, creed, and gender, as well as broad trends in the emerging popular culture, especially the growing prevalence of violence, that comprise the larger ambience of education. They should take advantage, creatively and innovatively, of the 'peace opportunity' in the treatment of every topic and subject. Such opportunities include, among other things, the scope for enlarging the awareness of students in respect of the ground realities.

India is a vast country with immense diversities. Special care needs to be taken to eradicate the rural and urban discrimination and reflecting the immediate contexts of students in their specificities. Textbooks, in the end, are as good as their fate in the hands of teachers. It should be possible for a teacher, trained from the perspective of creating peace, to make up for what textbooks lack in terms of contextual specificity. Training future teachers to do so should be the major thrust in teacher education for peace. Every textbook must be thoroughly and critically reviewed for its contents, treatment, and overall vision. On the negative side, textbooks need to be kept clear of anti-peace ideas, assumptions, and attitudes. From a positive angle, it needs to be ensured that they appropriate 'peace opportunities' optimally. Attention needs to be paid to the language used in textbooks so as to ensure that their sensibility is conducive to nurturing courteous, aesthetically-sensitive, and socially-aware human beings.

4.1.3 Media and Violence

The influence of media is pervasive. In rural India children have more ready access to the television than. In thousands of villages, there are reportedly more television sets. Children spend more time on watching television programmes. In the process the child is exposed to thousands of episodes of violence, including murder, rape, and riot. The media plays, a major role in spreading a culture of violence. Teachers need to engage this reality in their approach to teaching.

Informed teacher-parent partnership can go a long way in protecting children from media-induced orientation to violence. Under the given circumstances, the initiative in this regard has to come from the teachers. In these respects, education of children may have to include media literacy for parents as well, to enable them to discharge their role adequately. The battle is half-won if parents are made aware of the harmful influence that television and cinema violence has on their children. Good parenting is perhaps the greatest defense against the ill-effects of media violence on children. On their part, teachers can help children to relate to the media in a realistic and wholesome means so that its benefits are derived and its harmful effects minimised.

4.1.4 Teacher-Parent Partnership

The importance of the teacher-parent partnership in education continues to be emphasised. In practical parental participation does not survive beyond the few early years of a child's schooling. Burdened beyond the school hours by tuition and homework, children live like guests in their homes. Children are forced to live in academic framework, out of touch with reality and uninvolved with the flow of life around them. In this respect, education for peace can make a wholesome difference. It is impossible to integrate peace concerns into the learning process and keep it confined to the classroom. Teachers will know at once that they build on the foundations that parents lay. They will know, too, that parents are helpful and necessary allies. The peace values and problem-solving methods taught in classrooms have to be sustained and reaffirmed at home, if they are to be internalised by students. The rehabilitation of parents in the learning process of their children can prove excitingly beneficial in improving the relational and emotional quality of life at home as well. They are, thus, sure to welcome the opportunities afforded by education for peace, if only teachers know how to open the door to this temporarily misplaced but crucial pedagogic partnership.

4.1.5 Challenge of Integration

Since peace is an integrative and all-embracing concept. But this ideal approach is to be implemented in a system that is far from this. The ground realities concerning every constituent of education—from textbook writing to classroom transaction, from teacher motivation to the school setting—has to be integrated. The Indian school system is the most complex and multi-layered in the world, marked by diversities, inequalities, and inadequacies of various kinds. For education for peace to have a realistic chance to deliver within this system, it is important that the likely pitfalls and potholes along the route of implementation be remedially engaged. From a pragmatic standpoint, the preference for the integrative approach is dictated by anxieties about Policy Perspectives

A. *Assessment and Examination*

The current system of examination and evaluation, burdened by curriculum load, is vitiated by tension, instability, suffering; that may lead to violence. "Learning, which is meant to be a joyful experience, is degraded into something burdensome, even oppressive, by reducing its goal to examination-centric excellence that is expected to eventuate into employment in due course. Fierce competition—artificially kept red-hot through the denial of adequate opportunities for higher education—and the stigma it imposes on failure, keep millions of children in a limbo of suffering and drives a few to despair and suicide. These extreme reactions are startling statements on the toll that education now takes" (NCERT, 2006).

A misconceived pursuit of excellence has degraded the beneficiaries of education into its victims! The learning process, along with its system of evaluation, needs to be radically reorganised and made pro-peace and student-friendly. Education for peace is situated in the domain of affective learning, which is not measurable in a quantitative form. In a practical sense, however, the total absence of evaluation may erode accountability and cause education for peace to be neglected. It is quite possible and necessary, therefore, to evaluate a school's effectiveness in educating students to be active agents for peace. The International Schools Association, Global Issues Network, suggests the following indicators for evaluating the effectiveness of education for peace programme in educating students and the school community as a whole. The school's mission statement should contain aspirations to peace and related values and skills. It should be mandatory to ensure that schools are free from discriminatory attitudes and practices based on caste and gender. The mission statement of the school should be periodically reviewed, under the following main heads, by the whole school community (see flow chart i.e. on next page).

B. *Pedagogical Skills and Strategies*

The common pedagogic goal for teachers is syllabus and examination oriented. In peace-oriented pedagogy, the focus is not merely on retention of concepts, memorisation of texts, or achieving individual goals and excellence but on learning to reflect, share, care, and collaborate with each other. Every topic/ lesson has peace-laden (hidden or explicit) components, which need to be transacted with deliberate planning from a positive and humanistic perspective. The methods of teaching should be creative, child-centered, largely experiential, and participatory. These include creation of appropriate learning experiences, discussion, debates, presentation, and group and cooperative projects, depending on students' maturity levels and the subject content. The teacher and school may devise other context-specific strategies to develop among students a sense of openness and comprehension about diverse cultures, histories, and fundamental shared values (*Op. cit.*).

There is ample scope in the syllabi of various subject areas for teaching students the importance of adopting peaceful means of resolving disagreements and conflicts and eschewing violence; and teachers need to take full advantage of this. Presenting lessons from a humanistic and positive perspective is the basis of education. Teaching should awaken positive feelings and foster positive experiences, help in arriving at an understanding of the self, encourage openness to inquiry by raising questions, exploring, and discovering and constructing an understanding of values, and provide an opportunity for applying the knowledge of values the student has learnt. Strategies like

Indicators for Evaluating Effectiveness of Peace Education in Schools

Individual Practice	Classroom Setup	School Setup	Community Approach
Tolerance	Recognition of diversity and prejudice	A secure and non-threatening climate	Service Programmes
Truthfulness	Cooperative group work	Fair school rules	Outreach Programmes
Respect	Absence of discriminatory attitudes and practices	A caring approach and provisions for counselling	Demonstrating leadership
Equality	Open and Respectful student-staff relationship	Representation	Awareness of problems and contributions to solutions
Effective Communication	Seeking Peaceful Resolutions	Parent-teacher Partnership	Exchanges
Openness		Inclusion of appropriate educational activities related to peace	Partnerships with other schools
Reconciliation Compassion		Evidence of staff development programmes relevant to education for peace	
Freedom and Prejudice			

questions, stories, anecdotes, games, experiments, discussions, dialogues, value clarification, examples, analogies, metaphors, role-play, and simulation are helpful in promoting peace through teaching-learning. Some peace values may be more appropriately inculcated while teaching a particular subject at a particular stage or grade, while others are better integrated with other subjects in a different grade.

4.2 Conflict Resolution

Origin of peace lies in finding the root cause of conflict. Although resolution may not be possible for all conflicts, effective management is the best resolution. Non-resolution of conflicts is neglecting one's own concerns and others too. Management involves efforts for attaining diverse objectives simultaneously with minimum costs and maximum outputs. The objectives of different castes, cultures, societies etc. are different even within same culture, all individuals may not have similar objectives; all nations may not have similar objectives. While one nation is trying to control population, others are giving incentive for increasing population. Management demands clarity of objectives and clear listing of alternatives available for management of conflict. Different conflict management models should be discussed: Competitive collaborative, assertive as well as cooperative and accommodative models, which means assertive and cooperative attitudes; and compromising model which involves intermediate, assertive and cooperative attitudes. In order to manage conflicts the best way is to enable conflicting parties to understand and appreciate each other's stand, rigidity and stiffness cannot help management of conflicts.

Conflict resolution is an integral part of peace building. Conflict resolution requires skills and strategies, which should be known to be those interested in peace making by continuous conflict resolution and management of conflicts. Peace education cannot be visualised without understanding and developing skills of conflict resolution. Conflicts are here to stay but they need to be resolved amicably. The key idea was: Origin of peace lies in finding the root cause of conflict. Although resolution may not be possible for all conflicts, effective management is the best resolution. Non-resolution of conflicts is neglecting one's own concerns and others too. Management involves efforts for attaining diverse objectives simultaneously with minimum costs and maximum outputs. The objectives of different castes, cultures, societies etc. are different even within same culture, all individuals may not have similar objectives; all nations may not have similar objectives. While one nation is trying to control population, others are giving incentive for increasing population. Management demands clarity of objectives and clear listing of alternatives available for management of conflict. Different conflict management models were discussed: Competitive collaborative, assertive as well as cooperative and accommodative models, which means assertive and cooperative attitudes; and compromising model which involves intermediate, assertive and cooperative attitudes. In order to manage conflicts the best way is to enable conflicting parties to understand and appreciate each other's stand, rigidity and stiffness cannot help management of conflicts.

Interdependence is the way of the life, which necessitates understanding and knowing others, which can happen only when there is dialogue between people. Stresses and conflicts are created by unreasonable expectations and the gap between reality desires. It is the common nature of human being that sticking to own opinion and insensitivity towards others opinion. This attitude of lack of empathy gives rise to suspiciousness, intolerance, and communication gap, which crops up conflict in society.

Conflict—Concept

- Conflict arises when individuals or groups encounter goals that both parties cannot obtain satisfactorily.
- Conflict is the struggle between incompatible or opposing needs wishes, ideas, interests or people.
- Conflict comes about from differences—sometimes through these differences we complement each other, what sometime we conflict.
- Conflict is not a problem in itself. It is what we do with it that counts.

What It is?

- In simple words conflict may be understood as collision or disagreement.
- The term conflict refers to perceived incompatibilities resulting from some form of interference or opposition

Competition

When individuals or group have incompatible goals but do not interfere with each other—they try to attain their goals, e.g. Track Events

- Interference in others domain is absent
- Generally goals are same.

Conflict is, when individual or group have incompatible goals and they try to interfere with each other as they try to obtain their respective goal. e.g. Football, Hockey, Cricket etc.

- In competition one will not frustrate the attempt of the other.
- In conflict one will frustrate the attempt of the other.
- Interference in others domain.
- Generally goals are opposite.

Types of Conflict

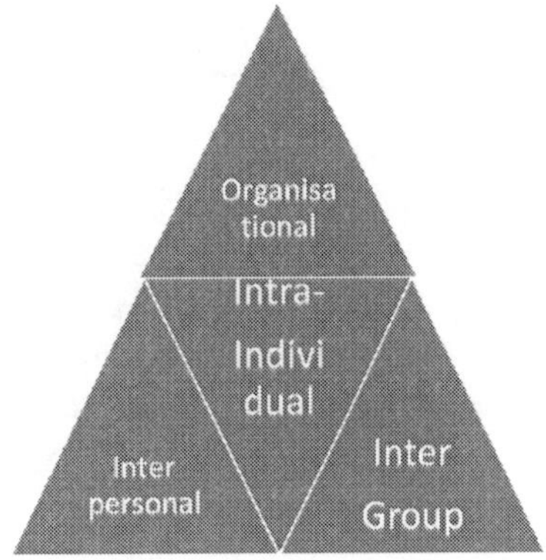

1. Intra-Individual Conflict

- Conflict within oneself.
- Micro conflict.
- Arises due to:
  - Frustration
  - Multiple Goals
  - Role ambiguity
- Conflict may be within an individual when there is incompatibility between his or her own goals or events.

2. Inter-individual Conflict

- Conflict between two individuals.
- Micro conflict in nature.
- Causes are:
  - Personal difference
  - Information Deficiency
  - Role Incompatibility

3. Inter-group Conflict

- Conflict between two or more groups within an organisation.
- Macro conflict in nature.
- Causes are:
  - Competition for resources
  - Task interdependences.
  - Status Struggles.

4. Intra-group Conflict

When conflict raises among the persons within the group due to various factors.

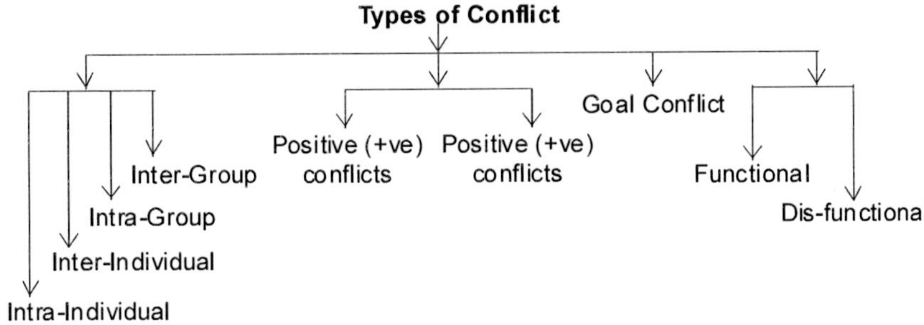

Other Types of Conflice

Moreover, there are also other types of conflicts we observe. They may be as below:

1. Functional Conflict

- Modern View
- Increases group effectiveness.
- Constructive in nature.
- Intensity of conflict is generally low or moderate.
- Stimulates creativity and innovation.

2. Dysfunctional Conflict

- Traditional View
- Hinder group effectiveness.
- Destructive in nature.
- Intensity of conflict is generally high.

3. Goal Conflict

1. Approach-Approach
   Two more positive but mutually exclusive goals.
   Decision Regret may occur
2. Approach-Avoidance
   Motive to avoid the goals is stronger than motive to approach it.
   e.g. Higher achievement in career Vs family responsibility.
3. Avoidance-Avoidance
   When individual is forced to choose between to mutually exclusive goals each of which progressive unattractive qualities. E.g. either resign the job or bear the bad boss.
4. Multiple Approach-Avoidance
   Several possibilities for action—each having several desirable and undesirable features—two alternatives—both involving +ve and –ve features

4. Positive Conflict

1. Increased involvement
2. Increased Cohesion
3. Innovation and creativity
4. Personal growth and change
5. Clarification of key issues
6. Organisational vibrancy
7. Individual and group identities.

5. Negative Conflict

1. Unresolved anger

2. Personality clashes
3. Less self-esteem
4. Inefficiency
5. Diversion of energy from work
6. Psychological well-being threatened
7. Wastage of resources
8. Negative climate
9. Disruption of group cohesion

6. Inter-personal Conflict

Interpersonal conflict occurs when a person or group of people frustrates or interferes with another person's efforts at achieving a goal. According to some researchers, conflict can consist of three different components.

The behavioural component of conflict involves someone interfering with the objectives of another person.

The cognitive component involves a disagreement between the parties that illustrates the differences between the interests and objectives of the conflicting parties.

The affective component relates to the negative emotional states of the conflicting parties. For example, conflict with a co-worker may make you feel anger, stressed, and frustrated.

7. Intra-personal Conflict

Intrapersonal conflict is the conflict humans face within themselves, it is a conflict between should and want. Should is always driven by the values, religious beliefs, upbringing etc. Wants on the other hand are driven by the environment which entices humans to indulge overlooking should. As a human component it raises at any moment. Conflict arises when any kind of decision needs to be taken.

The example of intrapersonal conflict may be between two choices: becoming a teacher at school level or becoming a lecture having appropriate qualification; my family tells me to abstain from alcohol/smoking, however my peers group instincts me to consume alcohol/smoking. "At times should wins and wants lose else wants win and should lose. Whenever should loses it leaves behind a sense of guilt, having consumed against the moral decree." Intrapersonal conflicts can sometimes have a damaging effect.

Anthony Robbins said in his book 'Awaken the giant within', "To overcome conflict humans need a very strong will power, as told by will and power are two words, the first step is to have the will and the leverage enough power to take a decision to battle the wants. Will power is like sitting in the car with an intention to drive and not stepping on the accelerator, no matter how much will you have the car will not move unless accelerated."

Transactional Analysis Model (TA)

Dr. Eric Berne during the 1960s created a model TA. It is developed about people and their relationships. TA is a very common model used in therapy. "It is based on two notions, first that we have three parts or 'ego-states' to our personality, and secondly that these converse with one another in 'transactions' (hence the name)."

Communications (Transactions)

When two people communicate, each exchange is a *transaction*. Many of our problems come from transactions which are unsuccessful.

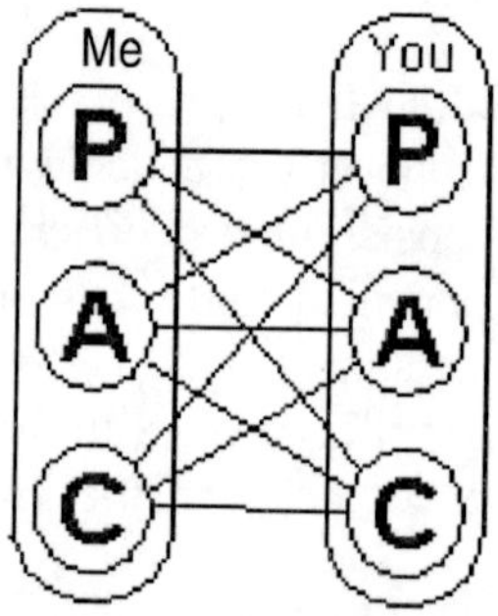

It is general event that parents naturally speak to Children, as this is their role as a parent. They can talk with other Parents and Adults, although the subject still may be about the children.

"The Nurturing Parent naturally talks to the Natural Child and the Controlling Parent to the Adaptive Child. In fact these parts of our personality are *evoked* by the opposite. Thus if I act as an Adaptive Child, I will most likely evoke the Controlling Parent in the other person." (*Op. cit.*)

We play many games through transaction, and there are rituals from greetings to whole conversations where we take different positions for different events. These are often 'pre-recorded' as *scripts* we just play out. They give us a sense of control and identity in positive direction. There are some games can be negative and destructive; if it is played out of sense of habit and addiction.

Complementary transactions: Usually such type of transactions occur when both people are at the same level. Ex. Parent talking to Parent, or children talking to children, or teacher talking to teacher etc. Here, both are often thinking in the same way and communication is easier. Problems usually occur in *Crossed* transactions, where each is talking to a different level. Ex. Teacher talking to children, parent talking to children etc.

When the author speaks to her daughter, her mother sometimes opposes; conflict arises due to misunderstanding. "The parent is either nurturing or controlling, and often speaks to the child, who is either adaptive or 'natural' in their response. When both people talk as a Parent to the other's Child, their wires get crossed and conflict results."(*Op. cit.*) 'The ideal line of communication is the mature and rational Adult-Adult relationship.'

Nature of Conflict

1. ***Cognitive:*** Problem solving, due to difference in perspective or judgments about issues—develop better ideas can air legitimate differences, +ve conflict.
2. ***Affective:*** Destruction, –ve conflict, emotional and directed at other people, anger, bitterness, goal displacement, poor decision.

Process of Conflict

Stage 1. Potential Opposition or Incompatibility

- Presence of condition that gives surface or opportunity for conflict to arise.
- Antecedent Conditions:
  - Communication
  - Structure
  - Personal Variable

Stage 2. Cognition and Personalisation

- Process where the parties decide what the conflict is all about.
- Only the parties become aware of the conflict.
- It can be of two types
  - Perceived Conflict
  - Felt Conflict

Process of Conflict

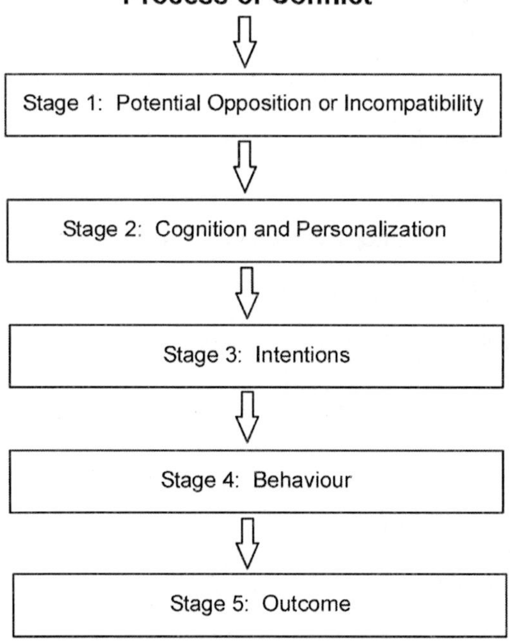

Stage 3. Intentions

- Intentions are decisions to act in a given way.
- Thin line between intention and behaviour.
- Behaviour does not always accurately reflect a person's intentions

Stage 4. Behaviour

- Conflict becomes visible.
- It includes the statements, actions and reactions made by the conflicting parties.

Stage 5. Outcome

The action-reaction interplay between the conflicting parties result in consequence.

The result can be of two types:

- *Functional outcomes:* increase in group performance;
- *Dis-functional outcomes:* Decrease in group performance

Functional Vs. Dysfunctional Outcomes

- Problems solving
- Strengthen relationship
- Make confident
- Enhance commitment to organisation
- Constructive Conflict
- Positive Outcome

Causes of Conflict

1. Task Interdependence
2. Task Ambiguity
3. Goal Incompatibility
4. Competition for Limited Resources
5. Competitive Reward System
6. Line and Staff
7. Intra Personal and Inter Personal Conflict

Strategies for Resolving Conflict

1. *Lose-Lose Strategy*

   Both Party Loses—(Compromise)

   Middle Ground

   Third party

   Arbitrator

2. *Win-Lose Strategy*
   One Party Wins—Other Loses (Competition)
   Superior subordinate conflict
   Line—Staff conflict
   Union—Management conflict
   Parties take short run view
   Emphasis on solution not problem
   Diffuse conflict—Loser will be bitter and vindictive
3. *Win-Win Strategy* (Collaboration)
   Desirable from organisational view
   Rewarding outcome
   Improved communication called management of conflict
   Complementary Transaction
   Bee Vs Flower

Style of Conflict Management

1. Competition
   1. Uses force, superior skill, or domination to win a conflict.
   2. Organisational development and effectiveness
   3. Competitive Spirit Basis.
   4. I Win/You Lose
2. Collaboration—Highly Effective
   - I Win/You Win
   - Conflict is resolved to everyone's benefit.
   - Strengthens relationships
   - Increases productivity
   - Long term solution
   - Responsibility Equation.
3. Compromise
   1. Mutual give-take situation.
   2. Neither a definite loser nor a distinct winner.
   3. Nobody gets what they want.
   4. Bargaining or Third party mediation.
   5. Establishes friendship.
4. Avoidance
   1. I Lose/You Lose
   2. Denying the existence of conflict and hiding one's own true feelings.
   3. Justifies situation, does not resolve.

Styles of Conflict Management

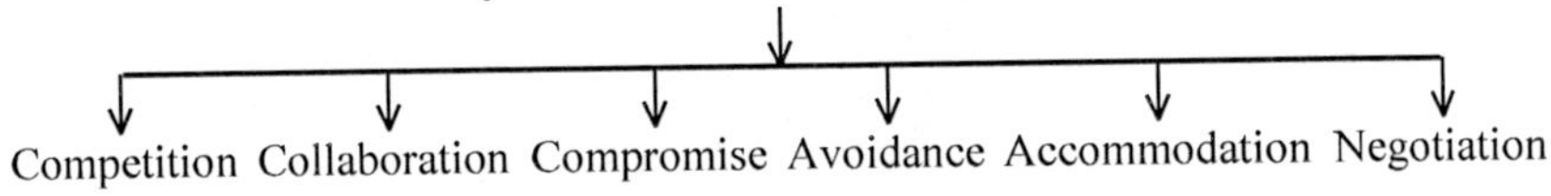

4. Weakens relationships
5. Loss of productivity

5. Accommodation
   - I lose/you win.
   - Playing down the conflict and seeking harmony among parties.
   - Emphasizing similarities.
   - Suppressing differences.
   - Short run solution.

6. Negotiations
   1. Acceptable Agreement combination of
   2. Compromise collaboration possibility
      (In this situation some disagreement and conflict exists.)
   3. Some degree of interdependence between parties
   4. Peaceful way of solving Conflict
   5. Opportunistic Interaction

7. Effective Negotiations
   1. Consider other parties situation and view point.
   2. Have a plan or concrete strategy
   3. Begin with positive note
   4. Address problem not personality.
   5. Pay little attention to initial offers.
   6. Emphasis win-win solution.
   7. Create a climate of trust
   8. Have open mind.
   9. Insist on objective criteria.
   10. Adapt to cultural differences
   11. Make clear agreement
   12. Be inventive about options
   13. Emphasis common ground
   14. Focus on needs not positions
   15. Be hard on problem and soft on person

Tips for Managing Workplace Conflict

- Double the dose of communication.
- Build good relationships before conflict occurs.
- Do not let small problems escalate; deal with them as they arise.
- Respect differences. Listen to others' perspectives on the conflict situation.
- Focus on solving problems, not changing people.
- If you can't resolve the problem, turn to someone who can help.
- Remember to adapt your style to the situation and persons involved.
- Acknowledge feelings before focusing on facts.

4.3 Brain Storming

What It Is?

In brain storming developed by Osborn, the individual is free to express his ideas readily, spontaneously and uncritically. According to him, there is greater chance of producing original ideas when brain is put under stress in order to attempt a solution to a problem. It should be discussed for their feasibility. Here ideational fluency is encouraged without fear on intervention or ridicule from the others. The method promotes self-confidence of the participants. The interplay of ideas sparks of far more good ideas than by the conventional problem solving technique. Brainstorming is a process for developing creative solutions to problems. Alex Faickney Osborn, an advertising manager, popularised the method in 1953 in his book, 'Applied Imagination'. Ten years later, he proposed that teams could double their creative output with brainstorming (Osborn, 1963).

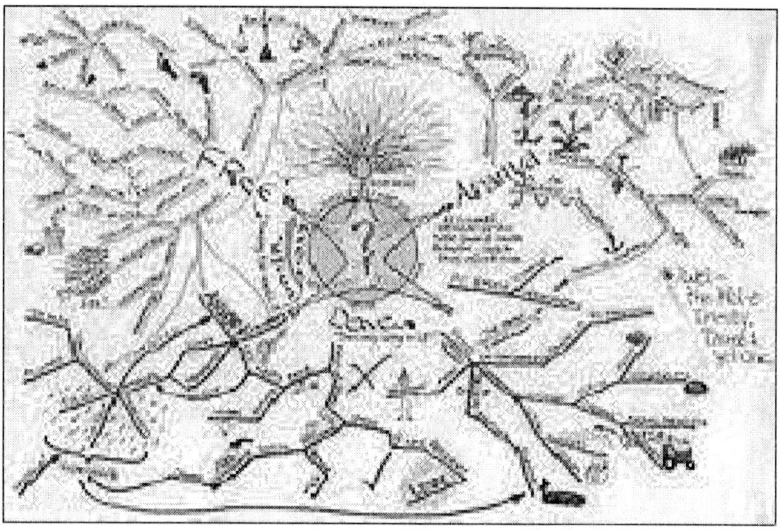

A Picture of Brain and its Neural Functions

Brainstorming works by focusing on a problem, and then deliberately coming up with as many solutions as possible and by pushing the ideas as far as possible. One of the reasons it is so effective is that the brainstormers not only come up with new ideas in a session, but also spark off from associations with other people's ideas by developing and refining them.

Procedure

We can divide the class into small groups. It is ideal to take five students in a group. There should be a recorder assigned for each group. Then the problem should be proposed to be brainstormed. Sufficient time should be provided to students to generate ideas. Then, list all the ideas for the whole class to see.

The Teacher should encourage "piggy backing" on one another's ideas. Discuss on different ideas and find the possible solutions.

"One approach is to *seed* the session with a word pulled randomly from a dictionary. Use this word as a starting point in the process of generating ideas. When the participants say they "can't think of any more ideas" then give them about 15 more minutes as the best ideas sometimes come towards the end of a longer thought process". (http://open-brainstormingblospot.com)

Brainstorming can either be carried out by individuals or groups. When done individually, brainstorming tends to produce a wider range of ideas than group brainstorming as individuals are free to explore ideas in their own time without any fear of criticism. On the other hand, groups tend to develop the ideas more effectively due to the wider range of diversity.

We should keep all the generated ideas visible. As a flip chart page becomes full, remove it from the pad and tape it to a wall as that it is visible. This "combined recollection" is helpful for creating new ideals. If the brainstormers have difficulty in coming up with solutions, we may have to restate the problem in a different context, such as using metaphors or linking it to own knowledge.

Generally the brain storming session follows following steps:

- Gather the participants from as wide a range of disciplines with as broad a range of experience as possible. This brings many more creative ideas to the session.
- Write down a brief description of he problem-the leader should take control of the session, initially defining the problem to be solved with any criteria the must be met, and then keeping the session on course.
- Use the description to get everyone's mind clear of what the problem is and post it where it can be seen. This helps in keeping the group focused.
- Encourage an enthusiastic, uncritical attitude among brainstormers and encourage participation by all members of the team. Encourage them to have fun!
- Write down all the solutions that come under to mind (even ribald ones)
- After completing the session of brain storming, the results of the session can be analysed and the best solution can be explored either using further brainstorming or more conventional solutions.
- "Do not censor any solutions, no matter how silly it sounds. The silly ones will often lead to creative ones-the idea is to open up as many possibilities as possible, and break down preconceptions about the limits of the problem."
- The leader should keep the brainstoming on subject, and should try to steer it towards the development of some practical solutions.
- Once all the solutions have been written down, evaluate the list to determine the best action to correct the problem.

Four Basic Rules of Brain Storming

There are four basic rules in brainstorming (Osborn, 1963) intended to reduce social inhibitions among team members, stimulate idea generation, and increase overall creativity:

- *No criticism:* Criticism of ideas are withheld during the brainstorming session as the purpose is on generating varied and unusual ideals and extending or adding to these ideas. Criticism is reserved for the evaluation stage of the process. This allows the members to feel comfortable with the idea of generating unusual ideas.
- *Welcome unusual ideas:* Unusual ideas are welcomed as it is normally easier to "tame down" than to "tame up" as new ways of thinking and looking at the world may provide better solutions.
- *Quantity Wanted:* The greater the number of ideas generated the greater the chance of producing a radical and effective solution.
- *Combine and improve ideas:* Not only are a variety of ideals wanted, but also ways to combine ideas in order to make them better.

Fundamental Principles

- The problem should be identified and presented in simple language.
- A small group (3-8) is suitable for catching of the ideas.
- All ideas should be recorded.
- Encourage the creative ideas.
- There should be some flexible time limit.
- Brain storming should be a part of problem solving process.

Successful Brainstorming

Effective brainstorming needs truly diverse thinking styles in a team. And when you get another member, ensure that person's thinking style is different than ours and the other team member. This is the first step in remaining competitive. Avoiding prejudice is better. Real team members should not be afraid to disagree, but once a decision has been made, they concentrate on getting there, not going back.

There are certain games that do a good job of using the various parts of the mind, which perform important function for reducing the fear factor by providing fun. Fear is a barricade for new ideals. By providing fun and laughter, we can create a pathway for radical ideals to emerge. Radical ideals come from creative activities. For example: drawing a card and then performing the activity before the timer runs out. For example, one team member might draw the word 'laughter'. Such drawing clues on a paper with her eyes closed; it may be direction, letters, word, picture or symbols.

The following points are very helpful for brain storming:

- Diverse thinking styles
- lively discussions
- Stimulus to spark the mind
- Fear prevention
- Fun games, friendly environment, and firm gestures that creates the feeling that everything is congenial

Come "out of the well" means as it provides an environment that uses everyone's thinking styles, rather than telling them to change their thinking style. When we provide a creative environment, instead of trying to change a person, we get the real person. When we get real persons into open, trusting environments with creative activities.

Conclusion

Brain storming is an effective technique for generating ideas. This technique may be used for solving any problem. It encourages students to come up with creative, exciting and fundamental ideas without fear of criticism. It creates a spontaneous reaction to the issue and finds solutions to specific problems. Effective brainstorming needs truly diverse thinking styles. Diverse thinking provides a creative environment, which provides real person. When we get real persons into open, trusting environments with creative activities.

4.4 Problem Solving Model

Problem solving is a good skill. Good problem solving skills are fundamentally important if we're going to be successful in our career. There are some persons who solve their problems by introspection, simulation, behaviour, computer modelling and experiment etc. The changing scenario of modern society dives mankind with various problems, which need effective solutions. Some people are born, some are brought up by experience and some are trained to solve problems quickly and effectively. Various researches such as Parnes (1958-60), Torrance (1959), Cavington, Krutchfield and Davis (1966) proved that cognitive skills like problem solving and creative thinking can be developed through special training programmes. Studies by Torrance (1960), Joyce Juntune (1979), and Shaw & Cliatt (1986) have proved the possibility of developing problem solving skills through deliberate effort.

We face a lot of problems in day to day activities. Among those, some are easily solved and some are felt difficult to solve. Some people have good capability to solve the problems and some are not able to do the same. Problems may be simple, complex, easy or difficult. A teacher's role is finding ways to solve them. So, being a confident problem solver is really important to success. There are number of processes to solve the problem. One can solve problems quickly and effectively by help of other.

There are four basic steps in solving a problem:

1. Defining the problem.
2. Generating alternatives.
3. Evaluating and selecting alternatives.
4. Implementing solutions.

Problem Solving Steps

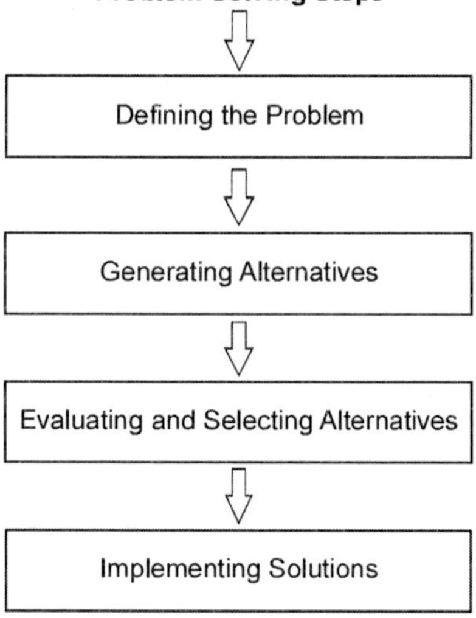

Defining the Problem

If we look a bit deeper of any problem, the real issue might be a lack of training, or an unreasonable workload. There are some tools which help one ask the right questions, and work through the layers of a problem to uncover what's really going on. At this stage, it's also important to ensure that looking at the issue from a variety of perspectives. There are various checklists which provide a powerful reminder to look at many elements that may contribute to the problem, and to expand your thinking around it.

Understanding Complexity

When the problem is simple, the solution is usually obvious; it is not needed to follow the four steps we outlined earlier. We follow that if the problem is likely to be complex and difficult to understand, because there's a web of interrelated issues. There are numerous tools developed to solve the problems. Many of these help you create a clear visual representation of the situation, so that one can understand about the event.

'Affinity Diagrams' are very helpful for organizing many different pieces of information into common themes, and for discovering relationships between these. Another popular tool is the *'Cause-and-effect Diagram'*. To generate viable solutions, we must have a solid understanding of what's causing the problem. Using our example of substandard work, Cause-and-Effect diagrams would highlight that a lack of training may be the cause of the problem, and they could also highlight possible causes such as work overload and problems with technology.

'Flowchart' and 'System Diagram' are also useful that help us to observe how various activities and inputs fit together. This will often help us identify a missing element that's causing our problem. The *'Drill Down'* technique will help us split our problem into smaller parts, each of which can then be solved appropriately.

Problem-Solving Processes

The four-step approach to solving problems that we mentioned earlier will serve well in many situations. Using established tools and techniques will help to improve one's approach to solving the problems that we face in our profession. We'll be more successful at solving problems and in consequence the work will be more successful. We can able to build a reputation as someone who can handle tough situations, in a wise and positive way. However, for a more comprehensive process, we can use *Simplex, Appreciative Inquiry* or *Soft Systems Methodology* (SSM). These provide detailed steps that we can use to solve a problem effectively. Whatever may be the problem, we must use a systematic approach of solving the problem.

Simplex involves an eight-stage process: problem finding, fact finding, defining the problem, idea finding, selecting and evaluating, planning, selling the idea, and acting. These steps build upon the basic process described earlier, and they create a cycle of problem finding and solving that will continually improve the organisation.

Appreciative Inquiry takes a uniquely positive approach by helping one solve problems by examining what's working well in the areas surrounding them.

Soft System Methodology is designed to help one understand complex problems so that one can start the process of solving them. It uses four stages to help one uncover more details about what's creating the problem, and then define actions that will improve the situation.

Managing the Problem

I have observed some experienced people, who do not stress the problem, they try to eliminate it. It may be good. But, we can find an easy solution of that problem. Some people manage it like a housewife manages her home by any means. Some people drive the direction in other way. To be an effective problem-solver, we need to be systematic and logical in our approach. This quiz helps one to assess our current approach to problem solving. By practicing this, would make better overall decisions. And as we increase our confidence with solving problems, it will easier to tackle.

Min Basadur's Simplex Problem-solving Model

To Min Basdur, This eight-step process follows the circular pattern shown below, within which current problems are solved and new problems are identified on an ongoing basis.

The different steps of the above system are mentioned below.

Step 1: Find the Problem

Some problems are very obvious and some are not so easily identified. As part of an effective problem-solving process, we need to look actively for problems—even when things seem to be running fine. Proactive problem solving helps us avoid emergencies and allows one to be calm and in control when issues arise.

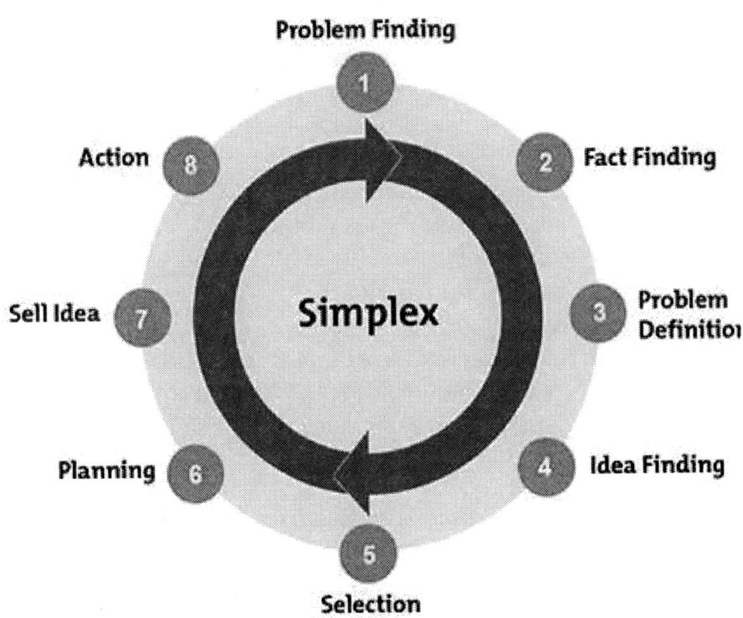

The Simplex Process

The following techniques may be helpful in solving problems:

- *Pest Analysis* helps us pick up changes to our environment that we should be paying attention to. Make sure too that we're watching changes in customer needs and market dynamics, and that we're monitoring trends that are relevant to our industry.
- *Risk Analysis* helps us identify significant business risks.
- *Failure modes and Effects Analysis* helps us identify possible points of failure in work process, so that one can fix these before problems arise.
- *After Action Reviews* help one scan recent performance to identify things that can be done better in the future.

Step 2: Find the Facts

After identifying a potential problem, it needs information. Hence, facts should be collected from various dimensions of the problem.

Step 3: Define the Problem

In this step, the problem should be clearly defined. Delimitation of the problem should be mentioned. It helps to stay focused on the main issues.

CATOWE is a good tool which may be used in this stage. By looking at a situation from these perspectives, we can open our mind and come to a much sharper and more comprehensive definition of the problem.

Cause and Effect Analysis is another good tool to use here, as it helps us think about the many different factors that can contribute to a problem. It also helps us separate the symptoms of a problem from its fundamental causes.

Step 4: Find Ideas

In this stage, ideas can be generated for finding a solution. The key here is to be flexible in the way one approaches the problem. One can see it from as many perspectives as possible. We can also use 'metaphor' and analogies to help analyze the problem, discover similarities to other issues, and think of solutions based on those similarities.

Traditional brainstorming and reverse brainstorming are very useful here. To generate a range of creative solutions of the problem, it is needed to involve people with different viewpoints to expand the volume of ideas.

Step 5: Select and Evaluate

In this stage, there are many ideas to be evaluated matching with criteria for a good solution. Decide what elements are needed for a realistic and practical solution. Paired 'Comparison Analysis', 'Decision Matrix Analysis' and 'Risk Analysis' are useful techniques which may be implied here,

Step 6: Plan

The problem solving process involves lots of planning and preparation. Here, it's important to know what to be prepared for as you begin to roll out your proposed solution. The type of planning depends on the size of the implementation project that we need to set up. For small projects, action plans are generally needed. It provides who will do what, when, and how. Larger projects need more sophisticated approaches.

Step 7: Sell the Idea

In this stage, we must convince other stakeholders that our solution is the best one. When we start communicating the plan, listen to what people say, and make changes as necessary. The better the overall solution meets everyone's needs. It has more positive impact.

Step 8: Act

When it is felt by the stakeholders that this is appropriate solution of the problem, we can move on to the implementation stage. This is the exciting and rewarding part of problem solving, which makes the whole process seem worthwhile. Once it is completed the implementation, we can move into the next cycle of problem solving.

Common Problem Solving Tools

- *Constructive Controversy*: Improving solutions by arguing for and against your options
- *Inductive Reasoning*: Drawing good generalised conclusions based on experience and observation
- *Failure Mode and Effective Analysis*: Spotting problems before a solution is implemented
- *Heuristic Method*: Using rules of thumb
- *Means End Analysis*: Identifying the steps needed to solve a problem

Problem Solving Approaches

There are various problem solving approaches we may follow to solve various issues in our profession. Some of them are given here under.

- *Plan-Do-Check-Act (PDCA)*: Implementing new ideas in a controlled way
- *Soft System Methodology (SSM)*: Understanding very complex issues
- Appreciative Inquiry: Solving problems by looking at what's going right
- *The Simplex Process*: A robust creative problem solving process

- *The Straw Man Concept*: Build it up, knock it down, and create a solid final solution
- *Hurston's Productive Thinking Model*: Solving problems creatively
- *Action Learning Sets*: Solving problems by doing and discussing

Finding Cause Techniques

There are several techniques used for finding the root cause for solving various problems. Among them some are given below.

- *Root Cause Analysis*: Tracing a problem to its origins
- *CATOWE*: Developing a robust problem definition
- *5 Whys*: Getting to the root of a problem quickly
- *The Drill Down Technique*: Breaking problems down into manageable parts
- *Cause and Effect Analysis*: Identifying the likely causes of problems
- *Appreciation*: Extracting the greatest amount of information
- *The Four Frame Approach*: Finding other ways forward
- *Interrelationship Diagrams*: Identifying cause and effect relationships

Conclusion

Problem solving is a unique important workplace skill. Being a competent and confident problem solver we can create many opportunities. By using a well-developed model like Simplex for solving problems, we can approach the process systematically, and can take concrete decision. Given the unpredictable nature of problems, it's very reassuring to know that, by following a structured plan, we can do everything and can resolve the problem to the best of our ability. There are number of such models developed. We can learn from those models.

4.5 Activity Performance

There are number of activities which can be performed to achieve peace and harmony in individual, group and society. A few among them are discussed below.

a) Reflective Thinking

What is Reflective Thinking?

Critical thinking and reflective thinking are often used synonymously. Critical thinking is used to describe:

> "...the use of those cognitive skills or strategies that increase the probability of a desirable outcome thinking that is purposeful, reasoned and goal directed—the kind of thinking involved in solving

problems, formulating inferences, calculating likelihoods, and making decisions when the thinker is using skills that are thoughtful and effective for the particular context and type of thinking task. Critical thinking is sometimes called directed thinking because it focuses on a desired outcome." Halpern (1996).

Reflective thinking, on the other hand, is a part of the critical thinking process referring specifically to the processes of analyzing and making judgments about what has happened. Dewey (1933) suggests that reflective thinking is an active, persistent, and careful consideration of a belief or supposed form of knowledge, of the grounds that support that knowledge, and the further conclusions to which that knowledge leads. Learners are aware of and control their learning by actively participating in reflective thinking—assessing what they know, what they need to know, and how they bridge that gap—during learning situations.

In summary, critical thinking involves a wide range of thinking skills leading toward desirable outcomes and reflective thinking focuses on the process of making judgments about what has happened. However, reflective thinking is most important in prompting learning during complex problem-solving situations because it provides students with an opportunity to step back and think about how they actually solve problems and how a particular set of problem solving strategies is appropriated for achieving their goal.

Characteristics of Environments and Activities that Prompt and Support Reflective Thinking

Mary (2014), in her dissertation has given following activities:

- Provide enough wait-time for students to reflect when responding to inquiries.
- Provide emotionally supportive environments in the classroom encouraging re-evaluation of conclusions.
- Prompt reviews of the learning situation, what is known, what is not yet known, and what has been learned.
- Provide authentic tasks involving ill-structured data to encourage reflective thinking during learning activities.
- Prompt students' reflection by asking questions that seek reasons and evidence.
- Provide some explanations to guide students' thought processes during explorations.
- Provide a less-structured learning environment that prompts students to explore what they think is important.
- Provide social-learning environments such as those inherent in peer-group works and small group activities to allow students to see other points of view.

- Provide reflective journal to write down students' positions, give reasons to support what they think, show awareness of opposing positions and the weaknesses of their own positions.

Why is Reflective Thinking Important?

Modern society is becoming more complex, information is becoming available and changing more rapidly prompting users to constantly rethink, switch directions, and change problem-solving strategies. Thus, it is increasingly important to prompt reflective thinking during learning to help learners develop strategies to apply new knowledge to the complex situations in their day-to-day activities. Reflective thinking helps learners develop higher-order thinking skills by prompting learners to:

a) Relate new knowledge to prior understanding,
b) Think in both abstract and conceptual terms,
c) Apply specific strategies in novel tasks, and
d) Understand their own thinking and learning strategies.

b) Concentration

Concentration has enormous power to act accordingly. For example; the sun rays spread on the earth in the scattering form, which has low impact. If those rays come through lens it burn the paper into ashes. Lens can converge the divergent sunrays in a singleton path. Similar activities mind can do through concentration. Enormous energy of mind acts tremendously in a single way through concentration. We realize that the curse of saints is the result of concentration implied in negative form. Concentrate on mantras or photos of great persons or scriptures have positive impact. It enhances the power of mind and helps to move in harmonious path. Habit of concentration enhances the will force.

c) Meditation

Generally mind is unstable and flickering in nature. We do meditation to make constant our mind. Constant mind is helpful to think and act positively. This stage leads to peace and harmony within individual and society. There are several techniques of meditation followed in different spiritual paths. Mainly the spiritual seekers do meditation, speculation, concentration etc. to enhance their consciousness, mind power, thinking ability, decision making and problem solving abilities. All the wise men do it as a good instrument. During mass meditation sharing of consciousness, spiritual power, energy, light possible. It is a good instrument for establishing peace and harmony in mind and among people. This technique has been prevailing in society for thousand years. This is also a means to unite with the divine. Major spiritual paths prefer meditation as good instrument.

d) Prabachan (Sermon)

'Prabachan' is generally known as holy speech. It charges the minds in positive manner. The messages of Gurus, Scriptures, Mythologies, and Saints are delivered to the common people for wellbeing of society. Some experts, saints, holy men shared their ideas and charge the masses to maintain a peaceful and harmonious life. When the modern society is moving with worry, tension, terror, murder, loot, vandalism, rubbery and disaster, at that time these holy messages provide calm and quietness among thousand minds. These conscious dialogues interact positively in the society. It shows direction to live a peaceful, harmonious and prosperous life. Hence, attend *prabachan* has a good meaning.

e) Yogasanas and Exercises

Yogasana and exercises are very meaningful for happy and peaceful living. It helps to recover the aberrations of the body and mind in one side and maintain balance, growth and development in other. It balances the different systems of body and helps to function properly the mechanism of body. Like food and water Yogasana and exercises are inevitable for healthy human engineering. In *Gurukula* system of education, it was mandatory for all disciples. After that it was limited in Ashrams or special institutions. Now it is seen that Baba Ramdev makes reach it at door to door. Well, it is a good symptom of making disease less society. To keep the body and mind healthy Yogasanas and exercises are immense helpful. All the conscious citizens are doing these regularly. It is part of our journey. Otherwise life will be miserable and disharmony. "Sariramadyam khalu dharma sadhanam". All types of activities will be done by body. Hence, body should be a fit instrument. It is possible only through Yogasana. The process may be understood by a single quote, "Sthira sukhamasanam." Doing yogaasana and exercises consciously helps to generate peace and harmony in body, mind and spirit.

f) Satsang (Religious Gathering)

'Satsangh' has immense value in our day to day life. It provides the art of living. When we are feeling sad, hopeless, despaired, troublesome, suffering, at that moment *satsangh* will provide us right direction to live peaceful life. It charges us positively to live a harmonious life. We feel sacred, holy, calm and quite mind when attend a *satsangh*. It is organised in the purpose of providing sanctity, positive living and happiness among participants. Value-oriented speeches are provided by experts and saints. It is also meant for sharing of consciousness, power, light, knowledge, peace, knowledge and goodness.

4.6 Sri Aurovindo's Integral View of Education for Peace and Harmony

Abraham Lincoln wrote to the headmaster of his son's school:

He will have to learn I know, that all men are not just, all men are not true. But teach him also that for every selfish politician, there is a dedicated leader and for every scoundrel there is a hero... Teach him that for every enemy there is a friend. It will take time I know, but teach him, if you can, that a dollar earned is of far more valued than five found...Teach him to learn to lose... and also to enjoy winning. Steer him away from envy; if you can, teach him the secret of quite laughter. Let him earn early that the bullets are the easiest to lick...Teach him if you can the wonder of books... but also give him quiet time to ponder the eternal mystery of birds in the sky, bees in the sun, and flowers on a green hill side (1864, May10). It is more relevant even today.

Education process of human being is different from other species on the earth. He is constantly learning, discovering, aspiring, progressing, growing in knowledge, acquiring newer and newer skills, rising on the wings of contrivance and complexity, and trying to rise higher and higher. To him, education is not merely an insurance against the uncertain challenges of the future; it is also a daring adventure into unknown possibilities (Iyenger,1976; Dhal, 2011; 2013). In each generation there is new excitement and expectancy. There was always the need to look beyond the formal education and to be in constant readiness to face and master the unexpected.

Education is a continuous process. It aims basically at awaking and developing the pupil's divers dormant faculties of observation, experimentation, and speculation. Within a broad framework of theory, the pupil should be encouraged to learn through doing-to experiment for himself-and the adventure boldly into the unknown. Children have to acquire, through self-effort as far as possible, the sort of competence and self-confidence that will train them to develop the necessary specialist skills to meet future contingencies and challenges. Education should try to provide the energy of body, alacrity of mind, and especially the deeper poise of the spirit that will develop the relevant skills as and when required. We should craft for learning with application of our knowledge in upliftment of down trodden and betterment of society. Noble values of caring and sharing, of service and sacrifices have made the society vibrant at all times. Our society is known for having great values for life and deep concern for human development. We should intensely aspire for deepening and broadening our knowledge, learn to experience the power of cooperation, collaboration and team spirit, and always be guided by supreme values we believe in.

According to Milton, a complete and generation education is that which "fits a man to perform justly, skillfully and magnanimously all the offices, both private and public, of peace and war". The circumstances of our technological society compelling a frantic multiplication of professional skills, and yet all have to be reared a sound basis laid in school and college by means of integrally harmonised scheme of education. Neither the horizontal (subjects, disciplines and courses) nor the vertical (nursery to post graduate), but the integral view of education holds key to success. In this system the centre is everywhere and the circumference is nowhere. From any point it can be started with integral consciousness. It is not enough to read Botany in relation to Zoology, or Economics in relation to History, or Linguistics in relation to Sociology; but everything has to be seen in relation to the whole, the very ground of Reality. Education should be related to each branch of knowledge to Reality.

The essential postulates of education would be the unity of matter and spirit in the universe, the unity of matter and spirit in the men, and the role of man to enact a visible efflorescence of the integrality, the wholeness, the light and puissance of unity. Hence, Sri Aurobindo writes (1972) in Savitri:

> "Matter shall reveal in Spirit's face
> Spirit shall lookout through matter's gaze
> This earthly life becomes the life divine."

The goal of education is verily to help the pupil to evolve into a noble specimen of the race, a witness to Truth in the four fold aspects of Love, Knowledge, Power and Beauty. The educational process would simply be the flowering of the human consciousness, ever more intimate and far reaching till it becomes knowledge, action and realisation in one. In education, therefore it is the utmost importance to awaken the veiled and withdrawn soul within.

Let us be clear as to what will be the right education in fast changing global situation today. A partial, personal or parochial view of education has to be replaced by an integral view comprising the needs of individual, nation and all humanity on the one hand and addressed, on the other. To utmost but harmonious development of body, vital, mind and soul, and the mobilisation of the enduring gains of the past, the thrust of the present and the possibilities of the unfolding future.

The formal education has to aim at helping the pupil to knowledge of the physical world, the biological world, the world of man's creations and institutions and of man himself in his solitariness and sovereign responsibility. There is both the need for horizontal and vertical integration of curriculum. The strivings of today being grounded on the achievements of all our yesterdays are pointing to the summits of future. The individual should be helped to realize his utmost potentialities, he should be enabled to find his proper relation with his social group and his nation; and he should be encouraged to find his true place in the global human community. There is thus a personal, a social or national and a global or racial dimension to education and these three should promote a living, evolving and progressively realizing dynamic of puissant consciousness. Also, with reversible movement of consciousness, the new man will be able at one end the same time to see the world in himself and see himself in the world.

In the Mother's words:

> 'The starting point is to seek in one-self that which is independent of the body and the circumstances of life, which is not born of the mental formation that you have been given, the language you speak, the habits and customs of the environment in which you live. You must find, in the depth your being that which carries in it the sense of universality, limitless expansion, term less continuity. Then you decentralize, spread out, enlarge yourself; you begin to live in everything and in all things; the barriers separating individuals from each other breakdown. You think in their thoughts, vibrate in their sensations, you feel in their feelings, you live in the life of all. What seem inert suddenly becomes full of life, stones quicken, plants feel and will and suffer, animals speak in a language more or less inarticulate, but clear and expressive; everything is animated with a marvellous consciousness without time and limit". (http://www.sriaurobindoashram. org/ashram/mother/writings.php)

Let us take two concepts like '*Para vidya'* and '*Apara vidya'*. Without the light of '*Para vidya'*, the higher spiritual wisdom all '*Apara vidya',* the lower knowledge gained through the normal academic curriculum in art and science, is mere '*avidya*' or false knowledge. Humanism itself, unless it undergoes initiations in the waters of spirituality, must prove a partial and limiting, and ultimately falsifying, experience. The education should not deal with other man just a brother, a fellow human being; rather the other fellow is my-self, ourselves-lit by the same spirit within, and marked for the same destiny of transformation from the human to the divine. The best approach to mathematics, physics, chemistry, biology, history, geography, poetry, music, art is to see them all as petals of one flower, notes of a single piece of music, tints of the same apocalyptic rainbow arc or rays that feed the same illumination. Para Vidya is the soul of education without which the body, however attractive in form and rich in raiment, is no better than show piece model.

Man, society, community, nation, race—have a soul, an evolving soul within, and as like to like, rapport at the level of the soul is easy to establish, whether between man and man, man and society, or nation and the global human family. On this foundation, and fed from this power-house of illumination, all other super structures and communication systems could be safely reared.

In this approach education is not isolated from life. If education were verily progressive self-knowledge, self-gathering, self-discipline, self-unfoldment, and self-realisation, education must be co-extensive with life.

All life is education, and with right sense of education and ascent of sincerity and dedication all life could be yoga. Life: Education: yoga-they are the same, only differing in the intensity of conscious effort, and the determined drive towards individual, collective or global perfection.

The whole of the discredited education of our time deserves to be thrown overboard. In this place let us encourage the pupil to exploit his innate buoyancy and curiosity and learn rigorously by his own efforts; to embark upon projects formulating his own objectives and seeking his own solutions through self-regulated programmes of work experience; and to engage in group activities or co-curricular work with his fellow, alike for gaining knowledge and skills and for community involvement and service. Flexibility and dynamism, rather than rigidity and uniformity should be the governing law of educational process; and teacher-pupil confrontation should be ended by making them both participants in the educational adventure.

The entire world is a school and all life is education. The educational institution could be a place of high concentration of aspiration and effort—even as a Temple, Church or Mosque is a house of God charged with an immediacy of presence, power and grace, because the entire universe itself is the House of God's omnipresence, organize by his power and glory. The two terms in education are: (1) the pupil, who seeks knowledge, and (2) God or Truth, the source of all knowledge. The teacher himself is but the link between the two, the channel of communication, the willing paraclete. A real teacher, enacting the power of divine love, helps the child's bud of consciousness to open out petal by petal, and to achieve environment of the academy.

A congenial environment is to be created, an ambience provided, that will facilitate the child's discovering and activating the psychic being within, and there by surpassing the ego's desire, establishing rapport with the soul or the psychic being in others, and progressively losing all sense of separativity, having become one with universal spirit. It is in effectively transcending his ego that the individual truly finds himself and also observes the common ground between him and others and all mankind.

According to Iyengar (1976), "the school atmosphere with intimations of the divine presence, the dedicated love of the teacher that gently opens the windows of the pupils' psychic self, the stimulating fellowship of the other pupils, the unending romance of life, the constant play of curiosity, the thrilled satisfaction of doing things on one's own or by spontaneous co-operative effort—these are among the elements of educational engineering that will temper and transform our children in to the 'hero warriors' of the tomorrow's world".

Modernisation of curriculum, elimination of deadwood, making pupil learn by themselves and take-up projects their own rather than be content with swallowing tabloid knowledge, encouraging pupils to cultivate a lively interest in the neighbourhood, promoting healthy teacher-pupil dialogues, all these will be very effective for our education. But all these will be valueless unless psychic awakening will take place. Through which enlargement of consciousness, the sense of the others and the living perception of the deeper unit will be possible. The emphasis is on education for growth of consciousness, education for tomorrow's free world and education for transformation of individual, society and global.

Hence, we would aspire:

> "*Om saha naavavatu sahanau bhunaktu*
> *Saha veeryam karavaavahai*
> *Tejasvi naavadheetamastu maa vidvishaavahai*
> *Om shantih shantih shantih*"
>
> The *Krishna Yajurveda Taittiriya Upanishad* (2.2.2)
>
> *Meaning*: May He protect us both (teacher and the taught)! May He cause us both to enjoy the bliss of Mukti (liberation)! May we both exert to discover the true meaning of the sacred scriptures! May our studies be fruitful! May we never quarrel with each other! Let there be threefold peace.

4.6.1 Education for Universal Harmony and Social Transformation

The general aim of education is to be attained is the advent of a progressing universal harmony. The means for attaining this aim, in regard to the earth, is the realisation of human unity through the awakening in all the manifestation by all of the inner divinity which is one. In other words, to create unity by founding the kingdom of God which is within us all.

This therefore, is the most useful work to be done:

1. For each individuality, to be conscious in himself of the Divine Presence and to identify himself with it.
2. To individualize the states of being that were never till now conscious in man and, by that, to the put the earth in connection with one or more of the fountains of universal force that are still sealed to it.
3. To speak again to the world the eternal word under a new form adopted to its present mentality. It will be the synthesis of all human knowledge.
4. Collectively, to establish an ideal society in a propitious spot for flowering of the race, the race of the Sons of God.

The terrestrial transformation and harmonisation can be brought about by two processes which, though opposite in appearance, must combine-must act upon each other and complete each other:

1. Individual transformation, an inner development leading to the union with the divine presence.

2. Social transformation, the establishment of an environment favourable to the flowering and growth of the individual. Since the environment reacts upon the individual and, on the other hand, the value of the environment depends upon the value of the individual, the two works should be preceded side by side. But this can be done only through division of labour. And that necessitates the formation of a group, hierarchies if possible.

The action of the members of the group should be three fold:

1. To realize in oneself the ideal to be attained: to become a perfect earthly representative of the first manifestation of the unthinkable in all its modes, attributes and qualities.
2. To preach this ideal by word, but, above all, by example so as to find out all those who are ready to realize it in their turn and to become also announcers of liberation.
3. To found a typical society or recognize those that already exist.

(*CWM*, Vol. 3, pp. 47-48)

4.6.2 Education for Human Unity and International Understanding

Education leads to the unity of all nations. It is the compelling future of the world. Thus, education has a definite role to play in educating the budding citizens of various countries for the realisation of this ideal. According to The Mother, "unity of the human race can be achieved neither by uniformity nor by domination and subjection, but by a synthetic organisation of all nations, each one occupying its true place according to its own genius and the part it has to play in the whole. In order to make this synthesis a living one, the grouping should be effectuated around a central idea that is as wide and as high as possible, in which all tendencies, even the most contradictory, may find their respective places. Education has a positive role to play in bring world union by making the children accustomed from a very early age not merely to the idea itself, but to its practice." (The Mother, 1978, Vol. 12, p. 40).The formation of an international institution for imparting education at Pondicherry is a step towards the achievement of this ideal. The creation of Auroville—a city of the future humanity is a glowing attempt to educate people for human unity and international understanding include, where people belonging to different nations and faiths would live a higher life that has spiritual principle as its base. This ideal has been envisioned to be the future system of education.

The SAIEC and Auroville, both are meant for human unity and International understanding through an innovative means of education i.e. Integral Education advocated by Sri Aurobindo and The Mother of Sri Aurobindo Ashram, Pondicherry. Whoever will go to this place, s/he can realise the peace and harmony everywhere. A supreme consciousness drives the organisations inwardly. The influence of this power can be felt everywhere of its environment, who wants to observe silently. This is inner peace. Would our education provide such type of peace!

4.7 Gandhiji's Concept of Peace

There are many philosophers and educators who have advocated peace and harmony as key ideas to be integrated with education. They are Mahatma Gandhiji, Sri Aurobindo, Rabindra Nath Tagore, Vivekanand, Gijubhai Badharika, Zakir Hussain etc. Gandhiji was the father of nation. His ideal of living is peace in this life, and not after life, through non-violence and truth. Industrialisation and modernisation have created dichotomies in the society, leading to tension and conflicts for everyone. These conflicts need to be resolved by developing right attitudes towards conflicts and their resolution through dialogues and discussions, and totally rejecting violent means. Industrialisation has also led to serious environmental problems, which have to understand by children as it concerns their future and through sustainable development. Peaceful life on this planet, clean and balanced environment resources would require that people resort to simple life. It was also pointed out that dialogue and discussion would not be so useful once wars and violence begins. Philosophy of '*Satyagrah*' and non-violence should be taught to children, which will help them to know the truth and work for it with determination when they take charge of their responsibilities as adults. Peace could prevail only if environmental awareness is created among all individuals. Creating awareness among pupil should form essential component of peace education programme. Arms and weapons today claim much more financial resources than is spent on welfare programmes.

Peace education is about developing responsible citizens who would respect others rights while claiming their rights and doing their duties as well. Various laws are formulated regarding human rights in national and

An Apostle of Peace Culture in the World

International levels. The violation of human rights in personal professional and social life is harmful. There are various instrument social and legal, institutions which help to protect rights of individuals. Gandhiji placed emphasis on every one doing their duties. The children should learn their duties along with their rights. Peace education should develop righteousness, sensitivity and values among children.

Education for peace is, in this sense, an essential component of holistic basic education that aims at the comprehensive development of persons. Peace is often equated with the absence of violence. To Gandhiji, exploitation was the most familiar and practical form of violence on an individual by the state, a group, another individual, or by machines; on women by men; and on one nation by another. Peace mandates the practice of values such as love, truth, justice, equality, tolerance, harmony, humility, togetherness, and self-control. Self-suffering, if need be, is to be preferred to inflicting violence on others.

Gandhiji's concept of peace includes:

(i) The absence of tensions, conflicts, and all forms of violence including terrorism and war. Peace implies the capacity to live together in harmony. This calls for non-violent ways of resolving conflicts. Diversity occasions conflicts but conflicts do not have to eventuate into violence.

(ii) The creation of non-violent social systems, i.e., a society free from structural violence. The duty to practice justice: social, economic, cultural, and political. Hunger is systemic violence.

(iii) The absence of exploitation and injustice of every kind.

(iv) International cooperation and understanding. This involves the creation of a just world order, marked by a willingness to share the earth's resources to meet the needs of all. That is, the need to shift from greed to need.

(v) Ecological balance and conservation. The adoption of lifestyles conducive to the wholeness of creation.

(vi) Peace of mind, or the psycho-spiritual dimension of peace. Peace begins with the individual and spreads to the family, to the community, to the nation, and to the global village.

Promoting a culture of peace involves a two-pronged strategy. The members of a society need to be oriented toward peace instead of violence. At the same time, social, economic, and political systems have to be reoriented to peace. The discipline of peace must shape our way of life. Education is vital for the effectiveness of both strategies.

Some Assignments

1. Write some peace related words and explain

2. Write the concept of peace explain by Gandhji and Sri Aurobindo
3. Explain some factors which are responsible for breaking peace in schools and colleges
4. How can a teacher help to resolve the conflict in educational institution?
5. Values implicit in different subject areas—elucidate it.
6. How does education support peace in the society?
7. Develop a lesson plan for developing peace in classroom.
8. Collect some documentary films on peace.
9. Write down the need and importance of peace in education.
10. Sketch a roadmap of peaceful living through education.

5
Strategies for Peace

> *"Peace education is skill building. It empower children to and creative and non-destructive ways to settle conflict and to live in harmony with themselves, others, and their world. Peace building is the task of every human being and the challenge of human family."*
>
> *—Fran Schmidt and Alice Friedman*

There is something in human nature that inspires us to rise above the violence. There is something that calls us to recognize and become aware of life rather than to be driven by it. Something which leads us to lay down in green grass to praise Creator and creation. There is something which draws us into awareness of power greater than ego—to see ourselves as part of the interconnected flow of life; something calls us to transcend old identities, fear and greed and something leads us to offer compassion to our enemies. That something is the force that gives meaning to our lives, it is the power that creates and sustains us; that is nothing else but Love; by which all creatures bind with each other.

We seek non-violent means to reach our goals. Non-violence requires us to act in a way that exemplifies our values and goals. Non-violence requires courage. It swears off actions which are motivated by anger and a desire to destroy. It requires us to maintain a respect for all life. Through love and peacemaking is truth discovered. Gandhi's word for non-violence, ahimsa means truth-force. In order to become peacemakers, we must become willing to be honest and look at our motivation to do violence. Try using violence without a rationalisation that distances from truth. This then is why worship of truth will lead us to a greater practice of non-violence. Untruth leads us away from ourselves, away from what is.

The Dalai Lama said that "unfortunate events, though potentially a source of anger and despair, have equal potential to be a source of spiritual growth. Whether or not this is the outcome depends on our response." Current events challenge us with an opportunity to live up to our principles and purposes.

Trying to maintain our peace values can be difficult in wartime. It is suggested that it might be nice to talk peace, but come on, sometimes there is no choice. Military action is the only thing that will stop the terrorists. This strategy hasn't seemed to work very well in Israel. We could unite diverse people behind common values if we value peace and justice rather than merely getting our own way.

It will take creativity to reverse the momentum of war. It will take holy joy to become peacemakers. Peacemaking is not only a practical task it is a spiritual one. It is spiritual because it calls us to grow in our awareness of truth and of divinity. Making peace, seeking peace, choosing peace, these tasks are essential to every aspect of spirituality. Being a peacemaker requires seeing the inherent worth and dignity in persons who have been deteriorated and devalued.

"To be peacemakers is to answer the spiritual call to love our enemies. To grow in skill as a peacemaker moves us to develop affinity for that which we perceive as foreign." Loving our enemies enables us to begin to love ourselves. Our enemies serve as mirrors reflecting back aspects of ourselves that need healing, aspects that we are unwilling to face. The judgments we hold against our enemies reflect judgments that we maintain against ourselves. In *Love without Conditions*, Paul Ferrini writes that "if we don't love our enemies we will not be able to receive the gifts they bring to us." Loving our enemies makes healing, peace and reconciliation possible.

To Phillip Scheelman (2009), perhaps the primary reason we exist is the purpose of making peace, of healing, of growing in the spiritual awareness of truth, divinity and our interconnectedness. It seems to me that everyone on this planet is suffering to one degree or another from a lack of peace. Each of us suffers from being out of sorts with life—suffers from lack of harmony with the source and unity of life. The problem is characterised if not caused by a lack of love and acceptance. Fear, hate and judgment keep us from truth. Lack of self-love inhibits our ability to love God, the Universe or Life itself. Each of us has so many ways that our ego, our separate sense of self struggles to assert its importance through separateness. Our egos, our attachment and our fear keep us suffering in separateness and keep us on the offensive against perceived threats.

As above, there are several strategies implemented for establishing peace in the society. A few among them have been discussed below. Those will be helpful for better understanding of strategies for peace.

5.1 Emotional Integration: Rapprochement, Storytelling, Narration of Scenario with Zest

Emotional activities are barriers in the pathway of peace and harmony. These are unstable in nature. If it can be integrated then fruitful result obtained. There are various emotional activities. A few among those are discussed here under.

(a) Rapprochement

According to Wikipedia, in international relations, a rapprochement, which comes from the French word *rapprocher* ("to bring together"), is a re-establishment of cordial relations, as between two countries. In the political scene of an individual country, rapprochement means the bringing together of diverse political factions as, for example, during metapolitefasi in Greece. It summarizes the following facts:

1. Re-establishing of cordial relations between two countries
2. The state of reconciliation or of cordial relations
3. An establishment or renewal of harmonious relations
4. cooperation—joint operation or action; "their cooperation with us was essential for the success of our mission"

Rapprochement means "reconcilation, softening, reunion, détente, reconcilement, restoration of harmony: the process of political rapprochement between the two former foes falling-out quarrel, antagonism, schism, dissension, exacerbation, resumption of hostilities." (Collins Thesaurus of the English Language—Complete and Unabridged 2nd Edition. 2002 © HarperCollins Publishers 1995, 2002)

As a good tool rapprochement can be taken for establishing peace and harmony between parties, agencies or nations. It will helpful for bilateral cooperation for success of mission.

(b) Storytelling

Generally children like story. Story creates interest among children. It helps them to enhance their natural inquisitiveness and imagination. As an effective technique it is widely accepted by all. It can be applied in primary and secondary level. Story telling may be used at the higher level also to create interest, curiosity and develop imagination and to manage the classroom. The subjects like: science, social science, language and mathematics may be taught through this technique. It is an effective method as well as technique for establishing peace.

We tell story of great scientists like Galileo, Marconi, Archimedes, Madam Curie, James Watt to create scientific attitude in science class. Teachers of History may tell the stories of Nelson Mandela, Mahatma Gandhi, Sri Aurobindo, Abraham Lincoln etc. to develop patriotism, self-determination, and ethics of life. The stories of different counties are told to teach Geography in classroom. The '*Panchatantra* 'stories of Vishnu Sharma, *The Ramayana*, and *The Mahavarat*, *Jatak Galpa*, etc. teach good lessons to humanity. The fables of different countries, fairy tales provide good lessons and enhance imagination power.

The story telling is a method, technique and a teaching skill. It must become a motivational device to develop curiosity, arouse interest and imagination in teaching-learning process. It should be followed by question answer to make the classroom active. The story should be prepared according to mental and emotional levels of children.

Story telling promotes interest among children in any subject of curriculum. The story teller should fit his story to audience as per subject matter. It develops an appreciation for and enjoyment of literature; enriches language and experiences. It develops listening skills and motivates students to read well. The story telling must be living by facial expression and body language. It must be in loud and clear voice with expression. Sometimes students may be provided opportunity to share short stories, amusing anecdotes in an informal setting to have a good experience. Guest may be invited to tell story occasionally.

To enrich story telling the teacher may use board or puppets or cartoons etc. The students may write his own story and share in his class. The teller should keep eye contact with the audience and speak directly to the listeners. He must convey enthusiasm for enjoyment of literature. He must attempt to introduce end and stories in creative, unique, and wonderful ways. The success of storytelling depends on body language, gestures, factual expressions, pace, delivery and atmosphere.

(c) Narration of Scenario with Zest

The narrative situations complement the potential level of emergency chart as tool for validating a collections emergency response plan against the many combinations of factors an emergency event might include. Because full-scale emergency response rehearsals are impractical for most institutions, these realistic scenarios are intended to be the basis for "table top" or "talk through" exercises to cross-check assumptions and response strategies. We set aside a couple of hours for a group of staff who are responsible for emergency preparedness and response to review one or more scenarios together, in the context of our collections emergency plan. Notes of our discussion and the assumptions and gaps identified, and modification of our plan to confirm or address them, will strengthen our preparedness for a real event. While institutions should pay priority planning attention to emergencies in direct proportion to the likelihood that they might occur, the unexpected is in the nature of emergencies. It can be useful to walk through even emergencies that are very unlikely for our context. That discussion can serve as a periodic staff reminder of our emergency plan contents, or as a "worst case" scenario to assess your plan's capacity to cover a variety of emergencies. Scenarios can't provide all details for all institutions, emergencies, or collections. Feel free to make them more reflective of our institution and collections. Where a question about conditions arises, use our imagination to fill in missing information as your collections or staff might experience a similar event. In some cases alternate scenarios have been suggested to allow a wider range of institutions to see themselves for the purposes of this planning exercise. Narration of scenario as a method may be implied to integrate the happenings in the path of peace and harmony.

5.1.1 Pedagogical Skills and Strategies

The focus is not merely on retention of concepts, memorisation of texts, or achieving individual goals and excellence but on learning to reflect, share, care, and collaborate with each other. Every topic/lesson has peace-laden (hidden or explicit) components, which need to be transacted with deliberate planning from a positive and humanistic perspective. The methods of teaching should be creative, child-centered, largely experiential, and participatory. These include creation of appropriate learning experiences, discussion, debates, presentation, and group and cooperative projects, depending on students' maturity levels and the subject content. The teacher and school may devise other context-specific strategies to develop among students a sense of openness and comprehension about diverse cultures, histories, and fundamental shared values. There is ample scope in the syllabi of various subject areas for teaching students the importance of adopting peaceful means of resolving disagreements and conflicts and eschewing violence; and teachers need to take full advantage of this. Presenting lessons from a humanistic and positive perspective is the basis of education. Teaching should awaken positive feelings and foster positive experiences, help in arriving at an understanding of the self, encourage openness to inquiry by raising questions, exploring, and discovering and constructing an understanding of values, and provide an opportunity for applying the knowledge of values the student has learnt. Strategies like questions, stories, anecdotes, games, experiments, discussions, dialogues, value clarification, examples, analogies, metaphors, role-play, and simulation are helpful in promoting peace through teaching-learning. Some peace values may be more appropriately inculcated while teaching a particular subject at a particular stage or grade, while others are better integrated with other subjects in a different grade.

5.2 Understanding Background: Survey, Action Researches

Problem rises due to miss-understanding. Understanding the background is more important to solve the problem. Survey and action researches provide sufficient data to get evidence of the problem. Day to day a good number of miss-happenings are occurring. These miss-happenings break the balance of society. To overcome these problems we have to go the background of the problem. Relevant data will be collected through survey. Action research as short period of study is more helpful to find the cause and effect of the problem. After getting the result necessary precautions may be taken to solve the problem taken for study. This is a good tool to find the cause and effect of the problem and provide proper solution.

Participatory Action Research (PAR) goes far beyond collecting and analyzing information. In fact, through its process character, it inherently provides the space for conflict stakeholders to reflect on and elicit their own understanding of the conflict situation, while also being faced with the perspectives of others. This understanding provides the critical foundations that are then further strengthened through incremental dialogue, starting from "single-identity" to inter-group dialogue. Dialogue then fosters interaction and collaboration, with the objective to address some of the divisive factors triggering conflict within and between communities. The actors involved in this PAR process were able to open traditional mechanisms to new ingredients and have also contributed to critical reflections on the approach taken, thus allowing it to adapt to contextual realities. As a result, traditional conflict resolution capacities have been validated and capitalised. Such community based peace building and reconciliation processes are needed to continue to provide avenues and space for those most directly affected by conflict, and therefore constitute a critical complement to a conflict-sensitive state building process.

5.3 Violence: Prevention and Intervention

5.3.1 What It is and What It Does?

We have become numb, desensitised to the violence in our culture. Our children spend huge portions of their life in front of TV and movie screens where they are entertained by violence and domination. In video games, our children are asked to score points by killing and destroying. Consumers of mass quantities of violence can hardly keep from viewing people as expendable. The entertainment industry has also made violence seem sexy. Violence does not bring about peace. It tends to lead to more violence. If we acknowledge in ourselves the tendency to do violence, we can more honestly and freely begin to figure strategies for peace.

- Modes of violence
  - Verbal
  - Psychological
  - Physical
  - Structural
  - Vulgarity in popular culture
- Frontiers of violence
  - Caste

  - Gender
  - Discrimination
  - Corruption
  - Communalism
  - Advertisements
  - Poverty
- Perils of violence
- Media and violence
- Peaceful resolution of conflicts
- Reconciliation after conflicts

5.3.2 Violence in School, Home and Society

a) *Violence in School*

School violence is increasing day to day. Students are taking arms to schools. They fight with each other and also with school staff. These numbers are alarming. As Report of America in 2001, students between the ages of 12 and 18 were the victims of two million crimes at school, but 62 per cent of those crimes were thefts. In part, violence receives more attention because it draws media coverage. Educators and policymakers take the issue very seriously.

School violence has identified several individual and social risk factors. Individual risk factors include a tendency to externalize problems, as well as developmental delays, low IQ, and reading problems. Social risk factors include an unstable home environment, violent neighbourhoods, and certain characteristics of a school environment. A home environment may contribute to school violence if, at home, students are exposed to gun violence, parental alcoholism, domestic violence, physical abuse, sexual abuse, or harsh parental discipline. All of these may teach children that criminal and violent activities are acceptable and may increase a child's tendency to respond to frustration with aggression. A neighbourhood environment may contribute to school violence if a community has high rates of crime or drug use. A neighbourhood may also expose students to deviant peers or to gangs who contribute to violence inside schools.

Prevention and intervention strategies may target individual students, families, the school community, or society in general. Individual-level strategies target at-risk or aggressive students and teach these students conflict resolution, problem solving, and social skills. Family-based solutions attempt to improve family relationships in order to improve students' experiences while they are at home. School-wide strategies are designed to modify school characteristics associated with violence. Examples of this would be classroom practices that encourage student cooperation and close interaction with teachers, or the presence of police and law enforcement in schools to discourage violence. Finally, society-level prevention strategies attempt to change social and cultural conditions in order to reduce violence, regardless of where it occurs. For example, society-level strategies might try to reduce the violence portrayed in movies or music. (https//www.boundless.com/sociology)

Bullying is a common occurrence in most schools. Bullying can be physical, verbal, and emotional. Physical bullying is the most easily identified and includes unwanted physical contact such as pushing, kicking, tickling, or the like, and may also include the use of weapons. Verbal bullying is any slanderous statements or accusations that cause the victim undue emotional distress. This can include insulting someone's appearance, laughing at someone, or directing foul language toward someone. Emotionally bullying is any form of bullying that damages a victim's emotional well-being, such as spreading malicious rumors, giving someone the silent treatment, or harassment. (*op. cit.*)

A congenial climate should be created. Education for growing consciousness has to implement in school. Cooperation, faithfulness, positive thinking, following truth, cleanliness, positive attitude, helpful, honesty, integrity, respect to others, compassion, forgiveness, soft skills, polite behavior, good character etc. should be practiced in school. Parent –teacher cooperation, Teacher - society relation, social order, and ethical issues must be encouraged. Hence, the teacher has to be a yogi, hero and example. Parents must be aware about this issue and guide their children accordingly.

b) Violence at Home

Violence at home can be transmitted at school. Brett Welch says, "she's noticed that kids who act out at school often come from tough home situations. Kids who witness domestic violence are more likely to get in trouble at school and have behavioral problems, including being aggressive and bullying their classmates."

Scott Carrel's (2010) data confirms Whaf Welch's has observed. Carrel examined that, domestic violence and restraining orders happen in all the schools. But they were 10 times more likely to happen in the school serving the poorest population compared with the school serving the wealthiest population. He says his biggest fact is that "society has a vested interest in helping those families that are struggling with domestic violence. The more we can help other households, the better off our children will be." He further says, there are three things that might account for this: First, the violence in the homes may have stopped. Second, adult has decided to make some positive changes in the child's life. Third, to get involved.

It is observed that the domestic violence is becoming more acute, but it continues to linger as a major problem in our society. As with most acts of violence, the causes are known and the solutions are attainable. Mass media campaigns should be organized to educate the public on the presence and long-term damage of domestic violence. Effort should be made to detect earlier and prevention training for those families at high risk, and provide more intervention and treatment for both victims and criminals of domestic violence.

In modern times, day to day the domestic violence is increasing. Due to erosion of value in society or family, juniors could not respect to seniors, even children cannot obey their parents. Similarly learners cannot obey their teachers. In each home there is politics. There is no faith, obedience, love, simplicity and gratitude among each other in a family. Each member in family suspects others and think about others in suspicious mind. So, there is intra family conflict everywhere. There is no good relation among brothers and sisters. Old parents are tortured by young sons or daughters. These are clear symptoms of disharmony and indiscipline. In this situation, value education or peace education is barely needed, however individual should be conscious about himself, his family members and neighbourhoods.

(c) Violence in Society

Kerby Anderson (1995) in his book *Violence in Society* has discussed about the following matter. Life has indeed become more violent and more dangerous for children. The innocence of childhood has been replaced by the very real threat of violence. "Kids in school try to avoid fights in the hall, walk home in fear, and sometimes sleep in bathtubs in order to protect themselves from stray bullets fired during drive-by shootings."

It is observed that the children are exposed to violence everywhere. Children see violence in their schools, their neighbourhoods, and their homes. The daily news is covered with reports of child molestations and abductions. War in foreign lands along with daily reports of murder, rape, and robberies also heighten a child's perception of potential violence.

Watching Television in the home is the greatest source of visual violence for children. Teenagers listen to more than 10,000 hours of rock music, and this impact is intensified as they spend countless hours in front of TV watching violent and sensual images that go far beyond.

It is observed that modern families are exposed to even more violence than previous generations because of the media. The film cities are most voilent place on the earth. Violence now has gone mainstream. Movie violence these days is louder, bloodier, and more anatomically precise than ever before. Children especially confront an increasingly violent world with few limits. As concerned parents and citizens we must do what we can to reduce the level of violence in our society through the wise use of discernment and public policy. We need to set limits both in our homes and in the community.

Children's greatest exposure to violence comes from television. TV shows, movies edited for television, and video games expose young children to a level of violence unimaginable. Various researches say "that heavy exposure to televised violence is one of the causes of aggressive behaviour, crime and violence in society. Television violence affects youngsters of all ages, of genders, at all socioeconomic levels and all levels of intelligence." (*op. cit.*)

Violent images on television and in the movies do contribute to greater violence in society. Sociological studies along with common sense dictate that we do something to reduce the violence in the media before it further damages society. Television violence affects both adults and children in subtle ways. While we may not personally feel or observe the effects of TV violence, we should not ignore the growing body of data that suggests that televised imagery does affect our perception and behaviour. (*op. cit.*)

Parents, programmers, and general citizens must take responsible actions to prevent the increasing violence in our society. Violent homes, violence on television, violence in the movies, and violence in the schools all contribute to the increasingly violent society we live in. We have a responsibility to make a difference and apply the appropriate principles in order to help stem the tide of violence in our society.

The experts have given some suggestions for dealing with violence:

1. *Learn about the impact of violence in our society*: Share the event with our parents, elders, and religious members. Help them understand how important this issue is to them and their community.
2. *Create a safe environment:* We must make our homes safe for our families. Providing care and protection are obvious first steps. But parents must also establish limits, provide emotional security, and teach values and virtue in the home.
3. Parents should limit the amount of media exposure in their homes.
4. Family members should watch TV with children.
5. Elder should try to develop holistic attitude among children.
6. We may discuss the reasons for pain and suffering in the world.
7. It is better to avoid to discuss the children about dangerous events in society. We need to balance our discussions with them.

Further, the Green Party (2001) proposes these actions to overtake the violence:

- All legal fire-arms, especially handguns or other concealable weapons must be registered. Selling of the above weapons must be restricted.
- Nonviolence and peaceful conflict resolution must be taught at all school levels. Corporal punishment in schools should be banned. Nonviolent parenting skills should be provided..
- Adequate funding must be provided as remedy the conditions that spread violent crime.

- Develop police training and procedures that stress the handling of situations through mediation and negotiation, while minimizing the necessity for armed confrontations.
- Controlling the sale of items that promote violence such as: media that display content with violence, weapons and products generally adjudged to evoke violence, keeping in mind content related to the freedom of speech and artistic expression protected. More tax may be collected to deter violence. The generated funds should be used to aid the victims of violence and to help fund counseling for the criminals of violence.
- "Advocate counseling/education programs/anger management/ medical care/healthcare as appropriate in a therapeutic environment for victims of violence and for the perpetrators of violent acts according to their separate issues— to include special communities like children, adolescents, men, women, seniors, ethnic minorities, the disabled, veterans, drug abusers/users, single parents, parents with jobs, the suicidal, and the homeless." (*Op. Cit.*)
- Discourage media glorification/sensationalism of violence through multiple non-Governmental rating systems, parental controls, and education.
- "The role of violence in the media needs to be addressed because scientific studies have shown that an environment of unchallenged violence is conducive to the practice of violence. We need to reduce the tools and glorification of violence, keeping in mind content related to the freedom of speech and artistic expression." (*Op. Cit.*)
- Attacks on the vulnerable need to be addressed through surrender.
- Gang violence may be addressed through community-based programs and public education.
- 'Violence due to militarism and nationalistic actions is covered in other Platform Planks such as Disarmament and Foreign Policy."

Violence is the curse of our society, but we can make a difference. We must educate ourselves about its influence and impact on our lives.

5.4 Crisis Management

What is Crisis?

It is commonly understood that a sudden and unexpected event leading to major unrest amongst the individuals at the workplace is called as organisation crisis. In other words, crisis is defined as any emergency situation which disturbs the employees as well as leads to instability in the organisation. Crisis affects an individual, group, organisation or society on the whole.

- Crisis is a sequence of sudden disturbing events harming the organisation.
- Crisis generally arises on a short notice.
- Crisis triggers a feeling of fear and threat amongst the individuals.

Why Crisis?

Crisis can arise in an organisation due to any of the following reasons:

- Technological failure and Breakdown of machines lead to crisis. Problems in internet, corruption in the software, errors in passwords all result in crisis.
- Crisis arises when employees do not agree to each other and fight amongst themselves. Crisis arises as a result of boycott, strikes for indefinite periods, disputes and so on.
- Violence, thefts and terrorism at the workplace result in organisation crisis.
- Neglecting minor issues in the beginning can lead to major crisis and a situation of uncertainty at the work place. The management must have complete control on its employees and should not adopt a casual attitude at work.
- Illegal behaviours such as accepting bribes, frauds, data or information tampering all lead to organisation crisis.
- Crisis arises when organisation fails to pay its creditors and declares itself a bankrupt organisation. (Nagarjun, AEJJST, 2016)

What is Crisis Management?

The art of dealing with sudden and unexpected events which disturbs the employees, organisation as well as external clients refers to Crisis Management. The process of handling unexpected and sudden changes in organisation culture is also called as crisis management.

Why Crisis Management?

The Crises Management Experts have given certain facts for need of the crisis management:

- Crisis Management prepares the individuals to face unexpected developments and adverse conditions in the organisation with courage and determination.
- Employees adjust well to the sudden changes in the organisation.
- Employees can understand and analyze the causes of crisis and cope with it in the best possible way.
- Crisis Management helps the managers to devise strategies to come

out of uncertain conditions and also decide on the future course of action.

- It helps the managers to feel the early signs of crisis, warn the employees against the aftermaths and take necessary precautions for the same.

Strategies of Crisis Management

Process of Crisis Management

Crisis Management includes activities and processes which help the managers as well as employees to analyze and understand events. It enables the managers and employees to respond effectively to changes in the organisation culture. It needs of effective coordination amongst the departments to overcome emergency situations. Employees at the time of crisis must communicate effectively with each other and try their level best to overcome tough times. Keep patience and become alert to overcome the crisis. During crisis situation the management should be in regular touch with the employees, external clients, stake holders as well as media. Be flexible and adopt to new situations.

5.5 Negotiation, Persuasion, Co-existence

a. Negotiation Skill

It is observed that time to time, whenever people are together, conflict and disagreement arise. It is natural instinct of men that, they have different needs, wants, aims and beliefs and sometimes they clash. Negotiation is a process that can be used to address and resolve disagreements among agitated people and find common solution. Without negotiations such conflicts may lead to argument and resentment resulting destruction. The process of negotiation is to try to reach agreements, however the both parties will not create any hindrance in future.

Negotiation is a process where two or more people or parties who have conflicting interests attempt to reach agreement when neither side has the formal power—or the desire to use it—to get its own way. In our day-to-day lives, we are facing with negotiation situations constantly, though we are sometimes not aware of them. In our villages, there are several gentlemen who do this activity always. They have had special such potentialities; for which they can negotiate better. In a family/institution, the head always try to negotiate to resolve the conflict in the family/institution. This a positive approach of technique for resolving conflicts.

Types of Negotiation

There are two types of negotiation: Distributive and Integrative. Distributive negotiations can be thought of as disputes over a "fixed pie." That is, when we see conflict, from a distributive perspective, we are negotiating to divide some limited resource—and whatever you win, I lose, and vice versa. Integrative negotiations, on the other hand can be thought of as disputes where there is an "expanding the pie." That is, when we see conflict from a distributive perspective, we are negotiating to try to expand resources so that everyone wins from the outcome we achieve. Integrative negotiations are based on a win-win perspective.

Mary Parker Follet (1924), an early management theorist cites an example of distributive and integrative negotiation. Two sisters are arguing over a single orange. One wants it for a cake that she is making. The other wants it because she is thirsty and would like to make some orange juice. The sisters decide to split the orange in two. One takes her half, peels it, and uses the fruit to make a very small glass of orange juice. The other takes her half, peels it, and uses the peel to bake a very small cake. This is an example of distributive negotiation, where they split a fixed resource between them.

"In the same situation the sisters could have used integrative rather than distributive negotiation. They could have each had the entire orange, but only the part each needed. The thirsty sister could have used the whole orange to make the juice she wanted, then given the peel to the other sister to zest for the cake she wanted to make." (Skills you need.com)

Types of Negotiation

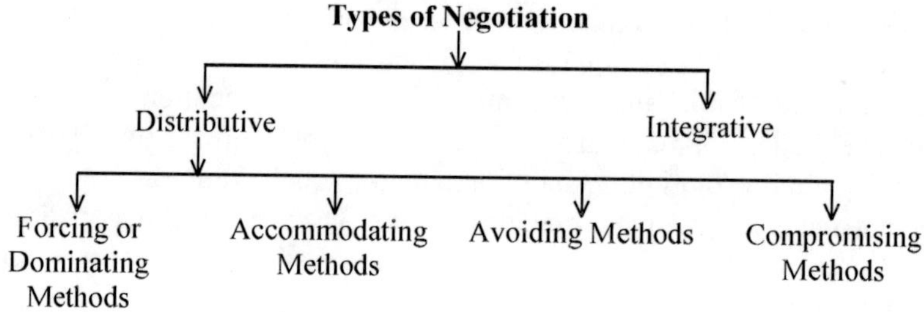

Distributive negotiations are characterised by "attempts to force a solution or to dominate a situation to get your own way, or by giving in to another person's wishes and accommodating to their desires, or by trying to compromise so that each person gets a little bit of what they want, but must also give up something they want, or even by trying to avoid the conflict altogether." (*op. cit.*)

Integrative negotiations are characterised by "collaboration where the parties try to find creative solutions that will fully satisfy both sets of desires. While such a win-win approach is probably a good perspective to take into any negotiation situation, they also take a great deal of time and effort and are the hardest to reach. They require everyone's active contribution and emotional participation." (*op. cit.*)

There are negotiation situations where distributive negotiations are more suitable courses of action to take. Taking a collaborative approach would be too time-consuming or where the outcome isn't really that important to either of the parties to the negotiation.

Forcing or dominating methods of negotiating are effective and very power-oriented. It dominates other rather respect. These negotiating methods are appropriate when we are confronted with an emergency that requires immediate, decisive action, or when we need to take unpopular action like disciplining an employee or enforcing unpopular rules. If we want to protect ourself against people who take advantage people who are less forceful in negotiating situations, this method may be applied.

Accommodating methods denote giving priority another person's desires in the negotiation. These methods are appropriate when we want to foster goodwill, or when we want to preserve the harmony of the relationship. In this case importance is given to the other person. Accommodating may be considered as a tool to aid employees in developing their own skills and to learn from their own experiences. Allowing employees to do a job in their own way and gives the opportunity to discuss with them and change accordingly congenial. This is a much better learning situation.

Avoiding methods involve sidestepping or postponing the negotiation process. They are applicable when the issues are inconsequential or unimportant, or when the tension in the negotiations are getting to great and people need to calm down. When we feel that we can't achieve our aim, and there is no reason to negotiate, in this case avoidance method may be applied.

Compromising methods provide a middle ground. Here there is give and take action, so that each person gets some, but not all of what they want. These are appropriate when we need to come to a temporary settlement to difficult matters, or when we don't have a lot of time, or if you can't find a win-win solution. "There are times when we try to come up with an integrative solution in our negotiating process, but just can't seem to get there. Have a compromise—give and take—fallback position allows us to still achieve something out of the negotiation. We can go into the negotiation hoping to fully satisfy both parties, but be willing to give up something to get something else." (*Op. cit.*)

Pillars of Negotiation

Steven Cohen (2002) notes the following negotiation skills are the Pillars of Negotiation. He feels these are very important in any negotiation situation: (1) separate the people from the problem; (2) focus on interests, not positions; (3) be creative (4) find supra-ordinate goals; (5) be fair; (6) be prepared to commit; (7) be an active listener; (8) be conscious of the importance of the relationship; (9) be aware of BATNAS.

(1) Separate the People from the Problem: This strategy may be applied when we need to view situation as problem that needs to be solved. We don't have to like the problem, but that doesn't mean that we have to dislike the other person.

(2) Focus On Interests, Not Position: This strategy encourages the interest of person not his position. Because, "Focusing on positions generates balkanization, while focusing on interests expands our freedom of action." We need to understand our and the other party's interests. Stress must be given on what the both parties want and why. Here, it will be seen the interest of both parties. The solution may be derived from mutual consent.

(3) Be Creative: Here, brainstorming techniques is more meaningful. Be open up to unusual and out of the ordinary proposals and unanticipated possibilities. If we are creative and do propose the unexpected, we can open doors to far greater opportunities and options. Create opportunities and solutions that lead to mutual gain.

(4) Find Supra-Ordinate Goals: It is more ideal to select goals that we can both agree on. Such goals may need to take into account broader perspectives. This will improve the chances of reaching an integrative, win-win solution.

(5) Be Fair: It is assumed that for sustainable development every business should be free and fair. That means there must not be any complexity. When people feel that the negotiation process has been fair and equitable, they will be more likely to make real commitment and less likely to reject the agreement.

(6) Be Prepared to Commit: After well preparation commitment may be given, otherwise don't make commitments. It is probably best not to make threats while negotiating. If it feels that one needs to do so, don't threaten any consequences.

(7) Be an Active Listener: Common people argue with the other persons. But it is wise do not argue with othes. Try to understand what they really want. Focus on what others say, both on their words and their underlying

meaning. This will help us understand interests upon which agreement can be based. Active listening can raise level of civility in the negotiation process.

(8) Be Conscious of the Importance of the Relationship: We are interacting and communicating with people during the negotiation process. If we will be conscious and understand the relative priority of the relationship, it can be easier to know when giving in on a particular point may yield a short-term cost, but result in long-term gains. Sometimes we care others than ourselves. This will make them feel that we care about them and their desired and it will build a good relationship for us for later issues that we feel are important.

There are also times when the harmony of the relationship is much more important than issue at hand. At those times pushing to get our way or even to take the time and effort to try to find an integrative solution might not be worth it. In this situation we may join in other's choice. It may reach us at appropriate negotiation. Always remember that the other person is also human. Treat them as if they have value and worth as a person, even if you might not agree with their point of view at the moment

(9) Be Aware of BATNAS: It stands for "Best Alternative to a Negotiated Agreement." It is the situation we want to improve by negotiating with a given party or set of parties. BATNA is an awareness of the relative value of negotiating a particular issue with a particular party. Here we may ask such question -Is the issue worth negotiating or do you want to fall back on better alternatives that you can obtain without negotiating?

b. Persuasion Skill

Persuasion is the ability to induce to undertake a course of action or embrace a point of view by means of argument, reasoning, or entreaty. Persuasion is explicit and direct, while manipulation is implicit and deceptive. Influence is the ability to produce an effect on someone else. To persuade others to our point of view we need to show what's in it for them. We need to highlight how our proposal meets their needs. Establish common ground with others and show how our ideas will lead to shared benefits.

Jay Conger (1998) in his article, "The Necessary Art of Persuasion," in the *Harvard project/programme purpose Review* talks about how to persuade and how **not** to persuade.

Conger's Four Ways 'Not to Persuade'

(i) *Make your case with an up-front, hard sell*: Push the person to accept what he is trying to get them to do. Don't back off; just keep pushing one's point of view? The reality with the ***hard sell*** *approach,* however, is that people don't really like it. They want to be able to think about the issues and have some time for ideas to generate.

(ii) *Resist compromise*: We know that our way is the best way. Don't give in to any of their idea. That will only show weakness. The *reality is that people like to feel that they can have input into decisions and tend to become defensive if someone else feels that their way is the only way.* When people become defensive, they hold on to their own position more tightly, rather than being willing to listen to other points of view. (Op. Cit.)

(iii) *Think that the secret of persuasion is in presenting great arguments*: It is the right statistical evidence, great examples, and outstanding support. Have a smooth, polished presentation style. The reality with thinking that the secret of persuasion is that while good arguments are important.

(iv) *Assume persuasion is a one-shot effort:* Imagine that we will never see the person again, so we don't have to worry about how they feel after we have persuaded them. Relationships aren't important, results are. "The reality of thinking that persuasion is a one-shot effort is that we do generally have long-term relationships with the people we are trying to persuade."(Op. cit.)

By utilizing Conger's four ways not to persuade, we are essentially telling people that are not of worth and value—that they don't really have the ability to hold their own ideas and opinions. We are treating them as if they don't count and as if their ideas are not worth much. Thus, by relying on the ways not to persuade we are not likely get others to go along with our persuasive attempt.

Conger's Steps to Effective Persuasion

Let's now look at some ways that we can follow when trying to persuade others. Conger feels that the best way to persuade others is by establishing credibility through expertise and relationship building, by providing the framework for common ground, by providing evidence, and by connecting emotionally.

a) Establish Credibility through Expertise and by Building Relationships: If an individual will grow his potentiality enormously, he can influence others. It will be felt by people that we know what we are talking about before they will be persuaded to adopt our ideas. To establish our own expertise educate our self so that we become knowledgeable about the issues, hire recognized outside experts to help us, and launch pilot projects so that we can demonstrate our knowledge.

If people trust us it will be much easier to persuade others. By building relationships with others we also build trust with them. We can build those relationships regarding issues we are trying to persuade others about by meeting one-on-one with key people you intend to persuade and by involving like-minded coworkers who have good support with the audience for your persuasive message.

b) Provide a Frame for Common Ground: To persuade others to our point of view we need to show what's in it for them. We need to highlight how our proposal meets their needs. We will create a common ground with others and reflect how our ideas will lead to shared benefits.

We have to acquaint with the audience and their needs. We have to analyze the audience and know them in order to be able to provide a framework for common ground. Then, we can interact with an audience to deliver a message effectively.

c) Provide Evidence: Good arguments may be helpful for effective persuasion. Sometimes evidences are more helpful to persuade others. "Use statistics and facts, but augment and enhance them with stories, narratives, examples, metaphors, and analogies. These will all humanize your evidence and help provide common ground."

d) Connect Emotionally: Reason is an important way to try to persuade others, but it is not the only way. Emotions also play a part in the persuasive process. When we are passionate about our ideas, people tend to be more willing to listen to them than when we don't really seem to care all that much about our ideas. It is not only our emotion about our ideas that matter. Our audience's emotional disposition, especially toward our ideas is also critical. Again, we need to analyze your audience to know how they are feeling so that we can adjust our persuasive message accordingly. Hence, sometimes emotionality has persuasive effect.

c. Peaceful Co-existence

Peaceful coexistence, in extending itself to all countries and social movements tied to the USSR's interpretation of communism, quickly became modus operandi for many individual communist parties as well, encouraging quite a few, especially those in the developed world, to give up their long-term goal of amassing support for an armed, insurrectionist communist revolution and exchange it for more full participation in electoral politics. (Wikipedia)

Khrushchev solidified the concept in Soviet foreign policy in 1956 at the 20th Congress of the Communist Party of the Soviet Union. The policy arose as a temptation to reduce hostility between the two superpowers, particularly in light of the possibility of nuclear war. The Soviet theory of peaceful coexistence asserted that the United States and USSR, and their respective political ideologies, could coexist rather than fighting one another, and Khrushchev tried to demonstrate his commitment to peaceful coexistence by attending international peace conferences, such as the Geneva Summit, and by traveling internationally, such as his trip to America's Camp David in 1959. The World Peace Council founded in 1949 and largely funded by the Soviet Union attempted to organize a peace movement in favour of the concept internationally. (Wikipedia)

During the late 1970s and 1980s, the concept of peaceful coexistence was expanded as a framework for all sovereign nations. In 1982 the Five Principles were written into the Constitution of the People's Republic of China which claims to be bound by them in its international relations.

The Five Principles of Peaceful Coexistence as promoted by China are:

- mutual respect for sovereignty and territorial integrity
- mutual non-aggression
- non-interference in each other's internal affairs
- equality and mutual benefit
- peaceful co-existence

There are three notable consequences of the Chinese concept of peaceful coexistence. First of all, in contrast with the Soviet concepts of the mid-1970s, the Chinese concepts include the encouragement of global free trade. Second, the Chinese concept of peaceful coexistence places a large emphasis on national sovereignty and territorial integrity, and thus moves by the United States to promote democracy and human rights are seen in this framework as hostile. Finally, as the PRC does not consider Taiwan to be sovereign, the concept of peaceful coexistence does not extend to Taiwan, and efforts by other nations, particularly the United States, to involve itself in PRC. (Wikipedia)

The above policies may be implied in other situation to establish peace. As a conscious citizen we have to follow this principle. In our country thousands year before the sages talked about this. For establishing harmonious civilisation its value is immeasurable. In Gurukula system peaceful co-existence was a vital principle. If we want a harmonious world, we have to follow this principle and make a better world.

5.6 Peace Values

The peace values can serve as vehicles for unity, solidarity and peace, as well as an instrument for democracy and sustainable development. Education, which has a fundamental role to play in personal and social development, has been used to create a more skilled work force, but often at the cost of the development of the whole person. The long-term goals of human values and moral principles tend to become less important when they have to compete with more immediate economic considerations. Furthermore, whether industrialised or industrializing, many countries in the region are still in the process of democratisation and require enormous effort in the dissemination of the principles of universal values, such as human rights for all, and in the promotion of a culture of peace and tolerance. To this end, education for peace, human rights and democracy should receive more attention and greater priority. Convinced that the changes and the challenges of the future require a better understanding of others and the world at large, and that they also demand mutual appreciation, peaceful interchange and harmony,

5.6.1 Peace Values for Personality Formation

- Love
- Truth
- Purity—both physical and mental (think, speak, and do what is right)
- Beauty and harmony—appreciating the unity in diversity of people and nature
- A spirit of appreciation (gratitude)
- A sense of responsibility
- Ahimsa—Not to harm other
- Humility—the willingness to be corrected and the courage to accept one's mistakes
- A spirit of service
- Leadership—initiatives make peace or to improve a given situation
- Positive thinking and optimism
- Discipline—self-control, concentration, hard work, and growth
- 'Other-orientation'—the skills to cope with 'otherness' and the ability to think for others and to help them
- Growth—both for the self and for the neighbour

5.6.2 Peace Values in Indian History and Culture

There are enumerable examples in Indian history and culture which have immense contribution for peace building in society and civilisations. Some of them are as following:

- Positive and negative understanding of peace
- Integrative vision (*vasudhaiva kutumbakam)*
- Diversity, plurality, and co-existence, with a special emphasis on customs and cultures
- Sri Aurobindo's views on peace
- Teachings on peace (ahimsa, truth and hospitality)
- Gandhiji's idea and practice of peace
- Peace movements (especially the Freedom Movement)
- Religion and Spirituality the means of peace and harmony
- Patriotism and dedication to the mother India
- Following the Dictums of ancient scriptures
- Parables and anecdotes

5.6.3 Peace Values and National Unity

In Indian constitution the following characteristics are enshrined to act:

- India—unity in religious, cultural, and linguistic diversity
- Human dignity
- Equality

- Social justice
- Protection of the rights of all people
- Participation
- Freedom of speech and expression

5.6.4 Peace Values and Globalisation

There are certain points we can think about peace values in global platform.

- Peace in the global context
- Peace movements and initiatives
- Ecological concerns—caring for nature and sustainable development
- Liberalisation, Globalisation and Privatisation—their implications for peace
- Globalisation and democracy
- Peace, development and social justice in international outlook
- Peace and gender biased
- Generation gap and peace
- Drug abuse and peace
- HIV/AIDS and peace
- Terrorism and peace

5.7 Peace Skills

It is expected that students will develop the skills (and attitudes) necessary to be proactive and effective peacemakers. These can be summarised under three heads: thinking skills, communication skills, and personal skills.

5.7.1 Thinking Skills

There are different types of thinking skills as per views of various experts. Some of them are discussed below.

Critical Thinking: The ability to distinguish between fact, opinion, and belief; to recognize bias and prejudice; to identify issues and problems as well as the assumptions in an argument; and to reason correctly

Information Handling: To be able to form a hypothesis and test it; to know where to look for answers and how to select and reject information; to effectively weigh up evidence; to hypothesize eventual outcomes and consequences in order to be able to choose the most appropriate action.

Creative Thinking: To seek novel solutions and answers; to think laterally and approach problems from multiple perspectives.

Reflection: To stand back from a problem and identify its component parts; to effectively monitor thought processes and produce appropriate strategies for dealing with any particular problem.

Dialectical Thinking: Thinking about more than one point of view;

understanding both points of view; being able to construct an argument from either point of view based on knowledge of the other.

5.7.2 Communication Skills

Communication and Listening skills are essential to enable teachers get sensitised to the area of communication and get insight on the impact of different communication styles on others. Communication and listening skills are basic skills, which are required for our learning, emotional, social, and personality development. How one communicates with others verbally and non-verbally determines the extent to which s/he is able to convey his expectations and needs to others, how s/he is able to impact others as an aggressive or polite individual. Awareness of one's own communication style and its impact on one's own self and emotional life will enable teacher to bring above improvement in their own skills. Knowledge of communication viz. listening to verbal, non-verbal messages and interpreting them, impact of attending to non-verbal messages and feelings enables one to become effective communicator. Some means of above skills are given below:

- *Presentatio*n: To be able to clearly and coherently explain ideas.
- *Active Listenin*g: To listen carefully, understand, and acknowledge the views of others.
- *Negotiatio*n: To recognize the role and limitations of compromise as a tool for the cessation of conflict; to carry on a productive dialogue towards the resolution of a dispute.
- *Non-Verbal Communicatio*n: Recognizing the meaning and significance of body language.

5.7.3 Personal Skills

There are number of personal skills one can follow for developing peace culture. A few among those are given here:

- *Cooperatio*n: To work effectively with others towards a common goal. Cooperation encourages peaceful situation.
- *Adaptability*: To be willing to change opinions in the light of evidence and reason. It is helpful for reducing conflict and tension.
- *Self-Disciplin*e: The ability to conduct oneself appropriately and manage time effectively. It can enhance for building peace culture
- *Responsibilit*y: The ability to take on and complete tasks in an appropriate manner; being willing to assume a share of the responsibility.
- *Respect:* Listening sensitively to others; making decisions based on fairness and equality; recognizing that others' beliefs, views, and ideas may differ from one's own.

- *Love:* 'Shradhaban lavate param'—means lovable person achieves Divine grace. Love is the key of peace.
- *Hard labour:* Every labour has reward at last. Dignity of labour is always productive and praiseworthy.
- *Truth:* Only truth in speech and action can provide value based peaceful society.
- *Respect to Various values:* Economic value, aesthetic value, political value, social value, cultural value, Artistic value, literary value, peace value, historical value, mathematical value, scientific value, work value, democratic value, human value, and environmental value etc.
- *Remaining Calm and Quite:* In calm and quite situation we can take proper decision.

5.7.4 Activities/Assignments

- Outlining framework of peace values and their behavioural manifestation at different stages-group work.
- Reflections on the original writings/practices/educational experiments and values of great Indian thinkers and educationists on peace-Library work.
- Developing a folder on key concepts and glossary on peace education.
- Plot a drama on related to peace and self-empowerment.
- Ideas generation for making collages/slogans on topics like: gender equality, human rights, child rights, save nature, intercultural understanding relevant to school education.
- Visiting websites on Peace Education.
- Visiting a few institutions/schools/places of significant for peace.
- Maintaining a daily reflective journal or diary

6
Peace and Education

Peace education is holistic. It embraces the physical, emotional, intellectual, and social growth of children within framework deeply rooted in traditional human values. It is based on philosophy that teaches love, compassion, trust, fairness, co-operation and reverence for the human family and all life on our beautiful planet.

—*Fran Schmidt & Alice Friedman* (1988)

The aims of education enunciated in the NCF include developing commitment to democracy and the values of equality, justice, freedom, secularism, and concern for others well beings. It is that children can be oriented towards peace and enabling them to make choices and decisions about what is right and best for common good, and promoting their ethical development that their capacity for value based decisions making could be developed. Education for peace is about empowerment of self so that individuals are equipped with knowledge, competencies and skills of conflict resolution; such individuals will have self-awareness, values of tolerance, compassion and competence to deal with crisis in creative manner. In order to develop these attitudes, skills and competencies among pupils, the institutions of family and school have to be oriented to make conscious efforts to promote peace related skills. Development of peace-skills and attitudes would entail inspiring the entire atmosphere of school, personnel and staff to nurture such attitudes and competencies for peace. Teachers being central to the entire gamut of all relationships at school, their orientation is most crucial.

Peace also encourages for self-development, identity and prejudice, conflict resolution, democracy, justice and human rights, sustainable economic development, gender equality etc. The teachers need to develop consciousness and insight, into their own role as peace educators, their attitudes and values, and the skills necessary for implementing peace education through activities in schools and classrooms.

Peace generates harmony at all levels within individuals, their families and inter relationships, working environments, with in neighbours etc. It is a dynamic concept related to human beings; who have recurrent needs, which are contextual, full of variety and urgency. Democracy, freedom and equality for all are not enough; social justice and inequalities have to be understood and attend to. Human rights and responsibilities need to be respected. Inner peace or intra personal peace is reflected in the behaviour viz. physical, social, emotional, health, productivity, and relationships. The outside changes in the productivity, relationships, however, begin from individual, who are pro-peace need for increasing one's own inner resources and extension of the meaning of peace to include health, yoga, meditation and fitness, communication skills, stress management, family relationships, democratic and constitutional values, ethics, justice, equality and equity.

Peace education was taken to enable teachers to become aware of the present status of violence and conflict in society, particularly in the school and enhancing of their consciousness. The peace disturbing elements in the school viz. child abuse, bullying, examination, stress among students, cultural intolerance conflict among staffs, parent and teacher at disagree etc. to be comprehended and understand by teachers. The teacher might be enable to understand that all the conflicts whether at school level, student level or staff level or where else are the result of a few sources. These sources may be obvious or hidden in the structure of society. They need to understand these sources and become aware how these few sources lead to series of small conflict, which eventually turn, into bigger and violent struggles sometimes. The teachers have to realize that conflicts are not outside the society but these are a part and parcel of our own system and cultures; without exploring and realizing these sources and different categories of conflict, effective action cannot be initiated.

Education fosters the culture of peace. The aim of education is to prepare children to live life as responsible and productive citizens and members of society. The requisites of citizenship and membership of society include humaneness, tolerance, and patience, the capability to develop ensure one's own well-being and that of others, critical thinking skills, capability to make rational value based decisions etc. The idea that Peace Education is an additional intervention to attain these objectives of education was to be realised.

Education aims at preparing children to grow into youth capable of living peacefully and constructively. Apparently this aim of education is not being fully attained. Peace education is the additional intervention to attain the objectives of education by developing their critical thinking skills, which have a bearing on their moral and ethical development. The objectives of education are not currently paid attention. Peace education aims at nurturing skills, attitudes and values, which enable individuals to resolve conflicts peacefully, and build a non-violent and just society. It seeks to develop healthy relationships.

Peace needs social justice. The members of the institutions should understand what social justice means and the attitudes, basic prejudices, which accompany injustice, were to be conveyed. The teachers have to realize the opportunities in school they which can capitalize on to help children acquire healthy attitudes towards needs and requirements of others. There are various ways in which justice is denied to vulnerable groups, particularly school children, girls, culturally, educationally or physically differently abled. It should be realised and proper actions might be taken accordingly.

The educational institutions must be identified with Inter Cultural Harmony and its nature. The understanding of overlaps across cultures and existing communalities among cultures, religions, communities and regions by teachers is important. The vertical and horizontal mobility in society causes great overlap and continuity in various dimensions of living rituals, practices, mores etc. these aspects remain elusive to people. The awareness of the communalities, the continuities and differences from past cultural structure is likely to change the mind sets of the teachers resulting in positive attitudes towards other cultures and sub cultures. The changed attitudes will lead to acceptance of inter-cultural differences and intercultural harmony.

The cultural diversity and inequality need to be reconciled peacefully. Understanding, respect and appreciation towards differences is needed for survival of democracy and peace. War and violence result when differences are highlighted and overlap and connectivity is over looked. Different stories and anecdotes should be included in curriculum to create the culture of peace.

The teachers must understand the issue of equity and equality especially in the context of gender. A wide variety of gender related inequalities are nurtured at school level. The teachers including female teachers are unaware of the structural, attitudinal naivety strengthening the gender biased attitudes and values. Gender equality involves that the women may be empowered to question, take charge of their own selves, and participate in decision making for which they need to be prepared. The women need to be prepared to take a front seat, and not to feel guilty for raising questions and demanding their rights. They should have decision-making power in matters related to their marriage, motherhood, financial, or any other personal issue. They need to be prepared to think critically, provided security, and freedom from traditions, which restrict their participation. There is need for mutual understanding among men and women, instead of competition and blaming each other; both men and women need to live in harmony. Data from researches, surveys, and articles show that 1/3rd women suffer nutritional deficiency, 300 women die every day during childbirth or pregnancy related problems. Those in the work force are employed in subordinate jobs and very few make it to executive positions. The teachers have significant role in developing healthy attitudes among men and women towards gender equality.

6.1 Education for Peace

'Education for peace' is a slogan requires for the time. This is an ultimate goal of human being. It seeks to nurture the knowledge, skills, attitudes, and values that comprise a culture of peace. It is a long-term proactive strategy to nurture peaceful persons who resolve conflicts non-violently. Education for peace is holistic. It embraces the physical, emotional, intellectual, and social growth of children within a framework of human values. Recognizing peace as holistic carries two major implications for education for peace. (*a*) Peace involves all aspects and dimensions of human existence in an inter-dependent way. Only those who are at peace with themselves can be at peace with others and develop the sensitivity it takes to be just and caring towards nature. (*b*) Peace implies reciprocity. Values like love, freedom, and peace can be had only by giving them to others. Peace for oneself that excludes peace for others is a dangerous illusion. Education for Peace, hence, has a two-fold purpose: (*a*) to empower individuals to choose the path of peace rather than the path of violence; and (*b*) to enabling them to be peacemakers rather than the consumers of peace. Education for peace is, in this sense, an essential component of holistic basic education that aims at the comprehensive development of persons (NCERT, 2006)

The following suggestions are given by various experts for establishing and enhancing peace through education:

- Set up peace clubs and library;
- Create a pool of films—documentaries and feature films regarding promotion of values of justice and peace.
- Media can be used as a stakeholder in peace education.
- Make provisions in schools and colleges to enable students to celebrate some significant days like: (a) Human Rights Day, (b) Day for the Differently-abled, (c) Girl Child Day, (d) Women's day, and (e) Environment Day etc.
- Organize district-level peace festivals for school students
- Organise workshops in peace education for teachers, principals and parents.
- A nationwide campaign to eradicate corruption in education.
- Peace education should be enshrined in educational review or reform of policy.
- Parents and teachers should collaborate in the process of promoting a peaceful approach to problems and conflicts arising in school.
- Curriculum design needs to be informed by a holistic approach to peace ducation.
- Syllabi and textbooks need to be reorganised to reflect the concerns of education for peace.
- Teacher education programmes at all levels to be reformed and radically re-organised in the light of the avowed goals of education and the specific requirements of education for peace.
- The school atmosphere must be kept free from violence of every kind. Students must be enabled to participate in maintaining and improving discipline.

- Peace education must be followed by each concern of educational institution.

6.1.1 Integrative Approach of Peace in Education

The peace values existed in the curriculum are heightened when the school atmosphere is imbued with the values and attitudes of peace. Teacher–pupil interactions, parent- teacher relations, lesson designs in textbooks, the pedagogies, practicum, organisational management and the total academic environment of the school must be oriented toward peace. Since peace is an integrative and all-embracing concept, the integrated approach is to be inculcated in the curriculum. Integration occurs when all the activities of the school, curricular as well as co-curricular, are driven toward education for peace. At the classroom, peace activities are intruded into the contents of the lessons, which are treated also as a means of helping students to imbibe peace values. The integrated approach of peace can be understood as various points of view, i.e. philosophical, psychological, motivational, and pedagogical. From the cognitive and developmental point of view, constructivist psychology has established that children construct knowledge holistically. When knowledge is embedded in appropriate contexts, it becomes more meaningful and enjoyable for the learner. In the integrated approach, the lessons and topics become the vehicles to convey peace messages in meaningful contexts. This approach not only makes the subject matter wholesome and situated but also motivates students to learn and to relate what they learn to their own settings. It provides contexts and enquiry to explore, think, reflect, and internalise positive behaviours. The integrated approach must be reflected in the whole of educational programmes in schools and must permeate the school to imply it curriculum and co-curriculum. Hence, every teacher has to become a peace educator. Teachers, parents, textbook lessons and the pedagogy for teaching them, the school management and administrative staff etc. all the components of school must be oriented to education for peace.

6.1.2 Introduction of Peace Education in School Curriculum

Peace education can be introduced in school through curricular and extracurricular activities. The conceptual framework of each subject should encompass the spread of universal values and enduring attitudes in the students' mind. We can adopt peace education in following context:

Language: Language shows the beauty and feeling. It may provide opportunities to understand the problem and its resolution, identifying values, diversities of nature, interaction with society. It encourages intercultural communications, social consciousness, and potential for interconnecting disciplines. Hence, language is a proper medium through which peace education can be implemented in the classroom. Peace education concerns with cooperative, interactive learning are also helpful for language learning. Pupils can be organised to work collaboratively with others. Peace education concepts such as respect, justice, democracy, rights, responsibility, negotiations, shared decisions critical thinking etc. can be infused in language teaching. It develops communication, expression of feelings and areas of agreement and disagreement, building international exchange and understanding, cultural awareness and appreciation of values in different societies. Writing short stories and playing dramas show cultural reflection. Debates on war and peace, Violence and non-violence, rights of women, education of refugee, boarder issues, cultural diffusion etc. enhance the peace culture. Language teacher may promote the understanding of peace and the language of non-violence. The capacity for reflective conversation and debate is acquainted with language acquisition, cross-cultural understanding and peace education.

Mathematics: Values in mathematics are so deep, affective qualities which education aims to foster through mathematics and are a crucial component of affective environment in the classroom. It is a powerful subject to express the topics of equity, global of wealth, economic development, expenditure in education, pollution, and environmental responsibility. The different data of the world can be expressed through charts, figures and graphs. Problem solving method can be effectively used by the mathematics teacher to teach peace through mathematics. Through mathematics we get information about war period, its expenditure, loss of lives and properties, use of nuclear energy, affected areas etc. in different countries of the globe. Mathematics provides opportunity to learn problem-solving skills, creative thinking and critical thinking skills and acquainted with environment.

Science: Science teachers can teach us peace by promoting environmental awareness and ecological thinking. Knowing science in day to day life and care of living beings and social responsibility needs awareness of ethics. The process of evaluating evidence and analysis of data and making prediction develop peace culture in society. The moon light teaches us peace and harmony. The sun provides power in positive direction. Electrons bind each other like social bond. Students can learn peaceful living in nuclear world. Students should learn alternative sources of energy like wind, solar, water etc. and its implications in social and political fields. The subjects like; greenhouse effect, climate changes, pollution free environment, nuclear waste and its management, sharing resources, deforestation, land, mines dams and their ecological impact and studies about war and its impact should be judiciously taught to students through science. The knowledge about plants, animals, birds should be learnt. Eco-consciousness and sustainability and interdependence should be included in curriculum for better understanding about environment. The students must be aware about the terrific consequence of war or conflict and its effects

Social Science: Social science teaches us experience of war making and peace building, skills of interpretation, enquiry and communication etc. Past events teach us about the cause and effect, sorrow, heroism and sacrifice. It also teach us about international organisation and political activities for peace and understanding. Lessons of rights of life and responsibilities, the role of UNO and its members during conflict, the failure of war and many peace treaties should be taught to learners through social science. The leadership quality of past heroes encourages learners to become good leader. Each culture has its own values. The principles of equality, justice, and solidarity are central theme of cultural diversity. It must be learned by the learners. Through social science the students must be explored the issues related to identity, cultural diffusion, comparison among cultures, cultural influence, bridge and boundaries, contributions to the world heritage, how cultural diversity threatens the world peace and contribution to enhancing world peace. Distribution of natural resources, material wealth, production and consumption of goods, eradication of poverty, role of international agencies and their agreement, responsibility of developed nations, trade affairs and measures of economic development in past must be known by the learners. Students must be aware about famine, flood, natural resources, environmental pollution, trade flows and migration etc. through geography. Population explosion, growth, migration refugee issues, demographic change and disaster must be understood by learners in making peace making process. Conflict resolution skills, cooperation, collaboration, gender equality, human rights, justice, women rights, social value, social ethics, multicultural issues etc. should be learned through social science.

ICT: ICT has great value in building of peace culture. It enhances global cooperation. It encourages in exchanging the ideas and experience with others across the world. It provides right information in right time at right people. It brings closer the world of civilisations. Peace ideas and thoughts of different countries can be disseminated through this multisensory media. Moral stories, lectures, blogs, poems, essays, letters, and information of different countries or cultures can be shared through ICT. The inspirations of great thinkers, research reports, writings, strategies of conflict resolutions and problem solving, world views and news, data can be obtained through ICT. On the whole it is powerful device in modern world for uniting the nations of the world and building a peaceful globe.

6.1.3 Fostering Culture of Peace through Education

The aim of education is to prepare children to live life as responsible and productive citizens and members of society. The requisites of citizenship and membership of society include humaneness, tolerance, and patience, the capability to develop ensure one's own well-being and that of others, critical thinking skills, capability to make rational value based decisions etc. Education aims at preparing children to grow into youth capable of living peacefully and constructively. Peace education is the additional intervention to attain the objectives of education by developing their critical thinking skills, which have a bearing on their moral and ethical development. Peace education aims at nurturing skills, attitudes and values, which enable individuals to resolve conflicts peacefully, and build a non-violent and just society. It seeks to develop healthy relationships.

6.1.4 Social Justice

The teachers have to realize the opportunities in school they which can capitalize on to help children acquire healthy attitudes towards needs and requirements of others. They should be enabled to explore the ways in which justice is denied to vulnerable groups, particularly school children, girls, culturally, educationally or physically differently abled. The repercussions of social justice being denied were also to be identified. The needs have to be satisfied, until there will be dissatisfaction, which may not become apparent for fear or lack of expression, peace cannot be expected in the midst of discontentment. Equity in distribution of profits and benefits i.e. to each according to their minimum basic needs and work as per their capacities is the preamble underlying of social justice. It refers to the balance between self-orientation and other orientation. The teachers were expected to identify the situations, which violate social justice in the class and school and initiate action and discussion so that children's attitudes could be guided in right direction.

6.1.5 Inter Cultural Harmony

The vertical and horizontal mobility in society causes great overlap and continuity in various dimensions of living rituals, practices, mores etc. these aspects remain elusive to people. The awareness of the communalities, the continuities and differences from past cultural structure is likely to change the mind sets of the teachers resulting in positive attitudes towards other cultures and sub cultures. The changed attitudes will lead to acceptance of inter-cultural differences and intercultural harmony.

Just like the cultural groups, there are social, economic and political groups. There are inequalities among economic and political group as well. These inequalities within society often lead to conflicts and violence. The interconnectivity and overlap among different social groups is increasing, for instance, caste differences have been overtaken by class differences, and regional differences are more prominent than religious differences among people. The cultural diversity and inequality need to be reconciled peacefully. Understanding, respect and appreciation towards differences is needed for survival of democracy and peace. War and violence result when differences are highlighted and overlap and connectivity is over looked.

6.1.6 Gender Equality

The issue of equity and equality especially in the context of gender should be realised. A wide variety of gender related inequalities are nurtured at school level. The teachers including female teachers are unaware of the structural, attitudinal innocence strengthening the gender biased attitudes and values. Genders are defined as social roles, which are naturally and normally assigned, to the men and women; however, in spirit the equality is denied not only to women but among general population too equality is misleading. In our society decision-making lies with those in power and women are powerless. They do not control resources; even over their own self they have no control. The decision on giving birth to a child is also a special right of men. Gender equality involves that the women may be empowered to question, take charge of their own selves, and participate in decision making for which they need to be prepared. The women need to be prepared to take a front seat, and not to feel guilty for raising questions and demanding their rights. They should have decision-making power. In matters related to their marriage, motherhood, financial, or any other personal issue, they need to be prepared to think critically, provided security, and freedom from traditions, which restrict their participation. There is need for mutual understanding among men and women, instead of competition and blaming each other; both men and women need to live in harmony. Developing healthy attitudes among men and women towards gender equality should be highlighted.

6.1.7 Self-Development

The theme of Self-development finds its place in the peace curriculum because 'self' is the locus of all thoughts, attitudes, or values, which give rise to a peaceful, or aggressive, or violent personality. If the individual self is calm, evolved and adequate without any insecurity, inferiority feelings or weakness or fear the peace comes, naturally to such a person since self exists in relationships. Improving communication skills,—both verbal and non-verbal could help develop the self.

Self-Development for peace included mainly three aspects Understanding and Developing Self through effective communication and listening skills, understanding prejudices and biases in Communication and developing positive social skills viz. cooperation. 'Know Your Self' is the key of self-development. The future teachers should be understood the concept of inner-self, and empowerment of self by opening to others, meditation and self-reflection, balance between inner self and outer self and how peace is possible through calming inner noise and conflicts within self. Yogasana is very important for improvement of physical, mental, and emotional health and staying calm and composed in daily life. Yoga is needed in day-to-day life for attaining peace in mind and body.

Communication and listening skills are basic skills, which are required for our learning, emotional, social, and personality development. How one communicates with others verbally and non-verbally determines the extent to which s/he is able to convey his expectations and needs to others, how s/he is able to impact others as an aggressive or polite individual. Awareness of one's own communication style and its impact on one's own self and emotional life will enable teacher to bring above improvement in their own skills. It encourages self-development

6.1.8 Identity

Identity was planned to convey the differences in the way the individuals perceive themselves. Perception of Self in terms of one's cultural ties, regional, professional and personal qualities have a lot of influence over the prejudices, biases and judgments one makes on others. Awareness of one's own identity enables one to be fair while judging others and making evaluations about them. In order to be fair and free from prejudices towards others particularly those from different culture/regional groups, it is important for any individual, especially teachers to be aware of their own identity. So, that they become aware of their biases and prejudices toward students and do not allow them to interfere in their teaching-learning relationship. Awareness is starting point in dropping the prejudices and developing tolerate and respect for cross-cultural populations. Intercultural harmony at school level could be nurtured by developing awareness on identity among teachers.

Identity and its role in persuasion and mediation, the nature of identity and the ways in which it influences our attitudes and values are to be understood. Persuasion and meditation of conflicts requires consciousness of identity. Mediation requires understanding clearly the source and nature of conflict and the biases, which hold the conflict in peace. If the mediator also holds some prejudices and biases as the conflicting parties, he will not be able to comprehend the real issue and mediate.

Identity is supported by our cultural ethos and gives rise to positive and negative attitudes towards others, at the same time it also enables us to relate with others and motivates us especially during childhood. The identity takes complete charge over our behaviour and thinking, it becomes our reference point for judging others right or wrong. It was discussed that awareness of identity is important so that it does not submerge the individual. The feeling of continuity, which is so characteristic of identity, needs to be understood in proper perspective in the sense that the subtle changes are accruing to all, which do not become apparent to the individuals. These characteristics of identity must be known to a person getting ready to mediate in conflict. Sense of continuity in the identity gives us distinction and a feeling of belonging but the changes in identity over time are significant and need to be understood.

Beside awareness of the nature of our identity, the time and place for mediation must be chosen with care. Mediation requires sensitivity and patience towards conflicting persons, their feelings, even prejudices, and biases need to be respected before any change could be expected. Mediation requires empathy with the people involved in conflict and respect for their concerns and points of view.

6.2 Policy Perspectives

The Report of the University Education Commission in India (1962) points out that, "education should not stop with the development of intellectual powers but must provide the student...a code of behaviour based on fundamental principles of ethics and religion." The Report of the Secondary Education Commission of 1952-53 is a significant landmark in the thinking on moral and religious education. It identified character building as the defining goal of education. "The supreme end of the educative process should be the training of the character and personality of students in such a way that they will be able to realize their full potentialities and contribute to the well-being of the community." The report prescribed moral instruction as the means to achieve this goal. In respect of "religious instruction", however, the report stipulated that it "may be given in school only on a voluntary basis and outside the regular school hours, such instruction being confined to the children of the particular faith concerned and given with the consent of the parents and the managements." The Report of the University Education Commission (1962) struck a more confident note. "If we exclude spiritual training in our institutions," the Report stated, "we would be untrue to our whole historical development." The Report then goes on to make a case, not for religious or moral education, but for evolving "a national faith, a national way of life based on the Indian outlook on religion, free from dogmas, rituals and assertions." The Education Commission of 1964-66 put the spotlight on "education and national development", from which perspective it identified the "absence of provision for education in social, moral and spiritual values" as a serious defect in the curriculum. The commission recommended that these values be taught "with the help, wherever possible, of the ethical teachings of great religions." Agreeing with the Sri Prakasa Committee Report it recommended "direct moral instruction" for which "one or two periods a week should be set aside in the school time-table." The National Policy on Education (1986) expressed concern over "the erosion of essential values and an increasing cynicism in society". It advocated turning education into "a forceful tool for the cultivation of social and moral values". Education should "foster universal and eternal values, oriented towards the unity and integration of our people". The Programme of Action of 1992 tried to integrate the various components of value education into the curriculum at all stages of school education, including the secondary stage.

The National Curriculum Framework for School Education (2000), echoing the National Policy on Education (1986), regretted on the statement "erosion of the essential social, moral and spiritual values and an increase in cynicism at all levels." In this context, the framework try to integrate value education into the curriculum. In this view it "is not religious education but education about religions, their basics, the values inherent therein and also a comparative study of the philosophy of all religions." The framework prescribed an integrative approach. Value education and education about religions should be "judiciously integrated with all subjects of study". The shift of focus, over the decades, from religious and moral education to education for peace, via value education, parallels the shifting sense and sensitivities in the larger context of education. The acceptance of education for peace as a necessary ingredient of holistic education in the western context was driven by deepening anxieties about the rise and spread of violence. A similar pattern is obtained in our context as well. For evolving "a national faith, a national way of life based on the Indian outlook on religion, free from dogmas, rituals and assertions." (NCERT, 2006)

6.2.1 Initiatives: International and National

In 1999, the United Nations (UN) General Assembly approved the promotion of culture of peace. The UNESCO declared the period (2000-2010) as the International Decade for Promotion of a Culture of Peace and Non-violence for the Children of the World. The UNESCO recommendations on education for international understanding, peace, human rights, and fundamental freedoms (1974) and UNESCO's 1994 action plan for education for peace, human rights, and democracy, endorsed by 144 countries, are two of the prominent landmarks in the globe. The net ASP was launched by UNESCO in 1953 to promote international understanding and peace. As ASP net includes 7500 institutions ranging from nursery schools to teacher training institutions in 170 countries up to 2003. The network is dedicated to the pursuit of peace, liberty, justice, and human development. An innovative pilot project on "peace and disarmament education" is being implemented in four countries: Albania, Niger, Peru, and Cambodia, by the UN Department of Disarmament Affairs (UNDDA) and Hague Appeal for Peace (HAP). The Centre for Research on Education for peace (CERPE) at the University of Haifa, Israel, which has been running since in 1998. It serves as an interdisciplinary and international forum for the scholarly study of education for peace. The center has undertaken a number of research projects on education for peace. The Earth and Peace Education Associates International (EPE), New York, is yet another organization which promotes basic values related to peace, viz., sustainability, non-violence, social justice, intergenerational equity, and participatory decision-making. Besides these, a number of other organizations around the world are also working for peace.

6.3 Peace Education in Different Stages

The primary stage of education is the ideal time for laying the foundation of a peace-oriented personality. These years comprise the formative period in the lives of the students. At this stage, students are comparatively less burdened. The number of students who could be exposed to education for peace is at the maximum during this phase. Thereafter, students begin to drop out. Therefore, this is the stage at which focused attention should be paid to laying the foundation for a culture of peace through education. As the saying goes, "It is easier to build a child than it is to repair an adult." The values that make up a peace-oriented personality include: hygiene both of the self and of the surroundings, respect for others and for elders, recognition of the dignity of labour, honesty, love, sharing and cooperation, tolerance, regularity, punctuality, responsibility, etc. Education for peace for primary school children is about helping them enjoy and celebrate diversity, beauty, and harmony in nature. They must be encouraged to develop the skills it takes to be at home with others, especially the art of listening and with nature—aesthetic sensitivity and a sense of responsibility. As children grow older and reach the middle school stage, they begin to grasp abstract thoughts. In a limited way they develop the capacity to think rationally and relationally about the various happenings in their surroundings. A crucial issue for children at this stage is that of relating to other children and their status in peer groups. Since, the school brings together children from multiple religious, cultural, and regional backgrounds, students need to be equipped with cognitive competence to understand the values underlying democracy, equality, justice, dignity, and human rights. They need to respond positively to cultural plurality and appreciate the importance of peaceful coexistence. This is the appropriate stage for developing the skills for handling information, thinking creatively, self-reflection, and self-discipline, which will enable them to participate in groups and relate to others responsibly, negotiate conflicts with understanding, and develop an informed aversion to various forms of violence like communalism and discrimination on the basis of gender, caste, class, and religion. Besides, they need to develop discernment, to respond with maturity to corruption, misleading advertisements, and whatever is violent and unhealthy in the media. Above all, they need to be educated in the basics of becoming responsible citizens of a socialist, secular democracy.

In the secondary and senior secondary stage students gradually become aware of their identity. During this stage, the students want to become independent, though still deficient in maturity. The resulting confusion leads to conflict with peers, parents, and teachers. During this phase, their skills for rational thinking, communication, and self-discipline are tested. They need training to resolve, through dialogue and negotiation, the conflicts they are sure to encounter in day-to-day interactions. They also need to develop awareness about inter-relationships and interdependence in the global and ecological contexts, so that they can form a wider perspective on justice, peace, and non-violence. It is important to enable them to be not only the recipients of peace but the active makers of peace, who can think for others and help them.

6.4 Peace in Teacher Education

The teachers are the real heroes in the educational enterprises. Hence, the success of peace education depends on the vision, motivation, skills, and awareness of teachers. Teachers who carry out peace have to cherish its values, hold comparable attitudes, and exhibit similar behavioural tendencies. The teachers have to engage the opportunities of their vocation with innovation and imagination. The teacher-educators are to be free from culturally prejudiced, intolerant, and pedagogically ill-equipped to transact the messages of the text in the classroom in a way that promotes peace. Teacher education institutions, in this context, have a very vital role to play as they are the centers that mould the teaching fraternity of the country through their pre-service and in-service teacher education programmes. The teacher education curriculum frameworks of 1978, 1988 and 1998 emphasised the role of teachers as catalysts in the process of promoting social sensitivity, tolerance, cooperation, democratic and secular values, national integration, international understanding, etc. through inclusion of relevant themes in the 'Foundation Course' and 'school experience' programmes. However, the existing realities and growing faith in violence among the teachers themselves in the form of corporal punishment given to students, caste and/or gender discrimination, religious prejudice, etc. indicate that teacher education programmes have not succeeded in equipping would be teachers with humane qualities essential for promoting a culture of peace in schools. Hence, it is essential to reconsider the teacher education programmes in order to equip teachers both through pre-service and in-service education to:

- Be acquainted with cultures and political systems of their own as well as of others.
- Organise their perceptions of caste, class, religion, other cultures, and national groups on Constitutional values;
- Be free from any prejudice or dogmatic belief.
- Be aware of the societal structures of oppression and their effect on peace as well as the techniques to promote the art of living together.
- Be trained in various pedagogical skills which may help in resolving conflicts, tensions, violence and aggression among students and promote peace.
- Be committed to the profession and its ethical code of conduct.
- Be aware of the factors that hinder peace within the country, such as,

gender disparity, prejudice, ideologies of conflict, violation of human rights, violence, harassment;
- Be vigilant against promoting inequality or discrimination;
- National identity from an international perspective;
- aking accountability of building the future of nation and the world peacefully;
- Establish congenial relationship among human resources.

Teacher education programmes, therefore, need to prepare teachers as peacemakers and peace builders through pre-service and in-service programmes. The following suggestions have been formulated by experts for modifying teacher education programmes.

Knowledge

- Core constitutional values
- Human rights and responsibilities
- Recognition and avoidance of prejudice regaring to cultural, racial, gender based, and religions
- Globalisation and its effects
- Environment/ecology and sustainable development
- International understanding
- Conflicts, wars, and nuclear armament
- Theories of conflict analysis, prevention, resolution, etc.
- Symptoms of violence in students' behaviours
- Participative learning methods
- Media images promoting violence

Skills

- Active listening, communication, and reflection
- Empathy and cooperation
- Critical thinking and problem solving
- Conflict resolution
- Identification and positive interpretation of textbook content
- Use of participative teaching-learning methods
- Leadership and decision-making

Attitudes

- Tolerance
- Respect for human dignity and difference
- Gender and caste sensitivity
- Environmental awareness
- Caring and empathy
- Impartial decision-making
- Social responsibility and accountability

- Self-respect
- Willingness to change with other schools

6.5 Peace in School Setting

The Report of the Education Commission of 1964-66 lays utmost emphasis on the importance of the school environment in inculcating values in students. "The school atmosphere, the personality and behaviour of the teachers, the facilities provided in the school have a large say in developing a sense of values." Some of the pertinent issues like: children's rights and needs, discipline practiced, decisions making and classroom transaction should be cared. School life needs to reflect peace values. Peace education demands and effects improvements in all relationships between: teacher-administration, teacher-student, teacher-teacher, student-student, or teacher-parent. Irrespective of diversity in function, all those who comprise the school community must be treated as members of the school family. Interpersonal relationships must be shaped by reciprocity, mutual respect, and a caring attitude. Unethical and unjust practices of every kind must be avoided. Students need to be made aware of the problems and needs in the local community and enabled. A systematic effort to nurture students in the culture of democracy must be made. Besides, students must be enabled to assume responsibility for maintaining school discipline.

Activities of Peace Education can also be realised through the co-curricular life of the school. A number of activities and projects embodying peace themes could be organised in school.

- Peace values can be imbued among students through discussions, debates, seminars, and films.
- Participation of students in various school events like—role-plays, dramas, composing peace poems, peace songs, etc.
- The observation of Human Rights Day, Children's Day, UN Day, Day for the Disabled, Girl Child Day, Environment Day, etc. should be followed by students.
- Children could be encouraged to visit homes for senior citizens, down trodden, disadvantaged groups, etc. and enabled to develop an interest to help them.
- Spiritual and religious festivals and national days could be celebrated in the school and in the neighborhood.
- Discussions on lives of great men, saints, Rishis and holistic discussions could be organised in school to acquire wisdom.
- Mass meditations have great value in generating peace.

Since learning takes place in many different contexts, all of which can be used to promote messages of peace, a number of activities as part of the after-school programme could be taken up. Some of these include:

(a) 'Solidarity camps' bringing together children of different cultural groups for recreational activities;
(b) Sports activities that build character and promote a spirit of teamwork, cooperation, sportsmanship, etc.; and
(c) 'Media' awareness to reduce violence and increase the peace-content in radio and television programmes for children.
(d) Help in awareness-building among children are: magazines focusing on peace themes, street plays using dance, drama, and songs to educate the community on peace values, puppetry and animation to popularize the values of fairness, non-violence, and social harmony.
(e) Television and radio sports and peace campaigns can also be used to raise public awareness concerning peace and conflict issues. (NCERT-2006)

6.5.1 Integrating Peace Concerns in Classroom Transaction

Teachers' ability to be authentic individuals, who think rationally and act responsibly, is taken over by powerful hidden interests. They are coerced into attitudes and actions dictated by others. The teacher can offer some reflections on the nature of violence. Violence suppresses one's moral sensibility, rational thinking and humane sentiments. The teacher may use the history lesson on the Mughal emperor Akbar to help students' reflect on Akbar's policy of religious tolerance. The points to emphasize: (a) religious harmony is basic to our cultural heritage; (b) the untruth and injustice in stereotyping certain communities and groups; (c) the need for religious tolerance today; and (d) The contrast between a culture of peace and culture of war. In the latter religions also become violent.

It may be pointed out that integrating peace-related values into the school syllabus should not mean that various subjects are to be treated only as vehicles of peace education, and not as mediums for cultivating a taste for the subject concerned. The Report of the Education Commission (1964-66) cautions us that, "the teacher need not draw out the underlying moral all the time, but if he/she has given some thoughts to the values underlying the scope of the subject and his work as teacher, they will imperceptibly pass into his teaching and make an impact on the minds of students."

6.5.2 Methodology of Peace Education

Peace education can be transacted through various methods. Some among those are given below. It may be curricular or co-curricular activities; but it leads to develop peace culture.

- Experiential expositions,
- Group discussions,
- Peer teaching

- Demonstrations supported by audio-video inputs,
- Study materials, and handouts for inducing reflection among teachers
- Theoretical exposition and practical activities.
- Feedback, Self-assessment
- Institutional visit
- Display of slogans, poems, play and a puppet show
- Planning future Action Plans and assessment strategies
- Cooperative learning
- Role-play
- Story telling
- Service learning
- Cultural meets
- Inquiry based teaching learning
- Organizing assembly
- Sports and Games
- Debate

6.5.3 Teachers as Peace Builders

Teachers are role-models for students. A teacher tries to help students to become good human beings. He helps to fulfill the potentiality of students and enabled them for the service of the nation and society. "It is for this reason that a teacher is compared to a gardener who plants seeds of knowledge and good values, waters them with care and kindness, and removes weeds of ignorance." Good teachers are models of peace values, such as, the art of listening, the humility to acknowledge and correct one's mistakes, assuming responsibility for one's actions, sharing concerns, and helping each other to solve problems transcending differences, even if they do not preach peace. A teacher who imposes "discipline" in the classroom only by intimidating children with blows and slaps is a role-model for violence as the sole problem-solving strategy. The teacher's role in creating a positive climate in the classroom is of paramount importance. It is his/ her attitudes, values, and relationships that determine the nature of the classroom climate as well as learners. A teacher who can critically evaluate his/her attitudes, habitual modes of thinking, and approach to teaching is an asset for education. Peace values are learnt better through examples or living instances. Hence, Sri Aurobindo says, 'teacher must be a yogi, hero and example'.

Teachers are real heroes in educational enterprises. A teacher who, from a peace perspective, can critically evaluate his/her attitudes, habitual modes of thinking, and approach to teaching—what one teaches and what are the carry-over values of what is taught and how it is taught—is an asset for education for peace.

They must take vital responsibility in peace building process. They must have good relationship with students, colleagues, parents and communities.

Teacher must be a good disciplinarian having self-control and free from prejudice. He should help the learners for developing good habits like: truthfulness, honesty, and tolerance, respect and appreciate others, being fair and open minded compassion and service to others etc. He must understand the multi-cultural, multi-ethnic and multi religious problems first and then try to combat the issues. A conscious teacher must influence others to live in harmony and unity with self, humankind and nature. In educational field the teacher must be helpful to implement the "unity in diversity". Teacher must cope with prejudices, conflicts, and violence in an increasingly diverse society. Dr. S. Radhakrishna said, we should "...will peace with our whole body and soul, our feelings and instincts, our flesh and its affections."

6.5.4 Peace Related Activities in the Educational Institution

- Peace campaigns and peace march in some localities,
- Group lunch by organizing teachers,
- Play, dramas and Showing Exhibitions etc.
- Cleaning of the school,
- Address in the morning assembly by the principal,
- Silence for two minutes,
- Thought of the day,
- Affectionate behaviour towards students,
- Developing relationships with families of students;
- Weekly activities were—singing, drama, creative arts, cultural programmes,
- Story narration,
- Peace related songs,
- Pledges by teachers and students,
- Peace news clippings,
- Sharing students' experiences,
- Yoga and meditation related activities,
- Special lectures,
- Inviting speakers to talk on peace related issues;
- annual activities were celebration of national festivals/days,
- Mass awareness in the community,
- Voluntary service to community,
- Celebration of peace week etc.

6.6 Family's Role for Peace

Family's Role in Peace Making is significant. It shows the importance of family in the life of individuals by predisposing them to peaceful or violent skills, attitudes and values. The sense of security warmth, love and care available to a child in the family may build pro peace competencies, while aggression, hostility or neglect may lead to violent ways of being. Although, teachers may not directly influence the family of their wards however their understanding of their own family environment and awareness of its impact on them and the understanding of the behaviour of school children as a byproduct of their family environment, will facilitate the development teacher-child relationships. The consciousness of the family impact is necessary to be able to identify the needs of children for interventions, issues for parent-teacher meetings, and areas of enrichment through school based outreach programmes activities.

Violence in the family and ways of dealing with it, was to make teachers aware of the ways in which adults' encourages and perpetuate to resolve violence in the family. As teachers they need to take care that they themselves do not model and promote violence-verbally or non-verbally. A lot of evidence where women are subjected to emotional and subtle forms of violence was presented for consideration of teachers. Three kinds of violence, verbal, non-verbal and sarcastic behaviour lead to a lot of temperamental problems, among individuals, which spoils family atmosphere and relationships. Violence results from indifference towards weak, women and powerless.

Family Communication Styles enable to understand how healthy communication styles result in development of different kinds of personal orientation towards others, which has implication for development of the child, and peace related skills. The various communication styles in the family, the different skills required for effective communication—attending, listening awareness of self, nonverbal listening, body language etc. were discussed with the participants. It awakes of how the family members speak in authoritative, suggestive and defensive manner. It reveals the dynamics of the two way communication process giving, as well as receiving communication, providing opportunity to others to speak, listening to others attentively, giving direct and avoiding indirect communication. It is stressed on communication with children, the role of parents and teachers in facilitating child development by listening and paying attention to them.

6.7 Role of Media in Peace Building and Conflict Management

Mass media has paramount role in progress of civilisations. We look its proof in history. The advancement of mass media, such as printing, the telegraph, the telephone, the radio, television, the computer, and the internet, however, were in large part also touted as promoting understanding and even peace. The responsibility of media to report the news accurately and objectively has good significance. A government could use the media to help defuses crisis, as the Kennedy administration did during the Cuban missile crisis.

History also proved that sometimes the media could be misled by an administration into promoting a war. We have seen two negative developments in the United States in recent years, despite the undeniable benefits of the information revolution: the increasing partisanship reflected in the media means prejudices are reinforced rather than reduced and it has muddied the public's efforts to learn. It is hard to claim, therefore, that technological advances in the media by themselves promote peace. "The close relation between the media and the promotion of peace is focused much more closely in radio and TV international broadcasting. Major reputable broadcasters, BBC being the best known, follow high standards of journalism in avoiding often inflammatory misinformation. In doing so, they also advocate through their type of reporting universal values such as democracy, human rights, and economic freedom." While broadcasting in local languages to countries where free media are banned or significantly limited, regional language also tries to strengthen civil societies, combat intolerance, promote understanding, and serve as a model for local media. I believe that such efforts are fully compatible with objectivity. In the case of All India Radio we give highest priority to tolerance, bringing all ethnic and religious groups on the air whenever possible to encourage peaceful outcomes. If the media cannot stop violence and war, they must give support to those local forces trying to do so.

The media are directly connected to the great communications inventions: printing press, telegraph, radio, TV, and now the explosive and still unimaginable spread of the internet. Each of these inventions in its turn was touted as a great advance of civilisation, heralding a new era of peace and tolerance. There is no denying the great benefits brought by these inventions, but they have not lived up to their billing. One could argue in fact that they have as often been used as a means to spread intolerance, violence, and even war. Radio, Newspaper, TV, and the internet are unparalleled as educational vehicles able to reach large numbers of persons. While we ourselves have seen in recent years that the media is designed in the growth of programmes more to reinforce existing prejudices, often with distortions or even falsehoods, there are many examples in the national media that inform, educate, and stir our cultural thinking.

The modern age is focusing today on media and peace; we should really look at the international media that have a wide reach, especially radio and TV. But we also have to realize the admirable effect that the internet is having in gravely weakening the control of authoritarian regimes over information content. This change has provided a much more fertile environment for radio and TV to exploit. It is asserted that, in their operations, promoting peace and tolerance is not incompatible with providing objective and balanced information to listeners. To keep the glory of Mass media, one can encourage universal values such as security of the person, political participation, human rights including women's rights, and uncorrupt free economies without professing a bias toward the specific policies of any outside national ideology. In this regard we can say, there are some praiseworthy international broadcasters like BBC, the Voice of America, and The Hindu daily are promoting peace and tolerance. It is thus our responsibility as media users to support those media elements which promote the values which make a better world.

Mass media has great importance for changing of civilisation. There are different types of media are used globally to distribute knowledge and idealistically. Free mass media is a tool and signpost for democracy. Freedom of expression is not only the core of a healthy media but also a fundamental human right and vital for a democratic culture. It stands for freedom of speech, the right to information and the representation of different opinions in a heterogeneous society. In any culture of prevention, effective and democratic media are an essential part and indispensable for societies trying to make a transition towards peace and democracy.

The transmission of ideas can be promoted through conventional media such as newspapers, TV or radio and new technologies, the internet and digital content. The ability to make informed decisions strengthens societies and fosters economic growth, democratic structures and the positive outlook on the future. Journalism does not need justification for its existence. Its service to society is justification in itself. Journalism can not only help to distribute information but also counter hate-speech and create an environment of balanced opinions, an information equilibrium.[1] For the media it can be problematic to find a balance between preventing harm caused by speech and protecting individual expression. Being able to find this balance, however is important especially in conflict situations. Responsible journalism does not just re-publish press releases but is truly concerned with a truthful, balanced and fair account of events. In order to achieve this journalists have to stay clear of judgmental representations and describe reality without embellishment.[2] If democracy is to work properly, society needs access to news and information; analysis of the status quo, debate, practical information and exchange as well as entertainment are needed and provided by the media. The definition of conflict and defining conflict areas is not easy and no two places are alike. Journalists need to know what they can expect on sight in order to define the objectives of their project.[3]

In case of a crisis or a conflict, the international media can attract worldwide attention. The mass media is a pervasive part of daily life especially in industrialised countries and thus able to shine a light on conflicts anywhere in the world. Since most armed conflicts these days have governmental and not territorial reasons; the parties are often concerned with making sure that the majority of people are on “their” side, which bears a lot of potential for misrepresenting facts and trying to seize control over the distribution of information. For this very reason the intervention of unbiased and free global media is important not only for the world public but also for the people directly affected. The number of conflicts, however, that gets international attention is small; therefore local media is vital in this context.[4]

Broadcasting news by using community radios can help reach people in different areas, even with different languages more easily. This way people can be addressed directly and their own personal experiences and lives can be incorporated much better, than with foreign media. The danger of manipulation and inflammation of ethnic tensions, however, cannot be ignored. Another advantage of local media, especially radio is that in border areas it is possible to convey peace messages to passing fighters and refugees alike.[5] Democratic media structures need more than this; it is vital that the use of information within a society is not solemnly passive but that the population gets actively involved in creating content and broadcasting it.[6]

Internal conflicts do not occur spontaneously but tend to have a history. Local media usually have a deeper understanding of the existing political structures, the participants of the conflict as well as the changes preceding the outbreak of violence. The media can therefore not only influence society before the conflict by recognizing and properly addressing the issue but also afterwards. Unlike international media covering conflicts, local media are a recognised part of society with the ability to accelerate and magnify fears or reduce them. One should not forget that journalism can play a role in escalating conflicts, which also demonstrates the potential for positive purposes. The media have the power to defuse tensions before they even reach a critical point and keep a critical eye on government, opposition and society. By supplying credible information and reaching a large audience, the media help in managing conflicts and promote democratic principles. In the aftermath of a conflict, reconciliation and societal development can be encouraged as well.[7]

A measure of peace-building can be enhanced through peace journalism. Peace journalists try to uncover the causes behind a conflict and true goals of all participants while making sure to humanize all victims of the conflict. Part of the ethical guidelines for this kind of reporting is to bring out people that use peaceful measures and speak out against war and violence and document the suffering and loss on all sides. Possible solutions and trying to prevent further escalation of the conflict are at the center of peace journalism as well. A suggested framework used by peace-building media can employ different strategies such as (1) Conflict-sensitive and peace journalism; (2) Peace-promoting entertainment media; (3) Media regulation to prevent incitement of violence, but also (4) Peace-promoting citizen media.[8]

Journalists can be considered the helpers of all human rights defenders to ethical and moral standards in reporting as well as to addressing important topics in way that can be helpful for everyone. Media and journalism can be a great assistance in conflict management and peace building. However, they will never be able to eliminate armed conflicts altogether but they can support for eradication. The media can be a good tool in a healthy and functioning environment but more is needed than ethical and responsible reporting to ensure peace and sustainable development.

6.8 Spirituality and Peace

Peace is a golden term. Everybody wants peace, but nobody gets it easily. Somebodies get its sparks. Some realised it and live in for long time. We search peace hither and thither. We go to temples, mathas, Biharas, Churches, and Mosques etc. to achieve peace. But where is peace? For thousand years human being has been searching it in various forms. It is neither a piece of meal available any market nor any manager, leader, politicians, bureaucrats can achieve it so easily.

Our experiences say attending satsangh, study circle, going to temples or church, saying truth, positive thinking, positive seeing, doing 'yogasana' and 'pranayam', taking '*satwic*' food, pray to the divine, living righteous path, remembering God etc. are very helpful in the path of peace harmony. Is not it the spiritual path? Yes! These activities provide us glimpses of peace and tranquility. If we will practice it continuously it will provide us immense feeling.

When man follows worldly (external) means, he will follow stir mind and become unstable. He tries to enjoy everything. He understands the Worldly pleasure as happiness. He stays there for whole life. He wants all achievements will come in a few moments like computer. Hence, he does mischievous activities like: theft, loot, rubbery, murder, riots etc. He relies on falsehood, crime, terrorism, and some misdeeds due to selfishness. This is mundane live. Everything looks like pretension. Here suffering comes more than pleasure. This is devil's path or path of ignorance.

In other way, there is a spiritual path, divine's path, which is conscious, sincere, harmonious, peaceful, truthful, and beautiful and creates goodness in life and society. Here we can get permanent peace. But it is very hard and stupendous task. Here no external journey, but inner journey is required. Shall we start this inner journey! Journey to the soul or psychic discovery! It can be done silently. No need to move to the sun or moon, but to go inward, search the core of the being, concentrate there, think about it, live in it, we will get eternal peace, knowledge, love, light and power. Inner harmony will establish. Individual harmony leads to social harmony and a progressive civilisation can be established. Hence, spirituality is the key for establishing peace and harmony. Choice is imperative! If we follow the previous path life will be mundane, and if we follow the later one we can feel a glorious eternal and peaceful life.

Om dyauh shantih/
Antarikhyam Shantih/
Pruthibi Shantih/
Oshadhayah Shantih/
Banaspatayah Shantih/
Biswedevah Shantih/
Brahmah Shantih/

Sha ma Shantiredhi//
Om Shantih Shantih Shantih//

Translation: Let there be peace in heaven! Let there be peace in the sky! Let there be peace in the Earth! Let there be peace in water! Let there be peace in herbs and trees! Let there be peace in Gods! Let there be peace in Supreme-abode! Let there be peace in Peace! Om peace! Peace! Peace!

6.9 Assignments

- Give a demonstration on showing respect to elders at home and in school.
- Write a story to explain the word 'cooperation'. (Language).
- Sketch a peaceful world (Social Science).
- Explain how we can create values in society.
- Write a story with peace messages (Language).
- Collect newspaper chippings, magazines, articles on different themes related to peace and values for making a wall magazine (Language).
- Improvise the solution to a problem affecting weaker students through teamwork, utilising available resources (EVS/Social Sciences).
- Write a poem or a song describing values like honesty, hard work, etc. (Language).
- Identify problem areas in nearby village that require immediate solution (Social Science).
- Organise field visits to local orphanages or old age homes to sensitise students to the loneliness, deprivation, and helplessness of these sections of society.
- Organize programmes, talks, workshops, film shows, etc. to inculcate in the students love and affection.
- Make projects on ecological changes over the years and their effect in the rural sphere.
- Discuss how environmental degradation affects the poor
- What is the role of mass media in peace building and resolution of conflict?
- Write-down the situation after a war.
- What are the impacts of nuclear war on this fine globe?
- Write any conflict resolution technique.
- Make a list of some value oriented words.
- Collect symbols of various religions and explain their meanings

6.10 Project Based Activities

- Encourage students to participate in community activities through which they can learn social skills.

- Undertake a survey on how many children below the age of 14 are not attending school in the village, town, or neighborhood in question, exploring also the reasons why they are out of school.
- Organize conflict resolution sessions on selected themes.
- Study the problems linked with violence. Students can share their experiences with violence, so that others in the class can also learn strategies for coping with fears and anxieties.
- Make a project on eco-conscious approach
- Make a project on peaceful world
- Trace the road map of a peaceful state.
- Make case study of a conflict
- Make a plan to organize an interfaith dialogue
- Give a concise picture of 'Gurukula' system of education

Endnotes

1. Koven, Ronald (2004). *An Antidote to Hate Speech: Journalism, Pure and Simple.*
2. *Ibid.*
3. Deutsche Welle—Global Media Forum (2009) *Conflict Prevention in the Multimedia Age.* p. 69.
4. United Nations Office for West Africa (2005) *UNOWA Workshop on Reporting for Peace.* p. 3 5.
5. *Ibid.*, p. 4.
6. Deutsche Welle—Global Media Forum (2008) *Media in Peacebuilding and Conflict revention.* pp. 59-61.
7. Westphal, Florian (2004) *The Right Information at the Right Time.* URL: http://unesdoc.unesco.org/images/0013/001389/138983e.pdf page 27-29.
8. Himelfarb, Sheldon and Chabalowski, Megan (2008) *Media, Conflict Prevention and Peacebuilding: Mapping the Edges.* United States Institute for Peace. URL: http://www.usip.org/resources/media-conflict-prevention-and-peacebuilding-mapping-edges

Bibliography

Abdul Kalam, A.P.J., (2016). *Indomitable Spirit,* Delhi: Rajpal and Sons.

Adams, Robert, (1999). *Finite and Infinite Goods.* New York and Oxford: Oxford University Press. chapter 3, "Well-Being and Excellence."

Aharoni, Ada, "Women in Pursuit of Peace", *Peace, Literature, and Art*, Vol. I.

Anderson, Elizabeth, (1999). "What Is the Point of Equality?", *Ethics* 109, pp. 287-337.

Ankerl, Guy (2000). Global communication without universal civilisation. INU societal research. *Vol. 1: Coexisting contemporary civilisations: Arabo-Muslim, Bharati, Chinese, and Western.* Geneva: INU Press.

Aquino, Corazon (1994). World Commission on Culture and Development.

Argenti, Paul (1997). *Organisational Communication*, Irwin/McGraw-Hill, New York.

Aristotle, (1941). *Nichomachean Ethics*, in *The Basic Works of Aristotle*, Richard McKeon, New York: Random House, pp. 935-1112.

Asimov, I. (988). *Book of Science and Nature Quotations*, New York: Weidenfeld & Nicolson.

Aung San Suu Kyi (November 21, 1994) address to WCCD in Manila Karve, I. Yuganta. Bachelor, M. and Brown, K. (eds.) *Buddhism and Ecology.*

Aurora, S. (2016). *Human Rights and Value in Education,* Belgium: Education International.

Bajaj, M. (2011). "Human Rights Education: Ideology, Location, and Approaches", *Human Rights Quarterly*. 33, 481-508.

Balasooriya, A.S. (2000a). *World Peace through School Manuscript.* Maharagama, Sri Lanka: National Institute of Education.

Balasooriya, A.S. (2000b). *Mediation Process.* Sri Lanka.

Basadur, www.basadurprofile.com/about.aspx

Bey T.M. and G.Y. Turner (1995). *Making School a Place of Peace*. London: Sage.

Brown, G. (1971). *Human Teaching for Human Learning.* New York, Viking.

Canfeid, J. (1975). *101 Ways to Enhance Self-concept in the Classroom.* Engle Cliffs: Prentice Hall.

Catherine Morris, *Peacebuilding in Cambodia: The Role of Religion* http://www.peacemakers.ca/research/Cambodia/Cambodia2000ExecSum.html

Catholic Contributions to International Peace http://www.usip.org/publications/catholic-contributions-international-peace

Cavington, Krutchfield and Davis (1966).

Christiano, Thomas, (1996). *The Rule of the Many,* Boulder, Colorado: Westview Press.

Christiano, Thomas, (2008). *The Constitution of Equality: Democratic Authority and Its Limits*, Oxford: Oxford University Press.

Cohen, G.A., (1988). *History, Labour, and Freedom: Themes from Marx*, Oxford: Oxford University Press.

Cohen, Joshua, (1989). "Democratic Equality," *Ethics* 99, pp. 727-751.

Cohen, Steven (2002). *Negotiating Skills for Managers*, McGraw-Hill Trade.

Cole, W.O. (ed.) (1991). *Moral Issues in Six Religions*, Oxford: Heinemann.

Conger, Jay (1998). *Winning Them Over: A New Model for Managing in the Age of Persuasion*, Simon and Schuster, New York, New York.

Coombs, P.H. (1985). "*The World Crises in Education: The View from the Eighties*", Oxford: Oxford University Press.

Cotrino Abrams, G. *Education for Peace.* Miami Beach.

Dalai Lama, H.H. *The Art of living and Dying in Peace.*

Damon, William (1988). *The Moral Child: Nurturing Children's Natural Moral Growth.* New York: The Free Press.

David Newton (2010). *The Role of the Media in Promoting Peace*, Middle East Institute; www.fethullah-gulen.org

Davies, W.H. (1925). *Leisure*. James R. Wells.

Deborah M. Kolb and Associates (1994), "Joseph Elder: Quiet Peacemaking in a Civil War," in *When Talk Works: Profiles of Mediators.* San Francisco: Jossey-Bass.

Delors, J. (1996). *Learning the Treasure within: Report of International Commission on Education for the21st Century.* Paris: UNESCO.

Descartes, R. (1979). *Meditations on First Philosophy*, in *The Philosophical Works of Descartes*, Volume 1, E. Haldane and G. Ross (trans. and eds.), London: Cambridge University Press, pp. 131-199

Descartes, R. (1979). *Principles of Philosophy*, in *Philosophical Works*, E. Haldane and G. Ross (trans. and eds.), London: Cambridge University Press, pp. 201 302.

Dewy, J. (1916). *Democracy and Education*, London: The Free Press.

Dhal, P. (2007). *Implementation of Integral Education.*1st ed., Balasore, MIRA, p. 132.

—— (2011). *Psychic Education*, New Delhi, APH Publication.

—— (2015, April). New Horizon and Vision of Teacher Education "SRJHSE", Vol. 4, Issue-2, Pune, pp. 2078-2085.

—— (2016, July). Quality in Education for Modern India on Indian Philosophical Foundation, "International Journal of Informative and Futuristic Research", Vol. 3, Issue-2, Ambla, pp. 4283-4292.

Dhammapada, I 5.

Dhand, H. (2000). *Teaching Human Rights: A Handbook for Teacher Educators.* Bhopal: Asian Institute of Human Rights Education.

Erickson, Richard J. (January-February 1973). "Development of the Strategy of Peaceful Coexisting During the Khrushchev Era". *Air University Review.*

Ferguson, J. (1977). *War and Peace in the World's Religions,* London: Sheldon.

Fishkin, James, (1983). *Justice, Equal Opportunity, and the Family*, New Haven: Yale University Press.

Fountain, S. (1988). *Learning Together—Global Education.* New York: Stanley Thrones Publishers Ltd., New York University.

—— (1999). *Education for Peace in* UNICEF. New York: Working Paper Education Section, Programme Division, UNICEF.

Fuller, R.B., and Kuromiya, K. (1982). *Critical Path.* Macmillan.

Ghose, A. (1992). *A New Education for a New Consciousness: Sri Aurobindo and the Mother on Education.* Sri Aurobindo International Centre of Education.

Giri, A. (2016). *The Calling of Global Responsibility: An Introduction and An Invitation to Adventures of Ideas and Transformative Movements.* Chennai: MIDS.

Government of India (1949). *Report of the University Education Commission, (1948-49).* New Delhi: Ministry of Education, Government of India.

—— (1953). *Report of the Secondary Education Commission, (1952-53).* New Delhi: Ministry of Education.

—— (1966). *Report of the Education Commission 1964-66 on "Education and National Development".* New Delhi: Ministry of Education.

—— (1993). *Learning without Burden.* New Delhi: Ministry of Human Resources Development (MHRD), Department of Education.

——. (1986). *Report of the National Policy on Education (1986).* New Delhi, Ministry of Human Resources Development.

Graham, Pauline, Editor (1999). *Mary Parker Follet: Prophet of Management: A Celebration of Writings from the 1920s*, Harvard project/programme purpose School Press, Boston, MA.

Halpern (1983). www.cs.cornell.edu/home/halpern/abstract.html

Hare, R.M., (1981). *Moral Thinking: Its Levels, Method, and Point*, Oxford: Clarendon Press.

Harris, I. and C. McCauley (2000). *Report on the International Workshop on Education for Peace.* Israel: University of Haifa.

Harris, I.M. (1988). *Education for Peace*. London: McFarland and Company.

Heise, L. (1998). Violence against Women: An Integrated, Ecological Framework. *Violence against Women,* Vol. 4, No. 3, pp. 262-290.

Henry O. Thompson, (1978). *World Religions in War and Peace*, (Jefferson NC: McFarland, 1988); John Ferguson, *War and Peace in the World's Religion.* New York: Oxford University Press.

Homer Jack, ed. (1968). *World Religions and World Peace: The International Inter-Religious Symposium on Peace.* Boston: Beacon.

http://www.mindtools.com/pages/article/newppm_89.htm

http://www.sriaurobindoashram.org/ashram/mother/writings.php

https//www.boundless.com/sociology

https://en.wikipedia.org/wiki/religion_and_peacebuilding#cite_note

https://www.peacefromharmony.org

https://www.religioustolerance.org/retz_0.1.htm

https://www.skillsyouneed.com/ips/negotiation-persuation-skills.htm/v

Iyengar, K.R., (1975). "*Re-Thinking on End and Means in Education*", New Delhi, Sri Aurobindo Ashram, p. 28.

Jackson, J. and Miller, S. (2009). *Let There be Peace on Earth: And Let it Begin with Me*, Random House Digital, Inc.

Jaygopal, R. (1990), *Human Recourse Development: Conceptual Analysis and Strategies,* New Delhi: Sterling Publishers Pvt. Ltd.

Jenkins, J. (1992). *Contemporary Moral Issues*, Oxford: Heinemann.

Jewkes, R., Levin, J., and Penn-Kekana, L. (2002). Risk factors for domestic violence:

findings from a South African cross-sectional study. *Social Science and Medicine,* Vol. 55, pp. 1603-17.

John Paul Lederach (1999), *The Journey Toward Reconciliation,* Scottdale, PA: Herald Press.

Johnson, Steve (1999). *Issues in Ethics*, Vol. 10, No. 1 Springer Publication.

Joyce Juntune (1979). joycejuntune.com

Kalam, A. (2010). *Indomitable Spirit,* Delhi: Rajpal and Sons.

Kaushik, N. (2010) The Role of Mass Media in Peace Building, Conflict Management and Prevention.

Kemson, Joshua, (2016). *Philosophy.*

Kerby Anderson (1995). https://probe.org/violence-in-society/

Kolb, Deborah M. *et al.*, (1994). "Joseph Elder: Quiet Peacemaking in a Civil War," in *When Talk Works: Profiles of Mediators*, San Francisco: Jossey-Bass Publishers.

Krishnamacharyulu, V. (2008). *To be Sure Teaching for Teachers of Today and Tomorrow*, New Delhi, Neelkamal Publications, p. 255.

Kulski, Wladyslaw W. (1959). *Peaceful Coexistence: An Analysis of Soviet Foreign Policy,* Chicago: Henry Regnery Company.

Kurvey, B. (1999). *Human Rights Education in India: Needs and Future Actions*, Vol. II.

Laing, R.D. (1964). "Sanity and Madness in the Family" in Andrewartha, G.P. *Objectivity and the Bell-shaped Curve*: 28-32.

——(1990). *The Divided Self—An Existential Study in Sanity and Madness*, Penguin Books.

Lederach, John Paul, (1999). *The Journey Toward Reconciliation.* Scottdale, PA: Herald Press.

Leo (2013). ABC of Harmony, Russia, GHA.

Leo, http//www.peacefromharmony.org

Lickona, Thomas (1991). *Educating for Character: How Our Schools Can Teach Respect and Responsibility*. New York: Bantam Books.

Lincoln, A. (1864, May10). *Letter to Headmaster of His Son's School,* USA.

Locke, John, (1690). *Second Treatise of Government,* C.B. MacPherson (ed.), Indianapolis: Hackett, 1980 edition.

Mahaparta, N. (2012, September). "Role of Education in Promotion and Protection of Human Rights", *Odisha Review*, pp. 26-30.

Mani, Gomathy (1991). *Education in the International Context,* New Delhi, Sterling Publishers Pvt. Ltd.

Marx, Karl, (1978). "Critique of the Gotha Programme," in Robert C. Tucker (ed.), *The Marx-Engels Reader*, New York: W.W. Norton, pp. 525-541 (written in 1875).

Mary Anderson (1999). *Do No Harm: How Aid Can Support Peace or War*. Boulder, CO: Lynne Reiner Publishers.

Maslow, A.H. (1968). *Towards a Psychology of Being,* 2e. Van Nostrand Reinholf.

Matthew, *The New Testament.*

Maxwell, J.C. (2013). *Sometimes You Win—Sometimes You Learn: Life's Greatest Lessons are Gained from Our Losses*. UK: Hachette.

Maxwell, N. (1984). *From Knowledge to Wisdom*, Oxford: Basil Blackwell.

Merry, Sally Engle, (2000). "Mennonite Peace building and Conflict Transformation: A Cultural Analysis," in *From the Ground Up: Mennonite Contributions to*

International Peace Building, Cynthia Sampson and John Paul Lederach, eds. New York: Oxford University Press.

Mill, John Stuart, (1979). George Sher, ed., *Utilitarianism*, Indianapolis, IN: Hackett Publishing. Originally published 1861.

Morgan, P. and Lawton, C. (1996) Ethical Issues in Six Religious Traditions Edinburgh: Edinburgh University Press.

—— (1996). *Ethical Issues in Six Religious Traditions*, Edinburgh: Edinburgh University Press.

Nadkarni, M.V. (4th April, 2007). *Inaugural Speech of Sri Auro bindo University*".

National Council of Educational Research and Training (NCERT) (2000). *National Curriculum Framework for School Education.* New Delhi: NCERT.

National Human Rights Commission, Faridkot House, Copernicus Marg, New Delhi.

NCERT (2006). Education for Peace, New Delhi.

——(2006). NCF 2005 Position Paper National Focus Group on Education for Peace, New Delhi.

Norman, A. (1996). "Teaching Wisdom," in Lehrer *et al.* 1996, pp. 253-265.

Nozick, R. (1989). "What is Wisdom and Why Do Philosophers Love it So?" in *The Examined Life*, New York: Touchstone Press, pp. 267-278.

Nozick, Robert, (1974). *Anarchy, State, and Utopia*, New York: Basic Books.

Osborn (1963). www.icre.pitt.edu/cbe/documents/Info Sheet PDFs/Teaching.

Panda, P. (2001). "Human Rights Education in Indian Schools", *Curriculum Development*, Vol. IV.

Pandey, S. (2004). *Education for Peace: Self Instructional Package for Teacher Educators.*

Pathak, C.K. (2004). *Human Rights Education*, Rajput Publication, New Dehli.

Pike, G. and D. Seiby (1993). *Global Teacher-Global Learner: Public Report on Basic Education in India*, OUP, (1999).

Plato (1978). *The Republic*, in *The Collected Dialogues of Plato*, Edith Hamilton and Huntington Cairns (eds.), Princeton: Princeton University Press, pp. 575-844.

—— (1978). *The Apology*, in *The Collected Dialogues of Plato*, Edith Hamilton and Huntington Cairns (eds.), Princeton: Princeton University Press, pp. 3-26.

Puri, Lakshmi (2014). A Culture of Peace Requires Participation of Women, UN Headquarter in Network, September 9.

Ranade, S. (1992). "Into the 21st Century", Sri Aurobindo Society, Madras, p. 18.

Rawls, John, (1999). *A Theory of Justice*, Cambridge: Harvard University Press.

——, (1999). *Collected Papers*, Samuel Freeman (ed.), Cambridge: Harvard University Press.

Raymond, G., Helmick, S.J., (2001). "Does Religion Fuel or Heal in Conflicts? In *Forgiveness and Reconciliation*, Raymond G. Helmick, S.J. and Rodney L. Petersen, eds. Philadelphia: Templeton Foundation Press.

Richard Arneson (2013). htts://Plato.stanfordedu/info.html#c

Robert Herr and Judy Zimmerman Herr, "Building Peace in South Africa," in *From the Ground Up: Mennonite Contributions to International Peace building*, Cynthia Sampson and John Paul Lederach, eds. (New York: Oxford University Press, 2000).

Ryan, S. (1996). "Wisdom," in Lehrer *et al.*, pp. 233-242.

—— (1999). "What is Wisdom?" *Philosophical Studies*, 93: 119-139.

—— (2012). "Wisdom, Knowledge, and Rationality," *Acta Analytica*, 27(2): 99-112.
Ryan, S. (2013). http://www.wisdompage.com/
SABCL, Vol. 14, Sri Aurobindo Ashram, Pondicherry.
Sakharov, Andrei (1968). *Progress, Co-ëxistence, and Intellectual Freedom*. Trans. by [staff of] *The New York Times*; with introduction, afterword, and notes by Harrison E. Salisbury. New York: W.W. Norton & Co. 158 p.
Sangiovanni, Andrea, (2007). "Global Justice, Reciprocity, and the State," *Philosophy and Public Affairs* 35, pp. 2-39.
Scanlon, T.M., (1998). *What Do We Owe to One Another?*, Cambridge, MA: Harvard University Press.
Schuler, S.R., Bates, L.M., and Islam, F. (2008). Women's Rights, Domestic Violence, and Resource Seeking in Rural Bangladesh. *Violence against Women,* Vol. 14, No. 3, pp. 326-345.
Semashko, L. (2013). *ABC of Harmony*, Russia, GHA.
Sethna, K.D., ed. (2009). "*Mother India*", Pondicherry, Sri Aurobindo Ashram, March.
Sharma, M.C. (2002). *Human Rights Education in Indian Universities and Colleges*, Vol. V.
Shaw & Cliatt (1986). *Journal of Creative Behaviour*, Vol. 20 no. 2, pp. 81-88.
Shukla, P.D. (1988). *The New Education Policy in India*, New Delhi, Sterling Publishers Pvt. Ltd.
Simmons, John (1992). *The Lockean Theory of Rights.* Princeton: Princeton University Press.
Smithwhite, M. (2006). "*A New Education with a Soul*", Coimbatore, ICPC Trust.
Sri Aurobindo (1917). *Arya*, August 15, Pondicherry: Sri Aurobindo Ashram Trust.
—— (1949). *The Human Cycle: The Ideal of Human Unity War and Self-Determination.* Pondicherry: Sri Aurobindo Ashram.
—— (1972). *Savitri*. "*Collected Works of Sri Aurobindo*", 28 (33-34). Pondicherry: Sri Aurobindo Ashram Trust.
—— (1972a). *The Life Divine*, Sri Aurobindo Birth Centenary Library, Vol. 18 and 19, Pondicherry: Sri Aurobindo Ashram.
—— (1996). *The Upanishads*, Pondicherry: Sri Aurobindo Ashram.
—— (1992). "*A New Education for New Consciousness*", Pondicherry, SAICE, p. 230.
——, (1949). *The Human Cycle The Ideal of Human Unity War and Self-Determination,* Pondicherry, Sri Aurobindo Ashram.
——, (1972). "*Collected Works of Sri Aurobindo*", Pondicherry, Sri Aurobindo Ashram.
——, (1972). *Savitri.* "*Collected Works of Sri Aurobindo*", Vol. 28, 33 and 34, Pondicherry, Sri Aurobindo Ashram.
——, (1972). "The Yoga and its Objects', Pondicherry, Sri Aurobindo Ashram Trust.
——, "Essays on the Gita", Pondicherry, Sri Aurobindo Ashram.
——, "The Yoga of Self Perfection", Pondicherry, Sri Aurobindo Ashram.
——, The Synthesis of Yoga, Part Four: The Yoga of Self-Perfection, Chapter 20, The Intuitive Mind, pp. 775-776.
Srivastava, Namit K., *Women Empowerment in India,* University of Delhi.
Sumner, L.W. (1996). *Welfare, Happiness, and Ethics.* New York and Oxford: Oxford University Press.

The Mother, (1978 Ed.). "*On Education*" (Collected Work, Vol. 12), Pondicherry, Sri Aurobindo Ashram Trust

The Mother, (1978b). *Collected Works of the Mother*. Pondicherry: Sri Aurobindo Ashram.

The Mother, *Collected Works of the Mother*, Vol. 4 and Vol. 12, Pondicherry, Sri Aurobindo Ashram.

The Mother. (2017). Retrieved from http://www.sriaurobindoashram.org/ashram/mother/writings.php

Thilagavathy, T. and Ayoub, A. (2016) Human Rights Education in India: Importance, Present Status and Future Actions, *Asia Pacific Journal of Research* Vol. I, Issue XXXVI.

Tiberius, V. (2008). *The Reflective Life: Living Wisely with Our Limits*, Oxford: Oxford University Press.

Torrance (1960). www.torrancememorial.org/About_Us/History/1925_1960s.aspx

Trivedi, Sonu (2003). 'Human Rights and Democracy', *Mainstrem*, Vol. XLI. No. 52, New Delhi, December.

UN Women Pacific. (2011) *Ending Violence against Women and Girls: Evidence, Data and Knowledge in Pacific Island Countries.* http://www.unwomenpacific.org/resources/uploads/embeds/file/UN%20Women% 20Ending%20VAW%20Literature%20Review%202nd%20Edition.pdf (Accessed 1 June 2013)

UNESCO (1996). 'Learning the Treasure Within'.

UNESCO (1998). *Learning to Live together in Peace and Harmony*. A UNESCO APNIEVE Source Book for Teacher Education and Tertiary Level Education. Bangkok, Thailand: UNESCO Principal Regional Office for Asia and the Pacific.

UNESCO (2001). *Learning the Way of Peace. A Teachers' Guide to Education for Peace*. New Delhi: UNESCO.

UNESCO, (1997). *'The Impact of ICT on Teaching and Teachers'.*

UNESCO, (2013) *Women's Empowerment for a Culture of Peace and Non-Violence in the Pacific Consultation Meeting Proceedings.*

UNESCO. (2001). *Learning the Way to Peace. A Teachers Guide to Education for Peace.* New Delhi: UNESCO.

UNICEF (1994). *I Dream of Peace.* New York: Harper Collins.

Van Vrekhan and Georges. (2000). *The Mother*. New Delhi: Harper and Collins.

Vergano, D. (2008). *The Lightness of Being*, USA.

Walzer, Michael, (1983). *Spheres of Justice: A Defense of Pluralism and Equality,* New York: Basic Books.

Watts, C. and Zimmerman, C. (2002). Violence against women: global scope and magnitude. *The Lancet,* Vol. 359, pp. 1232-1237.

Williams, Andrew (1998). "Incentives, Inequality, and Publicity," *Philosophy and Public Affairs* 27, 225-247.

Wood, Allen (1981). *Karl Marx*, London: Routledge and Kegan Paul, chapters 9 and 10.

World Health Organisation (2002). *World Report on Violence and Health: Summary.* Geneva, WHO.

www.dianahsieh.com

www.discovery.ucl.ac.uk/./1344128_new_vers_97%20Philosophia%20Arguing%20

www.selfdefinition.org/psychology/R-D-Laing-The-Divided-Self.pdf

Zagzebski, L. (1996). *Virtues of the Mind*, Cambridge: Cambridge University Press.

Index